Life's Daily
BLESSINGS

Inspiring Reflections
on *Gratitude* and *Joy*
for Every Day,
Based on
Jewish Wisdom

Rabbi Kerry M. Olitzky

For People of All Faiths, All Backgrounds

JEWISH LIGHTS Publishing
Woodstock, Vermont

Life's Daily Blessings:
Inspiring Reflections on Gratitude and Joy for Every Day,
Based on Jewish Wisdom

2009 Quality Paperback Edition, First Printing
© 2009 by Kerry M. Olitzky

Grateful acknowledgment is given for permission to reprint an excerpt from "Between Godliness & Immortality" by Rabbi Harold M. Schulweis, © 2006 Valley Beth Shalom; www.vbs.org

Library of Congress Cataloging-in-Publication Data
Olitzky, Kerry M.
Life's daily blessings : inspiring reflections on gratitude and joy for every day, based on Jewish wisdom / Kerry M. Olitzky.—Quality paperback ed.
p. cm.
Includes index.
ISBN-13: 978-1-58023-396-5 (quality pbk.)
ISBN-10: 1-58023-396-1 (quality pbk.)
1. Jewish devotional calendars. 2. Jewish meditations. 3. Spiritual life—Judaism. I. Title.
BM724.O45 2009
296.7'2—dc22
                                                            2009001701

Manufactured in the United States of America
Cover Design: Melanie Robinson
Cover Art: Judy Sirota Rosenthal, from "*Sheheheanu*" lithograph; www.sirotarosenthal.com; (203) 281-5854.

For People of All Faiths, All Backgrounds
Published by Jewish Lights Publishing
A Division of LongHill Partners, Inc.
Sunset Farm Offices, Route 4, P.O. Box 237
Woodstock, VT 05091
Tel: (802) 457-4000   Fax: (802) 457-4004
www.jewishlights.com

For
Rabbi Eliot Malomet—
colleague, teacher, and friend.

Contents

ACKNOWLEDGMENTS

Like so many other books whose motivation arose in the mind of Stuart M. Matlins, publisher of Jewish Lights, this book owes its birth to the same source. I've written or cowritten several other books in this category, such as *100 Blessings: Daily Twelve Step Recovery Affirmations, Exercises for Personal Growth and Renewal Reflecting Seasons of the Jewish Year*; *Sacred Intentions: Daily Inspiration to Strengthen the Spirit, Based on Jewish Wisdom*; and *Restful Reflections: Nighttime Inspiration to Calm the Soul, Based on Jewish Wisdom*. Following their success, Stuart invited me to put into words what I teach and what we both believe: we are able to look at the world around us and see how it is filled with opportunities for blessing. The book is thus designed to help others to do the same.

This book would not have been possible without the staff support at Jewish Lights Publishing. In particular I want to mention Emily Wichland, vice president of Editorial and Production, who has many times worked her magic with my words; Melanie Robinson, who designed the book cover; and Kate Treworgy, who is so helpful in getting the message of the book out to people so that they can hear it.

I also want to thank my friend Elliot Danto for reading each word with a critical eye from the perspective of an everyday Jewish believer who yearns for the spiritual connection within the context of the organized Jewish community. He asked me many important questions about my understanding of the texts that I chose for inclusion in this volume.

I also thank Rabbi David Levy for allowing me to use some of the material he gathered for his "meaning of life" project.

I must acknowledge staff and board colleagues at the Jewish Outreach Institute who provide me with support and encouragement, especially our president Alan Kane, who took up the reins during a difficult transition in the life of the organization and helped to guide it forward.

Finally, I thank my family, who nurtures me with blessings each day: Sheryl, Avi and Sarah, Jesse and Andrea. It is because of them that every word I write has meaning. I feel blessed every day because of them.

How to Use
This Book

This book is designed to be used as a lens for daily life. It follows the daily Gregorian calendar, because that is the primary calendar that most of us use to navigate our lives. But it is interwoven with the Jewish calendar and various events that mark the North American cultural calendar, as well. For those who regularly use the fixed blessings of Jewish religious life, you may find this book a helpful companion. Alternatively, it can be used on its own. Many of the entries are tied to the themes that emerge from the calendar. Sometimes dates that have become part of the fabric of North American society are noted. At other times, attention is given to the general season. Since Jewish calendar dates are generally not tied to the secular calendar, I have included them in the month or season in which they occur.

You may want to read an entry from the volume to start your day. Or you may find it a helpful way to reflect on the day's events at its end. As an alternative, you may want to consider taking a few moments out of your day—sometime in the middle—to read a selection as a means of helping you find an anchor in an otherwise chaotic world. Leave it near your bed. Put it in your briefcase or purse. Or keep it on your desk. You should feel comfortable reading it anywhere.

Don't worry about adhering specifically to the daily format. Read a section a day, or two. Look for an entry that reflects your feelings or need for a particular day. Flip through the pages. Read and reread entries that speak to you, whenever they speak to you.

Since this book is not written as an evolving narrative, it is not a book that you read quickly and then put aside. Rather, take time to read each entry slowly. Savor each word, especially the texts that begin each selection. You may find that some of them will serve you as a *kavvanah* (sacred mantra) for the day. Whatever approach you take to this book, let the blessings of the day buoy you and help you to shape your relationship with the holy and the sacred.

At the back of this small volume you will find additional resources, including a glossary of words and ideas, brief biographies of authors whose texts are quoted, and a glossary of sources for the quoted texts used throughout. It is my hope that these helpful tools will make understanding the material in the book more meaningful and accessible.

INTRODUCTION

Blessings abound in Judaism. Most of them are fixed pieces of liturgy that help to establish a relationship between the individual and the Divine by referencing a particular ritual or activity. So we say a blessing over wine or bread or Shabbat candles and dozens of other activities, all activities that are part of daily life or help to elevate secular days and make them sacred.

Judaism also contains in it the notion of blessing that is a result of our simply being in the world and appreciating the many blessings that God has given us. This is the blessing of the everyday. The notion of radical amazement, a phrase coined by twentieth-century theologian Rabbi Abraham Joshua Heschel to describe the ongoing experience of the sacred in the world, is the pivot on which this entire book is based. While some people spend their lives searching for the mountaintop experience on a regular basis, I believe that the experience of Sinai can be found in the everyday blessing of the world that surrounds us.

Jewish tradition suggests that we try to say one hundred blessings each day. We are provided with guidance as to how, when, and sometimes where these blessings are to be said. This book provides a lens through which we can see everything in our world as blessed and be motivated to say a blessing as a result, whether it is for one activity or for one hundred.

JANUARY

The Blessing of Beauty

JANUARY 1

I always want eyes to see the beauty of the world, and to praise this wondrous beauty that is without exception, and to praise the One who did it, so beautifully, fully, to praise fully, so full of beauty. *
NATAN ZACH

The Israeli poet's powerful words continue: "I shall not cease from praising. Indeed to praise, I shall not cease to praise. And when I fall, I shall yet rise, if only for a moment, lest they say, 'He fell but he rose again for a moment to praise with final eyes.' For that which is to praise, I shall not cease." What better way to begin the year and to begin this volume. It reflects a recommended posture for living—to look at the world around us in "radical amazement," a phrase coined by twentieth-century theologian Rabbi Abraham Joshua Heschel to describe how the individual should look at the world that surrounds us. This posture encourages us to praise the Source of all, recognizing that just to possess the ability to gaze upon such beauty, and being given the privilege to do so, is to live a life of blessing. So

*This poem is translated from the Hebrew by my friend Rabbi Shaul Feinberg.

we begin the year, as we begin each day, awestruck with appreciation and gratitude.

Sometimes it is not so easy to gain such a perspective on the world around us. Daily living can be difficult. And events do happen that darken our personal world, as well as the larger world in which we live. But that is what is so transformative about such an approach. Even amidst the sadness that constantly threatens to color things, our lives are filled with so much to appreciate. And when we forget, all we have to do is look outside and we will see so much to persuade us. Breathe deeply and say, "Thank you." It is a blessing to be alive.

God as the Source of All Things

January 2

The earth is Adonai's, as well as everything in it.
Psalm 24:1

As part of the morning prayer service, we recite a specific psalm that is identified with a particular day of the week. Each day has its own psalm. The verses of the psalm help to frame our outlook on the specific day—and on the days ahead—until we reach their peak on Shabbat. On first read, the verse that is cited above from one of these psalms seems straightforward: God is the Source of all things in the universe. Enough said. No news here for believers. It is what one would expect of a religious Judaism. But there is a spiritual lesson contained in the verse that is more than just the articulation of a fundamental tenet in Judaism. Through a deeper appreciation of its meaning, we may be able to bring ourselves closer to Shabbat—the end of the workweek—experience for which we may be preparing.

This verse teaches us that we really own nothing in this world. What we consider our possessions—even the wealthy among us who have acquired riches through long hours of hard work unassisted by others—are merely lent to us for the time that we are making our journey through this life on earth. We can even feel this in the Modern Hebrew way of expressing ownership: *yesh li*, it is mine but only for a limited period of time, only while it is in my temporary possession. On Shabbat, when no business is transacted, when we cannot acquire goods and call them our own, we learn about the way the world will one day be, when what we own will not distinguish us from our neighbors or separate us from them. Then it will be truly Shabbat and we will feel its blessing every day.

Entering into Dialogue with the Divine

JANUARY 3

Thank you, God, for making me according to Your will.
FROM THE MORNING BLESSINGS, SAID UPON RISING

The alarm rings and it is a new day, the beginning of a new week. Each day, our morning begins with a familiar routine, a series of activities that have become our a.m. ritual. Some people anticipate the morning by setting the coffeemaker on a timer the night before, so that the coffee might be ready even before we are. And the morning paper is delivered before many of us are even out of bed. Our morning ritual is perfectly timed, the result of our having gone through it so many times before, fine-tuning here or there, adding or deleting a step along the way as our lives have evolved and the constellation of our family has changed as well. Some things take less time as we grow older, and other things take just a little longer. The seasons impact as well. More clothing usually means taking more time to get dressed.

Before the tradition of Jewish liturgy became so fixed, each step in this routine was assigned an accompanying blessing so that before we were fully dressed in the morning and ready to leave the house, we might have already recited a couple of dozen blessings, well on our way to the Rabbinic goal of saying one hundred blessings every day. These blessings described individual activity in such a way as to make sure we realized the ultimate Source of the activity, regardless of how mundane the action. Slowly, most of these blessings lost their place as partners to our early-morning routine and resurfaced as part of the fixed liturgy for the morning prayer service—and are found there in the prayer book. For those who maintain a spiritual practice, such as praying each morning at home, these blessings are said in close proximity to where they were originally intended. But for those who pray at the synagogue or elsewhere in the midst of a community, they have taken on new meaning and transcended the original context. They don't seem to any longer mean what they were originally intended to highlight and acknowledge. Yet, through these blessings, we have established a new routine, for they provide us with a foundation on which to stand stalwart and firm as we enter into our daily morning dialogue with the Divine. The traditional formula of blessing (*Barukh atah Adonai*) is our way of entering that dialogue with the Divine, and its daily repetition helps us to maintain it.

The Holiness of Rest

JANUARY 4

Remember the Sabbath day and keep it holy.
EXODUS 20:8

This is a statement that is familiar to many people. Although we may not be able to locate its precise location in the Torah, we certainly know it is one of the Ten Commandments (the only holy day mentioned among them). Some people may read this statement from Exodus and think that it refers to Shabbat observance, however broadly it may be defined. Thus, divine instruction would be restricted to the period of time just before Friday sunset (eighteen minutes to be exact, according to tradition) to just after Saturday sunset (forty-two minutes by most people's reckoning, although some people wait an additional thirty minutes just in case). But this sacred obligation transcends any specific period of time. It is a mitzvah to be observed all the time. So we work toward it all week long.

How do we start out the morning, the first of a new week, remembering Shabbat? The answer is in the commandment itself. We remember Shabbat by keeping it *holy*, that is, wholly separate, and not allowing the mundane of the everyday to enter its precincts. Instead, we allow its holiness to infuse the rest of the week. Here is the way the spiritual logic works. One of the ways we prepare for the following Shabbat is by allowing the experience of the previous Shabbat to inform the everyday. So we slow down just a little bit. We take ourselves a little less seriously. We allow our work (what we were called by God to do with our lives) to take precedence over our jobs (the position that we hold).

Praise for Work

JANUARY 5

Let your deeds sing your praise.
RABBI PAUL STEINBERG

The tendency of people is to sing their own praises. It seems like just part of human nature, and we tend to do so without thinking much about it. After all, if everyone else does so, why shouldn't we? Weren't we taught to look out for ourselves—'cause no one else will? Perhaps we share our successes with others, or run the risk of bragging about them, because we are afraid that no one will know about them. They might otherwise be overlooked. We want to make sure that when we are compared with others, we don't come up short, as if it is some kind of zero-sum game. All of us want to be recognized and remembered for what we do.

The above bit of folk wisdom from a late colleague is spun from familiar sources. But it is something that he was fond of saying quite regularly. So I always associate it with him even if it is now part of the richly hued tapestry of common folk wisdom. For some, his approach may be difficult to follow. But it is really a simple thing to remember whenever we feel the urge to shower ourselves with praise: don't talk; just do. Let others do the talking. We have to focus on the doing. We will discover that the blessing we find is in doing the deed itself rather than receiving any praise for it. And others will be blessed as a result.

The Blessing of Strangers

JANUARY 6

What are you seeking?
GENESIS 37:15

This verse emerges from the section of text that is part of the extensive section referred to as the Joseph narrative in the Bible. It seems like a simple question without any particularly profound consequences. This is the kind of question that seems like it might come directly out of a Chasidic story. You know the genre—profound and somewhat elusive. It is also the kind of question I like to ask myself regularly that has the added emphasis of coming from a sacred—divine—source. Because of the specific context of the verse in the biblical story of Joseph, I like to call this text "the blessing of strangers."

At this point in the story, Joseph has been sent to look for his brothers, who are shepherding their flocks. Although their father, Jacob, knows of the antagonism that Joseph's brothers feel toward him, Jacob sends him out to look for them nonetheless. On the road, Joseph encounters a man, a stranger, and asks for directions. But the stranger insightfully asks him, "What are you seeking?" This is an existential question. Sometimes, the most profound questions, the ones that direct our lives in unpredictable ways, are asked by people whom we don't know, with whom we have momentary encounters. This one question sets Joseph on a path that changes his personal journey and all of Jewish history

The next time you ask for directions, the next time you encounter a stranger, be attentive. The answer you receive may change your life.

Partnership

JANUARY 7

*Two are better than one, for they shall
have a good reward for their toil.*
ECCLESIASTES 4:9

In an age of individualism, this note by the biblical writer named Kohelet (Ecclesiastes) is important for us to remember. It isn't that if you work together, your reward will be greater—although that might be so, since the effort is twice as much, or even more, than when an individual works alone. What Kohelet is trying to teach us is that when you work with someone else, the reward—which is the literal translation of the Hebrew word *b'rakhah* (blessing), according to my teacher Rabbi Chanan Brichto—is in the relationship that can evolve as a result of your working together. When you work with someone, when you share the intimacy of the creative act, unparalleled bonds can be forged between you.

This notion also teaches us a core value in Jewish life. Judaism is lived in community—even if that community is made up of only two individuals. That is why the study unit called *chevruta* (study buddy or cooperative learning) is a pair. It is better not to be alone. It is better not to study alone. It is better not to work alone. The solitary life may give us certain insights. It may help us to be reflective, but it is not to be prolonged or sustained as a lifestyle. Jewish tradition generally encourages us to retreat into activity, not away from it.

Kohelet's statement is not about romantic encounters. It is a statement about basic living. Just as Judaism suggests that the relationship between the individual and God can take us to the mountaintop, it also says that blessing can be found in the relationship we nurture with others.

The Simplest Pleasures

JANUARY 8

Eat honey, because it is good.
And the honeycomb will be sweet to your palate.
PROVERBS 24:13

While this teaching is contained in the book of Proverbs, it could have just as easily been part of a collection bearing the name of something like "the important things I learned in kindergarten." To me, honey is one of the simplest pleasures of life. We use it to sweeten our tea. We add it to cakes for the Rosh Hashanah holiday. Or, as kids, we just enjoy it like candy. While those who harvest it may have to be careful not to be stung by bees who are protecting their honeycomb, those of us who enjoy honey appreciate it for its basic quality: it is simple and sweet.

This statement encourages us to develop an appreciation for the simple pleasures in life. Moreover, it provides us with a motivation to actually go out and look for those simple pleasures—for they surround us. But too often we are simply unaware of them.

The author of Proverbs wants to remind us that such pleasures are out there. But it doesn't mean that we will benefit from their blessing. Instead, we have to go out and actively look for them. Once we start looking, it is they who will begin to find us.

What We Control

JANUARY 9

The world is not an illusion.
RABBI TERRY BOOKMAN

No matter what various secular philosophers might theorize, the world as we know it is real. As a result, it isn't perfect. But that is not news. We confront the challenges of daily living each day. And in the context of daily living, we reap the benefits and accept the burdens of our lives.

Rabbi Bookman goes on to tell us, "The pain brought to us by others and by the world itself is real. There are things we simply cannot change. And there are circumstances that are truly beyond our control. This is reality. But we can always choose our response. And we can change ourselves. How we

respond to a situation, any situation, is always our choice."*
And that is the important part of his lesson. We may not be in
control of the world around us, but we are in control of our
response. Just as the world is not an illusion, neither is our
ability to respond to it.

If when we see the world, we see its beauty and its blessings,
then that is the way the world is. And if we only see the under-
side of the world and its ugliness, then that is the only way the
world will be. Open your eyes and see what you can see. What
we see in the world is ours to behold.

The Blessing of Sacred Study

JANUARY 10

Praised are You, Adonai our God, Sovereign of the universe,
who makes us holy with mitzvot
and instructs us to busy ourselves
with the words and works of Torah.

DAILY BLESSING FOR STUDY

According to the Mishnah, most mitzvot (sacred obligations)
have specific parameters. But there are some that have no specific measurement. Among others, study has no limits. The regular study of sacred texts keeps us centered and focused. We
should do as much study of sacred text as is possible, for when
we study, says the tradition, the presence of God abides among
us. The Torah is a dynamic document. It becomes real when we
enter into it, when we become one with our ancestors, when we
live with them and struggle with them. And when we conclude our study, a bit of them is left in our soul, and we have
left a little of ourselves in the text.

*Terry Bookman, *The Busy Soul* (New York: Perigee Books, 1999), p. 98.

Some people begin their study with the traditional blessing noted above. And it is part of the regimen of daily prayer for those who follow the traditionally prescribed regimen of morning, afternoon, and evening prayers. It helps us to separate our sacred study from our everyday. And since the blessing is including in the morning, it is a way to prism the day ahead. Jewish tradition has offered us this formula that opens up the dialogue with the Divine and provides us with a sacred context for learning: "Praised are You, Adonai our God, Sovereign of the universe, who makes us holy with mitzvot and instructs us to busy ourselves with the words and works of Torah."

The Center of the World

JANUARY 11

When God returned us to Zion,
we lived as in a dream, then our mouths were filled
with laughter and our tongues flowed with song.
PSALM 126:1–2A, FROM THE PSALM SUNG BEFORE *BIRKAT HAMAZON* (GRACE AFTER MEALS) FOR SHABBAT (AND HOLIDAYS)

This psalm reflects the feeling of someone who has returned from exile. It specifically references the return of the Jewish people to Israel from the Babylonian exile. But it is also about the feeling of returning home after being away—especially for an extended period of time. Because I carry these words with me in my heart, they speak to me whenever I am fortunate to spend time in Israel or even when I read or hear about what is happening in that land of promise. It is an indescribable feeling of comfort and tranquility.

I have always considered Jerusalem to be the center of the world, certainly the center of my world. And it is this image, as articulated by the ancient psalmist, the one that introduces

Birkat Hamazon (Grace after Meals) on Shabbat and holidays, that best captures that feeling for me. It is even said that the Land of Israel is the place where heaven and earth touch. What better image could one desire to describe the feeling of being anchored in this world while reaching heavenward?

The psalmist's words also reflect a relationship with God, renewed, after a time of feeling distant and even abandoned. Upon realizing that the return to Israel is also reflective of a renewed relationship, the psalmist is overwhelmed by song and laughter. We can't always come back home physically, but we can all carry the feeling of home with us wherever we travel, wherever the journey of our lives takes us. May we be blessed with the knowledge and feeling that coming home awaits us all.

Waking Up

JANUARY 12

I am grateful to You, the living Sovereign,
for returning my soul to me as a result of
Your overwhelming compassion for me.
BLESSING SAID UPON RISING IN THE MORNING

Many people wake up, jump out of bed, and rush into their morning routine. Sometimes they have pushed the snooze button on their alarm one too many times and they are in a real hurry, so things are even more hectic than usual. A quick shower. Brush the teeth. Shave. Make-up. You know the rest. There are so many details to take care of before we leave the house. Few of us pause to reflect on the wonderment of waking up in the first place. Too many of us drop into bed at night totally exhausted and feeling overwhelmed, and yet we awaken to a new day renewed and refreshed. In our waking moments, we have the opportunity to express our gratitude to God, for restoring our souls to us, giving them back to us in better shape than they once were, certainly in better shape than they were when we went to sleep the night before. For those of us who are not great at constructing meaningful language in the early morning, the Rabbis have helped us out, urging us to recite these words upon rising: I am grateful to You, the living Sovereign, for returning my soul to me as a result of Your overwhelming compassion for me."

Some people whisper these words to themselves. Others recite them over and over as a *kavvanah*, a sacred mantra. And some softly sing them to themselves, growing in volume as they regain their strength and become fully awake, repeating them throughout the day. May a sense of gratitude and thanksgiving, whatever the shape of its expression, as well as the expression of wonderment at being alive, find a place in your thoughts throughout your day.

Loving the Stranger

JANUARY 13

The stranger who lives with you shall be to you like the native, and you shall love him [or her] as yourself; for you were strangers in the land of Egypt. I am Adonai your God.
LEVITICUS 19:34

I think about this text regularly. I wish that there was a better translation for the Hebrew word *ger* or a better way to express the sentiment of the text than using the word "stranger." Nevertheless, all of us know the feeling of being a "stranger," of feeling like we don't belong or are somehow out of place. This particular text—which is intentionally written in the form of a commandment—is repeated in the Torah more often than any other (over thirty times). We can therefore easily conclude that it is rather important, especially considering its ending. We should have no doubt that God is the source of this directive.

While this text finds its way into various other places in the Torah, it is intentionally included here in the biblical book of Leviticus, in what is called the *locus classicus* (the location that is well known). Leviticus is also known as *Torat Kohanim*, "the Torah [literally 'instruction book'] of the Priests." Elsewhere we are taught that the Jewish people should be considered "a nation of priests, a holy community" (Exodus 19:6). In other words, there are certain behaviors that are to set the Jewish people apart from the other nations of the world, and how it treats its newcomers should be one of the primary defining behaviors. In traditional Jewish circles, Leviticus (the third book of the Torah) is taught before Genesis (the first book of the Torah). Thus, the rules and regulations of Leviticus, including such statements, are considered of utmost importance.

So remember what it was like to feel like a stranger, and reach out to a newcomer with whom you come into contact. You will both be blessed as a result. The more you reach out, the more you will feel welcomed in.

Healing of Body

JANUARY 14

God, heal her please.
NUMBERS 12:13

This is Moses's simple but heart-wrenching plea to God to heal his sister Miriam. God, heal her please (*El na, r'fa na lah*).

Dr. Herbert Benson, well known for his work in mind-body medicine, suggests that we can ease our body's usual alert mode and—without undermining it—let it calm down and rest.

This is what he calls the relaxation response. In addition, he argues that the body and the mind "remember wellness." This "remembered wellness" can actually help heal the body when we are ill by bringing the wellness back—by "remembering" it: how we used to feel, the state prior to the onset of our illness.

Taking Benson's theory one step further and placing it within a religious context, we can "remember" our relationship with God even when—or especially when—in the midst of illness, or even facing the challenges of daily living, we may feel estranged from God, like God has forgotten about our relationship. In so doing, we can bring God's healing presence into our midst. Framed a little differently, God's presence seems to increase our own ability to heal. And we feel blessed as a result.

The Absence of Loneliness

JANUARY 15

Judaism teaches that loneliness is ultimate only in the absence of God. God can see inside us, can understand us at levels that elude our friends, our family—even our own selves. God overflows boundaries and assures us that we are not alone.

RABBI DAVID J. WOLPE*

The benefit of an ongoing relationship with the Divine is that we never feel alone. As a result, it is in the loneliest periods of the day that we feel so not alone. And it is in those loneliest places we frequent that we feel connected to God. This is the counterintuitive nature of spirituality. And whether we foster that relationship through traditional prayer and ritual or we do so in other ways that nurture the spirit, the challenge remains

*Shma 24/457, September 1993.

the same. We are still obligated to working on developing an ongoing relationship with the Divine.

I rise early most days, often before anyone in my home—or neighborhood—is stirring. And that is when I appreciate my daily routine of early-morning davening (praying) the most. It is because when I feel most alone I also feel most connected to God. So I gently place my *tallit* (prayer shawl) on my shoulders and wrap *t'fillin* (prayer box) around my arm and place it on my head. These acts awaken my spiritual sense and ready me for my prayers, which, in turn, help prepare me for the day ahead. And while praying in community is preferred, and I do so most days, Rabbi Wolpe's words speak to me more profoundly when I pray alone. It is then that I am blessed with the realization that I am not alone, that I will never be alone.

The Blessing of Love

JANUARY 16

*Streams of water can't put out love,
nor can rivers sweep it away.*
SONG OF SONGS 8:7

The biblical book called the Song of Songs is generally associated with spring. It is really more a series of extended love poetry than it is song, although poetry is sometimes referred to as song. The Rabbis required that the book be read as part of the Passover celebration in the synagogue. While scholars disagree, the Rabbis also tell us that it was written by King Solomon in his youth, when he was smitten by love. Regardless of when it is required reading, Song of Songs has always spoken to me in the middle of winter, especially when living in climes where it is particularly cold and the winter is long and dreary. The vision of this text—and the buoyancy of the love that is expressed in it—may be all we need to transcend the winter and anything else that might threaten to weigh us down. As the author of the above text exclaims, love is so powerful that nothing can stop it.

Love is a unique force in the universe. That is why an entire book of the Bible is devoted to it. While the Rabbis also teach us that it is an allegory—really reflective of the love between the individual and God—it is primarily a basic book on love between two humans. It is this kind of love, as expressed in the pages of the Song of Songs, that raises both individuals heavenward. It makes the possessors of such love feel like they are divine, that nothing can transcend the bond that they enjoy with one another.

Love is that kind of blessing. It provides us with a lens through which we see the entire world differently.

Chastisements of Love

JANUARY 17

God reproves the one who is loved just as
a parent might (do so) with a beloved child.
PROVERBS 3:12

This traditional notion of what the Rabbis call "chastisements of love" (*yissurim shel ahavah*) is a difficult notion to grasp and to accept. None of us like to be reproved. And we certainly don't want to think that we are deserving of such reproof from God. I am not suggesting that we understand our suffering as corrective punishment from God. Nor do I think that we should see it as a test of the one who is suffering. The traditional understanding is that by embracing the suffering without questioning, we are demonstrating our love for God.

This understanding does not resonate with my own, nor do I suspect that it speaks to yours, the reader's. We do, though, need to find a way to accept criticism and reproof, regardless of the source. It is only by learning from our mistakes and the corrections of them that we can improve as individuals, as human beings. When we were young, we may have resented the authority of our parents and rejected their discipline. It is only later in life that we begin to understand that, for most of us, our parents corrected us out of love—and we are able to see it as a blessing.

Good News

JANUARY 18

Praised are You, Adonai our God, Sovereign of the universe, who is good and who does good.
BLESSING SAID UPON HEARING GOOD NEWS

As we have learned, the Rabbis suggest that we should try to say as many as one hundred blessings each day. While they had this specific number in mind, it is also a metaphor. While it encourages us to utter many blessings, what it really suggests is that we need to open our eyes in order to see the many blessings that surround us and acknowledge them. Expressing our appreciation to the Source of blessing is the way we acknowledge the many blessings in our lives.

This blessing uses the traditional Jewish formula for blessing (*Barukh atah Adonai*—Praised are You, God ...) and then continues by naming the specific experience for which we are expressing our gratitude to God. In doing so, it opens up discourse with the Divine and refreshes our relationship with God. We are reminded to utter such blessings because we too often take good news—and its Source—for granted.

But we do not live an isolated existence in which we experience only the good. Unfortunately, we also experience that which is not so good—and sometimes even bad, evil, tragic. While it is easier to express our appreciation for the good that we experience in our lives, it is very hard to utter anything that acknowledges the Source of life when something bad happens to us. And yet, according to Jewish theology, the Source is the same and must be reckoned with—and eventually accepted: Praised are You, Adonai our God, Sovereign of the universe, the true Judge.

Natural Beauty

JANUARY 19

Praised are You, Adonai our God, Sovereign of the universe, who creates the fruit of the tree.
BLESSING SAID UPON EATING FRUITS OF TREES

This appears to be a simple, straightforward blessing, one to be said routinely before eating a piece of fruit. But it takes on particular significance this month, as it is often in January (or sometimes February) that the festival of Tu B'shevat (also referred to as the Festival of the Trees) is celebrated. The festival has a technical reason for its development: it was the time of year in which all trees were assigned the same birthday and thereby their ages were reckoned in anticipation of a property tax of sorts. But Tu B'shevat has evolved into a sacred celebration of nature with a mystical twist to it, for nature has a way of bringing us closer to the Divine. So this blessing acknowledges the importance of trees and the natural world—and their role in raising us to levels of holiness. It also acknowledges with appreciation and gratitude the fruit of the trees that helps nurture and sustain us.

But what is really special about this blessing—and we are reminded of this notion each time we utter it—is the intimate partnership between God and humanity to take care of the trees so that they may indeed bear fruit. While the blessing is to be said before eating a piece of fruit, it really extends beyond this simple act. Its intention is to stop us from eating without thinking. Thus, the blessing should not be taken lightly or uttered by rote. It teaches us that our survival depends on nature in all its complexity. Just as we should never take the Source of life for granted, neither should we do so with the earth or its fruit. We are stewards of this planet, charged with the responsibility of protecting it so that others—in generations that follow—may continue to share in its blessings.

The Broken Heart

JANUARY 20

The only whole heart is the one that has been broken.
RABBI MENACHEM MENDL OF KOTZK

Thus, one cannot draw close to God unless one has been broken. But then what is it that awakens the individual to God's healing? Some will argue that it is the confrontation with death, personified in the Jewish tradition by the *malach hamavet* (the angel of death). But it is more than just an experience with the limits of our own finitude that opens us up to healing. Perhaps God does reveal the divine self more forcefully to those who are in need of healing. Or perhaps those in need of healing are more open to God's presence.

Certainly, we are all in need of God's wondrous healing. And while we prefer not to have to take this path toward the sacred, illness awakens us to the world and the reality of living. According to Rabbi David J. Wolpe, "Suddenly God seems closer because we are awake [sensitive to God's presence and our illness]."

We will all confront illness in our lives—whether it is a serious illness of our own or the illness of someone we love. And we will be forced to confront the Divine as a result. But as the Kotzker Rebbe—as Menachem Mendl was also known—has taught, it is only in brokenness that we will discover our whole self.

Opening the Eyes

JANUARY 21

Look, we have examined it. That is how it is.
Listen to it and you will know something.
JOB 5:27

It is hard to find inspiration in the biblical book of Job, the central character who loses all that he has—his children, his spouse, and his possessions. And it is not his faith that inspires us, since it often feels unreal and suspect. But it is the realism of parts of the text that buoys us. The verse that is cited above is taken from the mouth of one of Job's friends, Eliphaz, who attempts to explain why the things that happened to Job indeed occurred. Since this is a book of wisdom (garnered from the experience of living rather than divinely revealed), the words of Eliphaz ring true in this case.

Take a look at the world around you. Don't go through life with your eyes closed. Open your eyes, your heart, and your mind to all that you experience. And remember to take the advice of others who may have something to teach you.

It is hard to take the advice of others. We want to learn from our own experiences. But when someone has taken the time to examine something, pay attention. There may be a blessing hidden among what you may learn. It is yours to discover.

Separating Out the Sacred

JANUARY 22

*Praised are You, Adonai our God, Sovereign of the universe,
who distinguishes between the holy and the ordinary.*

BLESSING FOR MAKING *HAVDALAH* (SEPARATION) BETWEEN
SHABBAT AND HOLIDAYS AND THE REST OF THE WEEK

For those who are traditionally observant, the distinction between Shabbat and the rest of the week is sharp. Shabbat is spent at home, at the synagogue, or with friends. There is no telephone to intrude, no Internet to surf; we cannot even touch objects that are related to daily work. (This is what the Rabbis refer to as *muktzah*.) The end of Shabbat means that all of the rules of Shabbat are lifted and we go back to the world of work, movies, phones, and cars. Even among those who are more liberally inclined in their observance, it is not unusual to find people who do not participate in anything that reminds them of their workaday world. Whether it is refraining from doing anything that has to do with money or staying away from anything relevant to a person's job, Shabbat observance for liberal and traditional Jews is about creating a major distinction between Shabbat and the rest of life.

So when it comes time to the end of Shabbat, we make an explicit separation between the sacredness of the Shabbat we have just experienced and brace ourselves for what we might anticipate in the workaday world ahead—and mark it with a ritual, to breathe a little divinity into the process. While this blessing makes use of the standard formula for Jewish blessing (*Barukh atah Adonai* ...), it reads more like an affirmation of faith than a prayer, as if to say, "With the extinguishing of this candle, we leave the holy, the sacred, and reenter the everyday, the mundane, the ordinary—with a renewed sense of optimism and purpose."

Nevertheless, this transition carries with it a measure of anxiety. We really don't know what the week will bring. So this final blessing reminds us—even as it seems to suggest the opposite—that once we have fully experienced Shabbat, we can never again leave the sacred behind. As a matter of fact, what the *Havdalah* ritual seems to teach us is how in the ordinary we must learn to find the sacred.

If we can take a braided candle, a bit of spice, and a cup of wine and transform a few moments of time on Saturday night into a sacred experience, then perhaps we might be able to do the same in the hours and days that follow. But don't worry: when we forget how to do so or get so absorbed in our daily routine that we forget the message, then Shabbat and the *Havdalah* that follows will come again to remind us.

Paying Attention

JANUARY 23

Whatever happens has already been destined and is known.
ECCLESIASTES 6:10

This is a tough notion for most of us rationalists to absorb and acknowledge. Such an approach seems to assume that God is responsible for directing the universe and our actions. Thus, we have little choice in the matter. We are simply doing what we are supposed to be doing, acting out someone else's plan for our lives. But said differently, the text takes on a different notion. As my wife, Sheryl, likes to say frequently, "Nothing is a coincidence." This is particularly true when we think about things that "were meant to be." This feels especially true in terms love and of relationships.

So when I am in those uncanny situations that seem to be orchestrated by a power beyond the self (whom I acknowledge along with Jewish tradition as God), I say to myself, "What am I supposed to learn from what is taking place? What is it that God wants me to pay attention to?" I don't want to miss what God has gone to the trouble of placing in front of me—since it is indeed intended to take place and not some random group of unexplained coincidences.

Perhaps the real challenge is not to find a theology in what is occurring. Rather, it is to take whatever happens and find the personal blessing in it for ourselves. That is what God placed in the event for us to discover. Maybe that is the only blessing that we need.

Written Upon the Heart

JANUARY 24

I will ... write it upon their hearts.
JEREMIAH 31:33

These words, penned by the biblical prophet Jeremiah, have always stirred something in me. As a prophet, Jeremiah speaks for God. Referring to the stone tablets of the law, Jeremiah tells the people that divine instruction has to find its way into the hearts of the people and not remain encased in stone. Law, which for Jeremiah is shorthand for Jewish observance, has to take on a human dimension if it is to have any real purpose and meaning. It has to be more than just learning a group of "how-tos" or a set of specific behaviors. This is a particularly important notion for those of us who tend toward the rational, who intellectualize everything, who seek only to acquire more knowledge, often at the expense of feeling. Knowledge is no replacement for the spiritual, although one may lead us to the other. But it is only the combination of both that will take us to the Divine.

Thus, we have to learn to reach beyond the letter of the law and immerse ourselves in its spirit. Of course, Jeremiah was not just talking about Jewish law and observance. He was referring to life itself. And like Jewish law itself, Jeremiah's teaching contains a model for daily living. So learn what you can. And then let what you have learned enter your heart. It is there that you will find life's blessing.

Distinguishing Light from Darkness

JANUARY 25

Praised be You, Adonai our God, who gave the heart understanding to distinguish between day and night.
FROM THE MORNING BLESSINGS, SAID UPON RISING

While this is how the text is generally translated and understood, a more literal translation might yield " ... who gave the rooster the ability to distinguish between day and night." Another way of looking at it could be " ... who gave me the ability to be a rooster." Why would the Rabbis want to capture such a peculiar notion and make it part of the fixed early-morning prayers?

Day is associated with waking. It is filled with light. And night is associated with sleeping. It is marked by darkness. And the body, like the rooster, knows when it is time to arise in the morning—often aided these days by an alarm clock. Then we go about our daily routine. So sleep is a semi-death. Thus, it is a blessing to get up each morning, to arise from such a state of being. And the measurement of a successful awakening is, in fact, the ability to distinguish between sleeping and waking, night and day.

Leaving Egypt

JANUARY 26

*In every generation, we are to look at ourselves
as if personally delivered from Egypt.*

FROM THE PASSOVER HAGGADAH

This text is usually associated with Passover, in the spring (generally celebrated in the month of April). It appears here in the month of January because of the recognition of the Reverend Martin Luther King Jr. and his understanding of the delivery of the ancient Israelites as a model for the civil rights movement in America in the 1960s and beyond.

The Hebrew word for Egypt (*Mitzrayim*) is often translated as "the narrow places," those places that constrict us, that limit our ability to soar. My friend Rabbi Lee Diamond understands *Mitzrayim* as the state of "narrowness" and of "being blinded." It is from that place of darkness that we all have to be liberated.

Perhaps the message of Passover liberation is so all-encompassing that it extends far beyond the limits of the holiday or even the month in which it is commemorated. It colors the entire Jewish experience. Its message of unending optimism also insinuates itself into the entire calendar. Thus, this text reminds us that it is a curse to be a slave, irrespective of the nature of the enslavement, and it is a blessing to be liberated. But what causes the blessing to soar heavenward, and take us on its wings, is the message of unyielding hope that is held aloft along the way.

The Wonder of Torah

January 27

If the Torah is an empty thing, it is because of you,
because you don't know how to expound it.
GENESIS RABBAH 1:1

This seems rather harsh. If the Torah doesn't have anything to say, is it my fault? Shouldn't the Torah speak on its own? Why do I need to interpret it? I often say that the Torah exists only when we engage the text. While most of us think of the Torah as a physical object, a rolled parchment on which is written the sacred history of the Jewish people and its encounter with God separated into five books, the Torah is really far more dynamic. It is an evolving dialogue between the Jewish people and God. Consequently, if we want to add our voice to the dialogue, then we too have to engage the text and enter into a conversation with it. And that is when the blessing occurs. When we leave the dialogue, even if it is only momentarily, we are changed and so is the text. For when we leave our engagement with it, we leave a little of ourselves in it as well. In doing so, we add our voice to the collective memory of the Jewish people.

So if the "Torah is an empty thing," as the writer of the selection from the midrashic collection Genesis Rabbah suggests above, if we have not found a place for it in our lives, it is because we have chosen not to allow its words to enter our hearts and minds—where it belongs.

Learning about the Self

JANUARY 28

Turn it, and turn it again, for everything is in it.
PIRKEI AVOT 5:22

This text from the collection of pithy sayings of the Rabbis called *Pirkei Avot* says it all. The selection above could really serve as the foundation statement for the study of all of Jewish sacred literature. It is what motivates us to continue to explore the same text over and over again. Each time we study, we learn something new. But the purpose of studying Torah is not to learn more about the text. Rather, it is to learn more about ourselves. And as we grow, we change. So there is always something new to learn.

Turning implies action. The meaning of the Torah text is accessible, but it will not come to us on its own. We are the ones who have to pursue it. It is our obligation to turn it over and over, that is, if we want to discern what it has to offer, what it has to teach us. Only in the probing of the text will its blessing be revealed.

The Center Path

JANUARY 29

Either/or questions are not good for the Jewish people.
RABBI HAROLD M. SCHULWEIS

I have always appreciated this comment by Rabbi Schulweis. The wisdom that is implied by this statement is overwhelming, for the Jewish community often sets itself up this way. We should spend money on either this or that. We do things either this way or that way. And that unfortunate approach gets translated into the life of the individual. These are my only two choices, so I better decide which is the right path to take.

In a sermon delivered for Rosh Hashanah, the Jewish New Year, Rabbi Jan Katzew, director of Lifelong Jewish Learning for the Union for Reform Judaism, considered the question this way:

> We live in an either/or world. Either you are for us or against us. Either you are right or you are wrong. Either you are good or you are evil. Either you are rich or you are poor. Either you are old or you are young. Either you win or you lose. Either you are in or you are out.... It may be simple to live in an either/or world.... An either/or world is inhabited by two types of people, friends or enemies, citizens or barbarians, members or infidels, brothers or others, people who have the truth and people who do not. In extreme cases, an either/or world is divided between people I would die for and people I would kill, people of God and people without God. We are all witnesses to an either/or world, but we do not have to accept it and live according to its norms.

Perhaps we need to do what the medieval philosophers have advised us to do: find the golden mean. They understood this to mean the path between the two extremes. While some may find this an unwelcome compromise, others will see it as the place to find centeredness. And in that center, we may be able to find tranquility and blessing.

Asking for What We Deserve

JANUARY 30

*Would that I would get what I ask,
would that God would give me what I hope for.*
JOB 6:8

How would our lives change if we were given what we asked for? Better that we should strive toward what we deserve—rather than simply receive what we desire.

But this is not the context of Job's complaint. The entire book of Job is decidedly disillusioning and understandably so. Its main character, Job, loses all that he holds precious in his life. As a result, he seeks the end of his own life—if only God would grant him that wish. Sometimes life does not seem so blessed. Sometimes we feel that we cannot raise ourselves beyond our current circumstances. And as a result, we become paralyzed, unable to see the potential in anything, let alone ourselves.

No matter what happens in our lives, the challenge remains the same—to see life as a blessing and to see blessing in all that we do. Understanding this notion alone is a major step for most people. Coming to this understanding itself may be all the blessing we need.

Listening for God's Voice

JANUARY 31

These and [also] these are the word of the living God.
BABYLONIAN TALMUD, *ERUVIN* 13B

This text from the Talmud has become an idiom that has entered contemporary Jewish discourse, transcending its origi-

nal context. In this section of the Talmud, there are two opposing schools of thought. This is not unusual for the Talmud—
although people sometimes find it hard to understand how two
opposing approaches to Jewish life can exist side by side in this
authoritative volume of Jewish law. Referring to the opinions
of Hillel and the opinion of Shammai on a particular aspect of
Jewish law, both are considered valid expressions of Jewish
thought. Thus, the text should be understood as "These [opin-
ions] and those [opinions] are both the word of the living God
[even though the law follows Hillel]."

This teaches us that opposing positions have a legitimate
voice in community dialogue even when one position is given
authority over the other. It also teaches us that we have to
understand that even those positions with which we do not
agree deserve our attention.

When we can hear God's voice in the words of someone
with whom we do not agree, then we may have found a place
of blessing in an otherwise fractured world and be able to put
the world back together—as it once was—one piece (peace) at
a time.

FEBRUARY

Finding Wisdom

FEBRUARY 1

*Let your ear incline to wisdom and
your mind to comprehension.*
PROVERBS 2:2

While the biblical book of Proverbs is considered a general book of wisdom—that which is learned from experience—it is also an instruction manual of sorts. It is specifically designed to teach the young reader, especially the one close to leadership, how to function in society. Leaders are usually understood as those who are in power or have authority over the lives of others. Perhaps the book of Proverbs is specifically for young people, because the author knows that they have yet to figure out some of these things on their own, since they do not have the benefit of experience. The author of Proverbs, whom Jewish tradition names as King Solomon, wants to save them from the pain that is also part of the process, even if it is part of the normal process of growth.

This text may be considered the foundation text for the entire book, but it also offers insight for our daily lives. If we are to lead a life of blessing, then we have to pay attention to all of our experiences and the experiences of others. This is indispensable to our learning and growth. Moreover, we have to attend to these experiences long enough to gain an understanding of what it is that we have experienced.

Finding the Sacred Level

February 2

I have one rule in my life and live by it.
And that is that if you're not prepared to
defend it in public, don't do it.
Alan Dershowitz

Some people think that there is a difference between private acts and public acts in the same way that they may feel that it is all right to use certain language in some contexts but not in other contexts. Alan Dershowitz would disagree. What is appropriate is not necessarily determined by context. He has a more universal sense of what is right and what is wrong.

Perhaps we might put it this way: if you can't say a blessing before doing it, then don't do it. That poses quite a challenge to all of us. It means that all that we do has to be elevated to a sacred level. This notion acknowledges that what we do—even the slightest act—takes on significance, especially as it involves other people.

Think about it. Consider the various things that you have already done today. Even if you started your day with morning prayers or a spiritual regimen of some sort, could you offer a blessing before each other act? Would they be acceptable in the sight of God? Would you want to be remembered for what you have done?

Reaching This Moment

FEBRUARY 3

Praised are You, Adonai our God, Sovereign of the universe,
who has kept us alive, sustained us,
and brought us to this moment.
THE *SHEHECHEYANU* BLESSING,
SAID UPON REACHING A SPECIAL MOMENT IN TIME

While this blessing is prescribed for specific occasions, it is also a more spontaneous form of expression. We say it when family gets together, when we have reached a certain milestone, or more simply even when we acquire a new article of clothing. Some people think that this blessing is overused since it is said so frequently. But for those of us who have faced life-threatening trauma or disease, each moment is indeed a blessing, and we are grateful that we are still alive to experience the moment.

When I was only sixteen, my mother was diagnosed with breast cancer. Years later, at my ordination as a rabbi, she confided in me that she really never thought that she would witness that day ten years later and was profoundly grateful for the opportunity just to be there. While not all occasions are as momentous, and we don't all have the perspective of a survivor, this modest blessing that is taken for granted by many people actually teaches us that all events are life changing and all perspectives should be as profound.

The Gift of Faith

FEBRUARY 4

*Hope in a renewed future is one of the
most profound gifts of faith.*
RABBI DAVID HARTMAN

We seldom think of faith as a gift. But belief in God and the relationship that evolves from it can be a gift when we allow it to illumine our daily life. Nevertheless faith is not easy. It usually doesn't emerge or develop on its own. It takes work to make it work.

We may want to add to Rabbi Hartman's statement that such hope is not only a gift that results from faith. The expression of hope in the future is a profound act of faith itself. Such faith assumes the presence of a benevolent God in the universe, a God upon whom we can depend with certainty. And it is the relationship that we have or want to develop with God that fuels such a faith. This kind of profound hope through faith has driven the Jewish people throughout its history. As a result, it is part of our collective memory as well. Faith allows us the privilege of taking this memory and making it our own. The steps to get there are found in living a holy life, one blessing at a time.

The Refracted Light of the Divine

FEBRUARY 5

*When I pray, I speak to God.
When I study, God speaks to me.*
RABBI LOUIS FINKELSTEIN

Rabbi Finkelstein's notion of prayer is rather straightforward and a commonly accepted notion of prayer. We pray to God for a variety of reasons. Mostly prayer is about gratitude, praise, and entreaty. But the notion of studying as a path to God is fairly unique to Judaism. The study of a sacred text, especially if it is considered to be of divine origin, that is, a revealed text, creates a specific context for our dialogue. It is a way in which we can discern what God wants of us, what our work is to be in this world. In the refracted light of the Divine that emanates from the text and our study of it, we are able to see more clearly—and our relationship grows and deepens.

While study can be a lonely pursuit, it is more commonly pursued with others—generally in the form of what is called *chevruta* (study buddy learning). That is why the Rabbis teach in *Pirkei Avot* (3:3) that when two sit and discuss Torah, the *Shekhinah* (God's indwelling presence) rests among them. What better blessing can there be than for God to dwell among us when we study?

The Blessing of Community

FEBRUARY 6

Praised are You, Adonai our God, Sovereign of the universe, Knower of secrets.

BLESSING SAID ON WITNESSING AN ASSEMBLY
OF SIX HUNDRED THOUSAND OR MORE JEWS

This is indeed an unusual blessing. What would motivate the Rabbis to include it in the list of required blessings? Why would they include it among the various blessings that when combined help us to reach one hundred per day? It is true that there is a special feeling that emerges when we are gathered in community. Understanding the number six hundred thousand is critical to understanding the importance of this blessing. For six hundred thousand is the number of people who assembled at the foot of Mount Sinai waiting for Moses to return from his ascent up the mountain. It is six hundred thousand who gathered together to receive divine revelation. So it is this number—which we understand as a metaphor for a large number—that emphasizes the importance of community. Look at what can happen when large groups of Jews get together.

The blessing also says something about God as the "Knower of secrets." This is an unusual appellation for the Divine, especially in the context of a large assembly. But it is a recognition that each of these individuals contributes to the community in his or her own way—including you. That is why the rabbis say the Torah was given in six hundred thousand voices, so that each person might hear according to his or her own ability to do so. As the Knower of secrets, God knows what is in the hearts of the entire multitude.

Even if you are someone who prefers solitude and avoids crowds, look for the opportunity to participate in large gatherings of Jews. Once you are able to say this blessing, you will understand that it is the gathering with those who are committed to the same ideals as you that is really the blessing.

The Path of Holiness

FEBRUARY 7

I look at holiness as a process.
We are never there but we are always reaching.
RABBI MICHAEL L. KRAMER

Holiness is both a path and a destination. It is the path that we have to follow if we are going to get there, if we want to reach a level of holiness in our lives. The destination seems to move forward just as we are about to reach it. Some people may find this frustrating. But it is part of the counterintuitive nature of Jewish spirituality that I find elevating. While holiness is a level to be reached and it brings us heavenward, because it seems to be composed of infinite levels, we are always reaching higher and higher.

Too often we are taught about setting goals and reaching destinations. Schooling is not about learning, it is about preparing our resumes. We rush our lives forward in order to reach our career goals. And then we push our children forward so that they can become adults. When we pause, we realize that we have wasted time, perhaps the holiest gift of all.

Rabbi Kramer teaches us that holiness can be found in the process of trying to achieve holiness, rather than in its destination. When you realize that truth, then you can stop and say a blessing for each thing you encounter during your day, which is why the Rabbis encourage us to say so many blessings in the first place. It forces us to stop rushing, to pay attention to the life that surrounds us, and to find the holiness that exists in our midst.

Reborn Each Day

FEBRUARY 8

Believe that each day the world is created anew and that you yourself are born anew each morning. Then your faith will grow, and every day you will find yourself newly eager to serve God.
BAAL SHEM TOV

I have always found this notion to be among the most powerful in Jewish theology. We are born anew each day. We go to sleep at night, tired and overwhelmed. And sleep approximates death. Then we wake up the next day renewed and refreshed, ready for the day ahead. Somehow while we sleep, we are transformed. And we are reborn.

Reflecting on this notion brings me closer to God. As I roll out of bed in the morning, I am motivated to express my thanks and appreciation for the new day and the new me. The Rabbis understood this predilection. That is why they built a set of morning blessings to be uttered upon waking (which eventually made their way into the more formal morning liturgy). And with each blessing that we utter, we—and our daily rebirth—are affirmed.

A Strategy for Righteous Living

FEBRUARY 9

Turn away from evil and do good.
PSALM 34:15

This is a long-term strategy for righteous living that depends on a two-step process—and one that appears to require a great deal of energy. The psalmist is telling us what to do, even though it is our responsibility to figure out how to do the "what" on our own, that is, once we figure out what it is that we are being asked to do. The psalmist's first point is clear. It is what might be called a non-action. We should avoid wrongdoing. But then comes the psalmist's second point: the required action on our part. We have to go out into the world and do some good. Now this sounds like a plan.

Even without any detail, I wonder why a plan for leading a life of blessing needs to be so complicated. Maybe there is a simpler way for us to reach the same goal. Perhaps if we spend our lives doing good, then evil might fall away on its own.

Becoming Who We Are

FEBRUARY 10

If I try to be someone else, who will be like me?
YIDDISH PROVERB

Like most proverbs, Yiddish folk sayings pack a powerful punch. They become even more powerful when we consider who is delivering them. In my case, it was often my Russian grandmother, of blessed memory, who towered at under five feet at her greatest height. Yet she stood taller than all of the other members of our family.

This notion acknowledges our uniqueness in the world and the opportunity we have to make unique contributions to the world as well. The morning blessings that are part of the daily liturgy are all about us thanking God for making us who we are as distinct human beings. We stand before our Creator and say, "Thank You for making me who I am—the way that I am." It is now up to us to demonstrate to God that it was worth the effort, because there is no one else to complete our work in the world, what we are supposed to be doing.

Lead Me to Blessing

FEBRUARY 11

*Fill me with Your spirit. Let me open my heart to You
that I become aware of Your indwelling presence.
I ask this gift in humility, trusting to
Your grace in the knowledge that the hungry heart
seeking You may find You within itself. Holy One,
give me tranquility of spirit and with it, the will to
work for righteousness with all Your might. So will
Your grace and power lead me to blessing.*

RABBI ISRAEL MATTUCK, ADAPTED BY RABBI CHAIM STERN

Whether you follow the traditional guidelines of daily prayer or you have your own daily spiritual routine, I find this *kavvanah* (sacred mantra) exceptionally helpful in directing my intention for the day ahead. So I repeat these words aloud and reflect on them, hoping that I am capable of having the words that leave my mouth then enter my heart.

Rabbi Mattuck's words invite God's presence into our lives. They also provide us with a plan for spiritual living. If we are successful in bringing God into our lives and humbling ourselves in the divine presence, then we might be able to find tranquility, righteousness, and blessing. With it comes the realization that it is not possible to achieve it on our own.

Leaving Fear Behind

FEBRUARY 12

The world is a narrow bridge.
The key to its crossing is not to be afraid.
RABBI NACHMAN OF BRESLOV

These words, especially when set in Hebrew song, may be familiar to many. They are perhaps the words for which Reb Nachman is best known. But seldom do we reflect on the idea that is inherent in his message. He offers us insight about the afterlife and our role in this world, but Jews don't talk much about the afterlife or the world-to-come.

Reb Nachman acknowledges this can be a difficult world in which to live. He speaks about life as a narrowness, the narrowness of the bridge that leads us elsewhere. This narrowness can be restrictive, confining, and limiting. As we navigate this bridge—which is our life—we encounter the challenges of everyday living. It is to be expected, for this world is not perfect. His central principle, and that of Judaism, is to confront the world and its challenges boldly, never to be afraid. The ultimate dissolution of fear comes from the realization that this life is only a passage into the next life: a messianic time when all those things that we fear, everything that causes us spiritual pain, will be removed from our midst, forever. Once we come to this realization, we might be able to see each day on this earth as indeed a blessing, for each day takes us further on the road.

The Blessing of Kindness

FEBRUARY 13

When I was young I admired clever people.
Now that I am old, I admire kind people.
RABBI ABRAHAM JOSHUA HESCHEL

This is the kind of insight that younger people may find hard to grasp. Yet it is readily apparent to those who are older. It is an especially difficult notion to grapple with, considering the fast-paced world in which most of us live. Employers are always looking for innovation from their employees. This is an important ingredient if we are to get ahead of the competition. And if we want to succeed, we have to be on the cutting edge, regardless of the discipline or vocation in which we work.

Perhaps it was Rabbi Heschel's age that brought him to this realization. Maybe the idea evolved as a result of the life he lived, beginning in Poland, and being rescued from the Nazis during World War II and brought first to England and then to the United States. Or maybe he gained this perspective simply by using a Jewish prism through which to view life.

See if Rabbi Heschel is right by performing a simple experiment. Today, don't spend the day being clever. Instead, spend today being kind. Then you will bring blessing into the lives of others—and, in return, you will find your life blessed, as well.

Freedom

FEBRUARY 14

*Being free means that I am in the place
I am supposed to be.*
RABBI SHLOMO CARLEBACH

We often think about freedom in terms of the various rights provided us by the U.S. Constitution. This boils down to looking at freedom as doing whatever we want. That is what is so intriguing about Rabbi Carlebach's comment. He is writing about a freedom that is profoundly spiritual. His "place" is not a physical space. Rather, it is a spiritual space in which he can find himself in relation to God.

Rabbi Lawrence Kushner likes to put it another way. He says that God puts us where we are supposed to be. And if we aren't where we are supposed to be, we shouldn't worry, since we won't be there very long.

The challenge, of course, is discerning that place. Maybe it is the special place that the Rabbis of the Talmud suggest is the place where heaven and earth touch. Once we reach that place, we can utter a blessing of thanksgiving for having arrived.

Helping God Finish the World

FEBRUARY 15

*Without human participation, God remains
incomplete, unrealized. It is up to us to actualize the
divine potential in the world. God needs us.*
RABBI DANIEL MATT

Rabbi Matt's conclusion is rather startling. We usually think of God as in need of nothing. That is what is so appealing about Rabbi Matt's mystical notion. Not only is the world unfinished without our partnership, even the divine self is incomplete without us.

That is quite a responsibility for us as humans. We have to complete the creation of the world, and we have to complete God. The latter is accomplished by making sure that the divine potential, which already exists in the world, is fully realized. And this can only happen when we are prepared to act accordingly. These are acts of kindness and goodness to those around us, those whom we know and love, and those whom we don't know and don't love.

Begin your day with blessing. Then make sure that all that you do in the hours that follow reflects what you have just uttered.

The Blessing of Strangeness

February 16

Praised are You, Adonai our God, Sovereign of the universe, who makes the creatures different.

BLESSING SAID UPON SEEING STRANGE-LOOKING PEOPLE OR ANIMALS

Some people may become indignant on the first reading of this blessing. We may even express outrage. After all, the Jewish tradition is supposed to be sensitive to all. And who are we to determine who is strange looking? We might be the strange-looking people in the eyes of others. Perhaps such a blessing may be appropriate for animals, but it does not seem appropriate for people.

If we are honest with ourselves, we know that we make judgments about people based on their physical appearances, as hard as we try not to do so. So we have to admit that the world is not always beautiful. Even creation has its dark side.

What this blessing forces us to acknowledge is that everyone is created by God, all in the divine image. But in expressing a blessing, we are affirming this perspective on life and reminding ourselves that all are reflective of the Divine—even the so-called strange looking among us.

Teach Me

FEBRUARY 17

Teach me, O God, a blessing,
a prayer on the mystery of a withered leaf,
on ripened fruit so fair,
on the freedom to see, to sense,
to breathe, to know, to hope, to despair.
LEAH GOLDBERG, TRANSLATED BY PENINA PELI

Sometimes the words of blessing spontaneously emerge from our lips. Unaided, they erupt from our hearts. But for most of us, such words do not always come easily. It is why the Rabbis have fashioned words of blessing for us—so that we are not left on our own to do so. But sometimes these words do not come at all, even when they are specifically written out.

These lines are part of a poem by the Israeli poet Leah Goldberg. In it, the writer beseeches God to help us form the words of blessing that express our appreciation for the world around us and all that we find in it. She is asking for more than just a writing lesson. She wants God to teach us how to see the world in such a special way. Goldberg acknowledges that it is hard to find the right words of blessing even when we are motivated to express ourselves. With the right words come an ability to hope and to despair, and to know. She concludes that this process is key to life itself—just to breathe.

Mending the World

FEBRUARY 18

*Blessed are You, Adonai our God, Ruler of the universe,
for giving us the opportunity to mend the world.*
RABBI RON KLOTZ

While this is not a traditional blessing—that is, not one of the list of blessings penned by the Rabbis to be among the one hundred that are to be said each day—it certainly contains what might be called traditional sentiments. We are each obligated to help repair the brokenness in the world, and in others. Of course, we may be simply motivated to do so because it is the right thing to do. But we also want to recognize that when we do so, we are contributing to God's work in the world. In repairing what is broken and working to bring perfection back to the world by healing it and those who inhabit it, we are acting as channels through which God's presence flows into the world.

The blessing that Rabbi Klotz wrote acknowledges the sacredness of such an act. It is a privilege to join with God in order to fix what is broken in the world. But the world is not alone in its need of repair. When we contribute to fixing the world, we often end up healing what may be broken in ourselves.

Making Peace

FEBRUARY 19

May the One who causes peace to reign in the high heavens let peace descend on us, on all Israel, [and all the world], and let us say, amen.

FROM THE LITURGY

This prayer is repeated in a variety of contexts in the liturgy throughout the day, because it is of utmost importance. Some people have added the words in brackets to the traditional text, because they believe that our prayer for peace should not be limited to the Jewish people. Such prayers need to be extended to all people throughout the world. And there is no greater gift or blessing than peace—whether it comes in the form of personal tranquility or the relationship between the nations.

I like to repeat it to myself throughout the day. It reminds me of the work that is ahead of me. The prayer and what it represents is not just about conflict between nations. It is also about the relationships between individuals—even family members. So if I can do one thing each day to limit conflict among people, then I have helped to bring peace from the heavens to the earth.

The Gates of Righteousness

FEBRUARY 20

Open for me the gates of righteousness;
I will enter them and give thanks to God.
PSALM 118:19

This text from Psalms has made its way into the liturgy as part of the *Hallel* psalms that are recited on festivals and at the beginning of new months. It represents a special plea to God. A less poetic version might read something like this: "If You, O God, direct me toward a life of righteous living, then I will indeed live such a life and express my thanks to You for doing so [for opening the gates] and allowing the privilege to live such a life."

This is often the way it is. We strive to lead a good life, but we cannot do so without some guidance. So we ask God for direction for our lives. When that direction comes, we have to be prepared to then live the spiritual life that we seek to live— to enter the gates of righteousness.

Transparent Prayer

FEBRUARY 21

Pray only in a room with windows.
BABYLONIAN TALMUD, *BERAKHOT* 34B

This is the basis for the architectural ruling that requires synagogues to have at least one window of clear glass in their sanctuaries. Some attempt to embrace the requirement fully. Others satisfy the law by simply including a small bit of clear (or translucent) glass among their stained glass windows. And, of course, there are some synagogues that don't take the issue seriously at all—or they may be basement synagogues or impromptu prayer spaces in which such an approach may be impossible.

It is true that God can be found anywhere. It is also true that prayer can therefore be recited anywhere. However, this text from the Talmud reflects an important posture to be undertaken for prayer. We may want to retreat in our prayers, to shut out the world around us. We may wrap ourselves in a *tallit* (prayer shawl) to try to do so and sing *niggunim* (wordless chants) to help us shut out all of the noise in the world. But both take us only momentarily to that place that transcends the rational world. We cannot pray without a direct connection to the outside world. Our prayers gain their footing in this world. The window allows us to see what is going on all around us, because that is the world in which we live and the world that we strive to perfect.

Letting Go of Anger

FEBRUARY 22

Bear in mind that life is short, and that with every passing day you are nearer to the end of your life. Therefore, how can you waste your time on petty quarrels and discords? Restrain your anger, hold your temper in check, and enjoy peace with everyone.

RABBI NACHMAN OF BRESLOV

Some may find this a depressing notion—the realization that our life on earth is time limited. But Rabbi Nachman is attempting to teach us a profound lesson that is easier to understand as we grow older. Those many things that seem so important—and seem worth arguing and getting upset over—are truly irrelevant. They have no lasting value. None. Rather, the relationships we have with others are what are most important. He goes so far as to say that fostering peace between people should be the most important guiding value for our lives.

If we do not let go of the anger that we have for others and the resentments that may be building up, we will be unable to pray. When our relationship with others is strained, especially when we are speaking of our neighbors, those with whom we work, or those in our synagogue community, our relationship with the Divine is also at risk. The solution? Remember Rabbi Nachman's three basic principles: Restrain your anger, hold your temper in check, and enjoy peace with everyone.

The Right Time to Pray

FEBRUARY 23

May this be an acceptable time for my prayer.
PSALM 69:14

Like so many texts that may be overlooked in the rapid flow of the liturgy, this psalm text has been taken into the liturgy during the Torah service for a holiday that occurs on a weekday. While it may seem out of place, since it is recited during a scheduled prayer service when the community is assembled, it is particularly poignant. It is we who have assumed the right time for prayer. We decide when it is time to pray and assume that it is also the right time for God to listen and respond. But we do so without any knowledge of the latter. So we hope that we have chosen wisely.

But there is more to this plea of the psalmist, for it emerges from the depth of the psalmist's being. We hope that we have chosen the right time and correct spiritual space to utter our prayers. Is it the right time for us to do so? May we find the proper *kavvanah* (sacred intention) so that our prayers may be heard in the spirit in which they are offered.

The Blessing of Inner Peace

FEBRUARY 24

Great is peace, since all blessings are in it.
LEVITICUS RABBAH 9:9

Usually we think about the variety of blessings that we are to offer during the course of the day. We think about their content as related to a specific task. Blessings for food. Blessings for ritual acts. With very few exceptions, we say the blessing and then perform the task. And the traditional form of blessing (usually "Praised are You, Adonai our God ... ") helps us place the act in the midst of our relationship with God. This raises what is often a mundane act to a sacred level. Morsels of food become part of heaven's bounty. The act of blessing thus is either a result of God's instruction to us or praise to God for sharing earth's produce with us.

This text reminds us that peace is a comprehensive blessing, because it contains all other blessings in it. Moreover, all blessings lead us to the same place: a place of peace. Living a life of blessing will provide us with a special kind of peace—inner peace.

The Gift of Love

FEBRUARY 25

*The whole value of a benevolent deed
lies in the love that inspired it.*
BABYLONIAN TALMUD, *SUKKAH* 49B

This reads sort of like this bit of oft-repeated folk wisdom: it is not the gift that is important but the sentiment behind it. This is a lesson that we are taught as children. We certainly appreciate this notion as parents when our children offer us something—when we know it comes directly from their hearts. Such gifts may be as simple as a plucked flower or a drawing. Nevertheless, some of us still have a hard time with the idea. We spend too much time approximating the value of a gift rather than its intent.

When we do good deeds, we are indeed giving gifts to others. Sometimes the gift is simply time—perhaps the most precious commodity of all. So when someone takes the time to do something for someone else or to select a gift for someone else, this is what gives it value. When we do for others, we are given a gift in return. That gift, the gift of love, inspires us to do the good deed in the first place. As a result, both giver and receiver are blessed.

Foresight and Ability

February 26

The difficult we do immediately.
The impossible takes a little longer.
David Ben Gurion

This quip was made by the first prime minister of Israel. He was speaking of the early pioneers who built the modern State of Israel. They indeed accomplished difficult tasks that seemed impossible. The early settlers of Israel drained the swamps in the north and caused the desert to bloom in the south. And they rebuilt the majestic city of Jerusalem. Their actions were manifestations of the drive that has perpetuated the Jewish people throughout its history. It is this drive that can motivate us, as well.

If something can be done, do it now. Don't put it off. If something is impossible to do, then do it tomorrow. Use today to plan how you are going to do it. And then when you have concluded the impossible task, thank God for giving you the ability and the foresight to do so.

The Beauty of the Unknown

FEBRUARY 27

The most beautiful thing we can experience is the mysterious.
ALBERT EINSTEIN

Some people like to figure everything out. They want rational explanations for everything. They feel like science has an answer. They may delude themselves into believing that if we can describe a phenomenon, such as an illness, then we will understand it. We would assume that a scientist like Einstein would have wanted the same, since he sought to understand the essential nature of things.

While Einstein surely found beauty in the simple things in nature, he understood them to be among the most mysterious. And those he found the most beautiful of all. So as you go about your day today, don't try to figure everything out. Instead, luxuriate in the mysterious, in the things that you do not know, that you may never know. And realize that just because you don't understand the mysteries of life and the world that surrounds you, it doesn't mean that God didn't have a plan for it. Your wonderment may indeed be part of the plan.

The Proximity of Redemption

FEBRUARY 28

*Peace comes to us in the recognition that even in
our weakest and most fragile moments,
redemption can be achieved.*

RABBI EDWARD FELD

In this text, Rabbi Feld offers us an important lesson about the challenges of daily living. It may be easy to speak of the peace between nations, of the absence of war and armed conflict, even if we have little control over it. War may feel distant from our lives when it is fought on foreign soil. But Rabbi Feld is not speaking of world peace in this text. He is speaking about an inner peace, a sense of tranquility and centeredness. Thus, he puts to rest, at least momentarily, the struggle of faith that has become the hallmark of much of Jewish theology.

Nevertheless, theological work demands that we open our eyes—his term is "recognition"—to what is taking place around us. He thus argues that the ultimate goal of our spiritual work should be personal redemption. And the only way to achieve it is through a recognition that even when we feel most distant from God, perhaps precisely when we feel most distant from God, it is then that God is near and close at hand. The recital of daily blessings—for food, for sustenance, for all else—brings us even closer to the Divine.

MARCH

Mighty Acts and Wonders

MARCH 1

Although the Holy One of Blessing is not visible to the human eye, God is discernible by virtue of mighty acts and wonders.... By virtue of the renewal of the months, God is revealed to humanity; it is as though they were greeting the Divine presence, the Shekhinah.

RABBI JONAH GERONDI

When we use terms like "mighty acts and wonders," we usually imagine the miracles of the past. We think of the Hanukkah and Passover stories, for example, where God entered into human history, according to Jewish tradition, to save the Jewish people. But Rabbi Jonah (as he was called) is speaking of much more subtle experiences of God.

While Rabbi Jonah was undoubtedly referring to the Hebrew months and the implied change process in the lunar cycle in the statement above, it is no less relevant to the succession of months in the secular calendar. With each passing month, as we move from one season to another, we see great change in the world around us. This change is evidence of the presence of God in the world. Thus, when we greet a new month, according to Rabbi Jonah, it is like welcoming the presence of God in our midst.

In each month is revealed new knowledge of the Divine. That is its blessing.

The Memory of Hope

MARCH 2

*I try to maintain hope—or at least the memory of
hope—when I am consumed with fear or despair.
I believe that hope is part of the will to live.*
PAUL COWAN

These words were penned in the midst of Paul's struggle with leukemia, a battle to which he eventually succumbed. While his words provide us insight into his soul, they also offer us direction for our daily lives. While we may not be facing a life-threatening illness—although some among us undoubtedly are indeed doing so, as are some whom we love—these words nevertheless teach us how to approach the challenges of daily living. Paul defines hope for us as the will to live. When we lose that will, we have lost hope. Thus, it is our responsibility to nurture that will in ourselves and in others.

The text in Deuteronomy says it all: "Therefore choose life" (Deuteronomy 30:19). And others have said, "Where there is hope, there is life." But Paul is offering us one more note. When hope eludes you and you are enmeshed in despair, recall the memory of hope in order to keep it—and you—alive. Every day alive, each moment we breathe, is indeed a blessing.

The Words of Our Prayers

MARCH 3

Every word of one's prayer should be like a rose that is plucked from a bush. One gathers rose upon rose until a bouquet is formed and can be offered to God as a beautiful blessing.

RABBI NACHMAN OF BRESLOV

Prayers come from words that are brought together to express what is in our hearts. These words emerge from letters floating in our souls, waiting to be used to serve a divine purpose. Such letters and words have the potential to express many things. What they ultimately say is up to us.

Reb Nachman teaches us that the words we use to form prayers should be carefully chosen, just as one would tenderly choose a flower to be given to a lover or friend. When brought together, these flowers form a bouquet, offering beauty and fragrance to all who choose to enjoy them. Such a process should not be rushed. It may take some time. On occasion, we are able to quickly find the right flower, find the right word. But just as we shouldn't hurry to choose a rose and we should take time to absorb its beauty, we should not offer our prayers in haste. Nor should we mumble our way through them.

We may be able to gather together a bouquet of flowers and allow its beauty to speak for itself. But when we bring together the bouquet of our prayers, it is the flowering of our soul that we present to God.

Finding Wisdom through Living

MARCH 4

If you call for understanding and shout for comprehension, if you seek it like silver and search for it like a hidden treasure, then you will understand the fear of Adonai and you find the knowledge of God.

PROVERBS 2:3–5

The biblical book of Proverbs is part of what is called wisdom literature, that which is gained through the experience of living. Thus, much of the book of Proverbs is written from the perspective of the teacher (who has the experience) to the student (who has not yet benefited from experience). These few verses present a change in direction in the process of ethical instruction. The verses that immediately precede this selection of text in the book of Proverbs suggest an answer given by the teacher. Conversely, this verse suggests the question asked by the student. In the mind of the writer of Proverbs, the student is calling aloud for the teacher to help him or her to understand. And when the student does not get immediate help, he or she begins to shout out for help. Thus, we learn that it is not just what we seek—in this case, an understanding of the Divine—but it is also how we seek it.

To enter into a dialogue with the Divine, it is not enough to simply utter words of prayer. A relationship with the Divine, suggests this writer of Proverbs, comes only through assistance from others and a deep digging into the self.

Helping Ourselves

MARCH 5

Call upon Me in the day of trouble.
PSALM 50:15

The psalmist is speaking for God in this verse. This is a posture we usually expect more from a prophet than from a psalmist. But the words that the psalmist brings us couldn't be clearer. God invites us to reach out when we are troubled, regardless of the nature of our pain. This is an invitation from God. What more could we ask for?

The words of the psalmist and God's invitation don't mean that there isn't more for us to do. We are given the opportunity for prayer. We have been given the privilege of presenting God with our burdens. And the dialogue of prayer itself may help to alleviate some of them. But we are not freed from our responsibility. The petitioning of God comes with a price. If we want God to help us, we have to be willing to start the process on our own. Get started and perhaps God might finish the job.

The Length of Our Prayers

MARCH 6

*In prayer there is a time to be brief
and a time to be profuse.*
ELIEZER BEN HYRCANUS, *MEKHILTA* TO EXODUS 14:15

This reads like the wisdom of Ecclesiastes: "A time to be born and a time to die ... " (Ecclesiastes 3:2). Perhaps Eliezer ben Hyrcanus was even thinking of the Ecclesiastes text when praying. He understood that the nature of particular situations places different demands on us. But the author of this midrash is not saying that the time that you have available to pray should dictate whether you should be brief or abundant with the words of your prayers. Rather, there are other elements that should dictate their length. After all, one of the most powerful prayers in the entirety of Jewish tradition was only five words in length. When the biblical Miriam suffered from leprosy, her brother Moses asked God to heal her by crying out, "*El na, r'fah na lah*—God, heal her please" (Numbers 12:13). He probably didn't think much about the words he would choose. They simply erupted from the depths of his soul. But he knew that there was nothing else to be said. No bargaining. No obsequiousness. And no need for additional words.

Similarly, most blessings are rather short even when they serve as introductions or endings to longer prayers. So when you pray, consider the context of your prayers. Only use the words that are necessary. Don't worry about impressing someone else who may be praying alongside. Remember that you are engaging divine time—and not just your own.

Absorbing Shabbat

MARCH 7

[Shabbat is a] realm of time where the goal is not to have but to be, not to own but to give, not to control but to share, not to subdue, but to be in accord.
RABBI ABRAHAM JOSHUA HESCHEL

This is the lesson from Shabbat that we carry into each week with us, particularly as we are driven to make more money, to increase company profits, and to get ahead—sometimes at the expense of others. Since those of us who spend time at the synagogue in prayer do so more on Shabbat than on other occasions, it is important for us to understand how the liturgy is supposed to work. But this is not about a lesson in liturgy. Rather, the idea is simple. We are supposed to take the values presented to us and then absorb them into our lives, into the way we behave, into the way we interact with others. If we are not able to do so, then the liturgy may be a failure.

The Torah said it best: We should thank God for all that we have. All that we own, all that we have acquired is a divine gift from the God who brought us out of Egypt—and continues to bring us out of every Egypt that we face. This is the God "who leads you through the great and awesome wilderness—of snake, fiery serpent, and scorpion, and thirst where there was no water—who brings forth water for you from the rock of flint, who feeds you manna in the wilderness, which your ancestors did not know, in order to afflict you and to test you, do good for you in the end. You may say in your heart, 'My strength and the might of my hand made me all this wealth.' But then you will remember God, that it was God who gave you the strength to make wealth in order to establish God's covenant that God swore with your ancestors as this day" (Deuteronomy 8:15–18).

So what values are you taking from your Shabbat worship this week? And if you don't pray on Shabbat, if you don't turn your heart to God, then perhaps this is the place to start.

Opening the Gates of Prayer

MARCH 8

The gates of prayer are never closed.
DEUTERONOMY RABBAH 2:12

Usually we reflect on the notion of closed gates in the fall, around Yom Kippur. Actually it is the theological construct that forms the basis for the final service on Yom Kippur called

N'ilah (literally, "closing of the gates"). This is exactly why I include the text during this month of March and not in September or October. Its placement here reminds us that it doesn't have to be Yom Kippur or any other designated time to approach God in prayer. Any time is an opportune time to present God with our burden or to approach God in thanksgiving and appreciation.

Sometimes we may feel like the gates of prayer are barely ajar and we have to use a great deal of spiritual strength just to force them open enough for our prayers to pass through. The result is that we then feel too spent to find the right words to express what is in our hearts and on our minds. Take your time. It is possible to express your prayers at any time. Prayer is always possible.

Divine Purpose

MARCH 9

Even those things that seem superfluous
have a divine purpose.
GENESIS RABBAH 10:7

As I look at the world around me, I am constantly amazed at its detail. I wonder about the purpose of everything, especially those things that seem to have no purpose at all. But then I am reminded that everything in the Torah, which Jewish tradition suggests is the blueprint for creation, has a purpose. Those things that seem to be superfluous in the Torah, and therefore have no meaning at all, often are more meaningful than those that have explicit purpose. Everything is there to teach us something. Our challenge is to discern the meaning. And if it eludes us, it is our responsibility. The text simply speaks; we have to be able to listen.

So I take this lesson out into the world with me and say a blessing for it all—even for the annoying gnat that bothers me constantly or the weeds in my garden that threaten its beauty. And I feel blessed that I am the beneficiary of such detail, knowing that it brings mystery to the world and the stamp of divinity along with it.

Disturbing the Silence

MARCH 10

In quietness and confidence shall be your strength.
ISAIAH 30:15

I am not sure that the prophet Isaiah was speaking to me when he penned this text. After all, I am not quiet. I usually remark that the decibel level of my voice is a direct result of growing up with a father who was hard of hearing. Yet my mother reminds me that I was loud for years before my father's hearing diminished. As a result, the childhood home in which I was raised was rather noisy. I had to compete with two older brothers. And the home that we shaped for our children has always been similarly noisy. When people come to visit, they are amazed at the constant din that pervades the house, especially at mealtime. It is something to which our daughters-in-law have had to grow accustomed, especially if they wanted to participate in the conversation.

But there are, in fact, times when I am quiet, when I look for such quiet confidence to engulf me, when I seek it unabashedly. These are mostly times of prayer. In community, I allow my voice to be swallowed by those around me. Or private prayer, when I can barely utter the words written in the prayer book so as not to disturb the holy silence of the sacred space that I have created just for that moment.

So maybe Isaiah was speaking to me, after all. His words are a constant reminder to me that I will not find my strength in loud brashness. Rather, I will find it in quiet reflection. And there will I find his blessing for me and for others.

Finding Real Love

MARCH 11

We see our reflection in water only when we bend close to it. So too your heart must lean down to another's. Then it will see itself in the other's heart.

CHASIDIC TEACHING

This teaching is about the blessing of love. Perhaps what girds it from underneath is the covenantal relationship between human beings and God. But this is a text about human love— a love that brings people close together and can blossom into lifelong companionship. While the Chasidic master who taught this idea is not identified, his intention is clear. We can only see ourselves in the reflection of another if we are willing to bring ourselves down to the other. If we keep our distance, hold ourselves above others, then we will never be able to find a love that is real.

Baal Shem Tov said it more directly: "It is not good to be alone, for one cannot know one's defects." Love does not find itself in the pursuit of perfection. Rather, one finds love in the acknowledgment of one's imperfection and the reality that one can only be completed, perfected with the other.

Moving Forward

MARCH 12

Everything is exhausting. You can't speak.
The eye can't see enough. The ear can't hear enough.
ECCLESIASTES 1:8

The writer of Ecclesiastes wrote many things about life. Much of what he wrote appears to be expressive of a depressing view of the world. We know the feeling Ecclesiastes is articulating. We know what it feels like at the end of a long day. We are tired, hungry. Perhaps we have not slept enough and have eaten too much or too much of the things that are not good for us. We may feel disillusioned by our jobs. And so we wonder what life is about, whether the path we have chosen is the right one. What we do is never enough. There is always more to be done. But we don't know what to do about it all. So we keep at it, whatever the "it" is. So what is Ecclesiastes trying to teach us amidst such a fatalistic outlook?

No matter. We are not ready to call it quits. Our eyes may never get enough, nor will our ears. We may try to understand the world around us, and we may never be satisfied by what we learn. Nevertheless, because of the divine spark that rests inside each of us, we are motivated to go on living, to work hard to build a better world, to express our creative self. Being alive is blessing enough to motivate us.

The Wisdom of Silence

MARCH 13

Silence is a fence for wisdom.
PIRKEI AVOT 3:13

We usually think about fences as protective devices. They protect what is inside them from whatever or whoever is outside. But fences work in two ways. They prevent what is inside from getting outside. In some cases, one fence is not enough. In prisons, for example, one fence prevents prisoners from reaching the second fence. The Rabbis of *Pirkei Avot* are constructing yet another kind of fence—a fence of silence. This fence may prevent wisdom from escaping. It is also suggesting that too many words can have a deleterious effect on wisdom.

If wisdom is gained through reflecting on our experiences, then we have to be quiet enough to listen to what the experience is teaching us. Then after we realize what we have learned, we can offer a blessing of thanks to our teacher, whoever that may be, and to God for giving us the ability to discern it.

Being Lucky

MARCH 14

My first piece of advice is to be lucky. That is not always easy, but one of the tricks is to recognize opportunity when it knocks.
EDGAR M. BRONFMAN

It is always better to be in the right place at the right time than it is to be in the wrong place at the wrong time. The key to opportunity, suggests Edgar Bronfman, is to discern one from the other.

But that is not all. We have to seize the opportunity when it is presented. We never know when or if it will be presented again. Often this is the stuff out of which heroes are made. They are usually everyday people who did not seek out heroism. They simply rose to the occasion when it was presented—and did not run the other way.

We usually don't think of the Purim narrative in this way. Perhaps its heroes, Mordecai and Esther, were not "lucky," since their community was in danger of being destroyed. But they did seize the opportunity to save the Jewish community in ancient Persia. As a result, the community survived and we tell the story of their heroism each year around this time in the spring.

Be on the lookout. While you may not be in the position to save an entire community, the opportunity to be a hero presents itself to us every day.

Holiness Blessings

MARCH 15

Praised are You, Adonai our God, Sovereign of the universe,
Creator of the fruit of the vine.
BLESSING SAID OVER WINE

This blessing is sometimes referred to as the *Kiddush* (or sanctification, as it is usually translated; it is one of several blessings that might be called "holiness blessings"). In most cases, it introduces the *Kiddush*, but it is not the *Kiddush* itself. Technically, it is the blessing over the wine that is either an independent blessing or the blessing over which *Kiddush* is spoken. That is why it is longer in the evening than in the morning when it is recited for Shabbat and holidays.

The Rabbis say that as we chant the *Kiddush*, we are witness to the original perfection of divine creation. Perhaps it is because creation took place by separating out things and giving them independence: water and dry land; light and darkness; man and woman. Thus, each time we recite *Kiddush*, and with it the blessing over wine, we are participating in the reenactment of creation.

The Straight Path

MARCH 16

The realization of great ideas is not accomplished without travail and woe, deep sorrow and repeated disappointment.
RABBI SOLOMON SCHECHTER

The route to great things is never a straight line between two points. And it is certainly often not the shortest distance between those two points. Perhaps that is part of the definition of something being a big idea. They don't come easily nor are they brought to fruition quickly. We have to work hard at them. And oftentimes, we are still frustrated and disappointed when the results we seek are not immediate and forthcoming. Some will respond to such circumstances by walking away. Our response has to be continually working at it.

For Schechter, this was not a classroom conversion, emanating from the towers of learning. His great ideas emerged from his own experience as the major architect of Conservative Judaism in North America. But he was also speaking about the journey of the Jewish people throughout history. He understood that Jewish history is not the simple recording of events over time. Jewish history has a mission and goal—to create a more perfect society in what is known as messianic time. But he also understood that such a time would not come on its own. We all have to participate in bringing it forward. Every act we perform contributes to its acceleration or its delay.

Loving the Basics

MARCH 17

Love tastes sweet but only with bread.
YIDDISH PROVERB

Maybe it is because I miss my grandparents—who all spoke Yiddish—or the era of our family's life that they represented, but I have always been captivated by Yiddish folk sayings. They offered them to me regularly and freely. I have to admit that I didn't always understand them. And I still don't always understand them. But they are alluring nonetheless.

Like my grandparents who were simple people, these sayings represent the richness of their basic folk wisdom. This particular bit of Yiddish wisdom is indeed a recipe but not the kind that you find in the kitchen. Rather, it is part of the recipes for living that they learned and sought to pass on to subsequent generations—often shared in the kitchen mixed among the fragrances of the old world. This proverb suggests that it is hard to love when you are struggling to survive. It might be politically incorrect to say so today, but that is what the Yiddish clearly says. Maybe my grandparents could say it because they came to this country from Russia with nothing. And they struggled most days of their lives. So maybe they understood love as a luxury or even a privilege that could only be afforded once there was bread on the table. Then they were motivated to express that love and to offer a blessing of thanksgiving for providing both: the food and the love.

The Light of the World

MARCH 18

Praised are You, Adonai, who gives light to the world.
FROM THE MORNING LITURGY

Light. There is much to be thankful for—when it shines forth.

There is something about light that is transformative. It may seem obvious, but light pushes away the darkness. As such, it offers us comfort and even support. When the sun rises, its light helps to allay the fears that often rise up in the night and threaten our well-being. Its spread of warmth in the morning provides us with reassurance and inspiration for the day ahead.

Light is also a symbol for knowledge, as it is a symbol for the Divine. Both knowledge and the Divine illumine the world. Together they help to eliminate hate and ignorance in the world. Thank You, God, for the light that brings brightness to my world. "In Your light, do we see light" (Psalm 36:10).

The Bright Side of Darkness

MARCH 19

You will not attain what you love if you do not endure
much that you hate, and you will not be freed
from what you hate if you will not
endure much from what you love.
MOSES IBN EZRA

We often speak of love-hate relationships with people, but we may also have the same with places and even things. We usually think of it as a way to express the dynamism of our emotions. I kind of feel that way about New York City, in which I spend much of my time. I appreciate its greatness, but

I also tire of its noise and grime. Moses ibn Ezra is providing us with a different kind of insight. At first, he suggests that we endure that which is negative in our experience because of the positive that comes along with it. Some people call this "the dark side," for even bright light casts a shadow. It seems that we can't have one without the other.

When we love, we are able to endure what is unpleasant in this world. Love has a way of protecting us, buoying us, supporting us so that hate can't fill us with its poison. When we love, we will be freed from the burden of what we hate—because it becomes transformed. For the brightness of love indeed illumines even the darkest side.

Letting Go

MARCH 20

My heart is not proud, Adonai,
and my eyes are not haughty;
on things beyond my scope
no more I brood.
But I have calmed and quieted my soul,
like a child at its mother's breast;
my soul is like a comforted child.
PSALM 131:1–2

I have never imagined the psalmist as someone who is writing for the purpose of creating liturgical poetry. I know that the psalms, which were attributed to King David, were sung on the steps of the ancient Temple by the Levites. But I have always seen the psalmist as someone who is simply expressing emotion and writing for himself (or herself). This selection from the biblical book of Psalms offers us a lens through which we can navigate our daily life.

In this poetry, the psalmist is suggesting what my wife, Sheryl, is fond of saying: "Control the controllable." In other words, recognize what is beyond your control, or "beyond your scope" in the language of the psalmist. Stop longing for things that are beyond you. Stop trying to fix things that you cannot. Just let them go. Spend your energy on those things that are within your orbit. Just let the rest go. That is what will bring you calm and tranquility. There is where you will find comfort and serenity.

Finding Strength

MARCH 21

Praised are You, Adonai,
who gives strength to the weary.
FROM THE MORNING BLESSINGS

This is one of the blessings that was originally said upon waking and has been moved into the more formal morning liturgy. It is a raw expression of emotion—even if it is cast into the traditional form of these morning blessings. I am thankful when I get up that I get up. I am thankful that I am able to face a new day with renewed vigor, even if the previous day was challenging and exhausting. I am thankful that God has given me the strength to do so.

Sometimes, I add my own personal expression of thanksgiving and gratitude to the morning blessings that are assigned in the prayer book. I think about what the previous day has wrought and the promise of the new day. I think about the blessings of family, of friendship, of love. I think about personal and professional achievements. And I say them out loud.

Once I have said all these things, only then am I ready to begin my day.

Sabbath Light

MARCH 22

Praised are You, Adonai our God, Sovereign of the universe, who has made us holy with mitzvot and instructed us to light the Shabbat candles.

BLESSING SAID UPON LIGHTING THE SABBATH CANDLES

Traditional blessings usually include the instruction for the action. Thus, in the context of interaction with the Deity, we express our thanks for instructing us to fulfill the act that we are about to do (or have just done in the case of Shabbat candle lighting). This time, the time of candle lighting, is a powerful moment for me each week. We follow the traditional candle-lighting times and are conscious of their change each week (according to the change in the time the sun sets). I leave my work behind entirely. No telephone. No computer. Nothing that intrudes on this special period of twenty-five hours. So the lighting of the candles represents a threshold over which we cross into sacred time.

Between the lighting of the candles and the uttering of the blessing, just after we have brought forth the light into our souls by enveloping the flames with our arms, we offer a few words of personal prayer, particularly for our children and parents. In the eastern European tradition, these were called *t'khines* and only offered by women at candle lighting.

Shabbat is also considered to be a time that offers us a glimpse into paradise—what the world once was and what the world will yet be. The candles are lit and I am swept away into paradise. I welcome you to join me there each week.

Forgiveness

MARCH 23

*The most beautiful thing one can
do is forgive a wrong.*
RABBI ELEAZAR BEN JUDAH OF WORMS

Just as we have noted that we don't have to wait until Yom Kippur to do *t'shuvah* and right any wrongs for which we are responsible, we shouldn't wait until that time of year to forgive anyone who may have hurt or wronged us. Most of us will wait until someone approaches us and asks that they be forgiven for something that may have happened. We look for an "I'm sorry" and then, sometimes begrudgingly, we accept the apology.

Rabbi Eleazar ben Judah is implying something else, something more active, because he knows that such actions have the potential for bringing *mashiachzeit* (literally, "messiah time") more rapidly. So don't wait for someone who may have offended you to approach you and ask for forgiveness. Seek out those people. They may not even know that you have been offended. They may have forgotten about what happened. Tell them that they offended you, that you are hurt, and that you forgive them. Do so with a full and open heart. Then let go of what had taken place. Purge your soul of it. In so doing, like Rabbi Eleazar, you will be hastening that special time for which we all long.

Finding God in Everything

MARCH 24

If I ascend to heavens, you are there.
If I make my bed in the lowest depths, you are there.
PSALM 139:8

This is a statement that suggests that God is everywhere. But the text also teaches us that God accompanies us wherever we go, whatever we experience, whether it is to the heights of ecstasy or the depths of despair. I remind myself of this statement by the psalmist particularly when I feel the presence of God lacking in my life. But I also try to remember it when things are going well and I feel that God is close at hand.

Levi Yitzchak of Berditchev composed a one-syllable melody using the Yiddish word *Du* (You). It was his way of expressing to God that God is everywhere. Everywhere he went, everything he did, anything he experienced, he felt God's presence and saw God's imprint on the world. May we learn to experience the presence of God in everything we do, as well.

Raising the Hands

MARCH 25

Praised are You, Adonai our God, Sovereign of the universe,
who has made us holy with mitzvot and
instructed us concerning the washing of hands.
PRAYER SAID UPON WASHING HANDS PRIOR TO EATING BREAD

While there are a variety of customs concerning how hands are ritually washed, they are not washed the way you would normally wash your hands. And, of course, no soap is used. Rather, water is poured gently over one hand at a time using a two-handled washing bowl that is held in the other hand. Generally, this is done three times, starting with the right hand. While the translation above captures the essence of the activity, the Hebrew phrase at the end of the blessing actually means "the raising of hands." The ritual itself assumes that one's hands are ritually impure and must be cleansed prior to completing a ritual act. In the ancient Temple, the priest would raise his hands while a Levite poured water over them.

When I raise my hands after I have washed and before I recite the blessing over bread, I imagine myself raising my hands to God in recognition of the Source of the bread that I am about to eat and enjoy. Whenever I raise my hands in this way, I am reminded of the ever-present Source above me.

Forgetting Fear

MARCH 26

Adonai is with me. I shall not fear.
FROM *ADON OLAM*, THE PRAYER SONG
THAT CONCLUDES MOST PRAYER SERVICES

This is the text that concludes most prayer services. It is also at the beginning of the printed edition of most traditional services, but it is generally not intoned at that point. Its placement is critical and often overlooked. It is often overlooked because people have generally started to leave at this point, disconnecting with the service, talking to friends, putting away their *tallit* (prayer shawl), stowing their prayer books. *Adon Olam* is included at the end of the service—and at its beginning—to indicate the path that the liturgy should be taking. In other words, the entire liturgy, the entire service with all of its elements including the Torah reading and the sermon, is included for one message alone. When you leave the synagogue, it is this message that you should take with you: Adonai is with me. I shall not fear.

If your liturgy does not take you to this place, then reconsider the words of your prayers. Armed with such a notion, what else to do we need?

Hearing God's Voice

MARCH 27

God's voice speaks in many languages, communicating itself in a diversity of intuitions. The word of God never comes to an end. No word is God's last word.
RABBI ABRAHAM JOSHUA HESCHEL

This is a fascinating notion. We realize that God speaks to us in a variety of ways. We also recognize that not all communication is verbal. The Rabbis suggest that God gave the Torah in seventy languages (since that was the presumed number of languages spoken at the time). Thus, the word of the Divine has to be spoken in many more languages today.

And we also realize that the giving of Torah on Mount Sinai, although fixed in time and space, was not finite. Its echo is heard throughout history. The challenge is not in the giving of Torah; it is in the receiving, the hearing of God's voice in the world today, amidst the noise that threatens to prevent us from hearing it. But anytime we hear the divine word, even in response to our prayers, Rabbi Heschel is teaching us that it is not the end of the communication or response—it never is. God always has something more to say to us. All we have to do is continue to listen.

Raising Ourselves Up

MARCH 28

As I raise myself up to you
[or attempt to leap; literally, "dance toward you"]
but cannot reach you, so may those who attempt to
injure us be unable to reach us.
FROM THE *KIDDUSH L'VANAH* LITURGY, BLESSING OF THE MOON

This is a custom initiated by Rabbi Isaac Luria, who is known as the Ari. As part of the *Kiddush L'vanah* ritual, which has historically been a men's ritual (as opposed to Rosh Chodesh, which has evolved into more of a women's ritual), participants are encouraged to dance outside. Some may consider this "a moon dance." Others might see this as an expression of joy and communion, much like dancing in the synagogue or on Shabbat has become.

While it may seem awkward or even artificial at first, this "heavenly dance" is a way of expressing our attempt to reach and understand God, things that we ultimately cannot fully do. Among some communities, while the prayer leader is saying "As I dance … ," it is customary to actually jump three times while asking God for these basic things: "May I have no toothaches this month, no headaches this month, no pain at all."

Try it. You may discover the path to dance your way heavenward.

Sharing What Is in Our Hearts

MARCH 29

Let everything that breathes praise Adonai. Halleluyah!
PSALM 150:6

This has become a popular text among many of us seeking a more personal Jewish spiritual life. It both concludes and summarizes the entire book of Psalms. For many it has become a *kavvanah* or sacred mantra. It may even be somewhat onomatopoeic. The entire psalm text describes various instruments that we may use to express our praise of God. We gather all of our inner resources in order to commune with God. We open up our mouths and this is what issues forth: Adonai (Yah, in the Hebrew), our name for God, and our expression of outreach toward the Divine.

But this text also has an activist message to it, one that is often overlooked. Perhaps this lack of emphasis is a result of its controversial nature. If every living being has a responsibility to praise God, and every part of each being has that responsibility, then we have to make sure the message is sounded to all those willing to hear it. This is not something that people easily or comfortably do. Are you prepared to share what is in your heart with others—as the psalm suggests?

The Principles of Faith

MARCH 30

Modeh ani lifanecha, *I give thanks to You*
Who wakes me into soft morning light
Who spreads our the tent of the sky
Who flames the day with sunflower faces.
RABBI JAMES B. ROSENBERG

These words could form an extensive introduction for your morning prayers, beyond the first line, which is, in fact, taken from traditional liturgy. Such an approach may be especially appropriate for those less likely to engage the traditional context entirely for such communion with the Divine. These words certainly reflect some of the basic principles expressed in the morning liturgy. But at the end, to make sure that all are in accord, we would add the common statement of agreement: amen. Amen to God as Creator and Sustainer. Amen to God's presence among us. Amen to the ability to teach this notion to others and be taught as well.

But now what do we do after we have assented to these thoughts? Is it enough to accept them as principles of faith? Is it sufficient that they form an introduction to our prayers? Our task now is to turn these ideas from thought to action, from belief to deed. Then we will surely bring the presence of God into our lives and the lives of others.

Running toward Our Responsibilities

MARCH 31

When there is smoke, there is smoke.
YIDDISH PROVERB

Sometimes what we perceive as reality is just as we perceive it to be. Nothing more, nothing less. We are often tempted into reading more into situations, even drawing out conclusions as a result. I used to call these catastrophic expectations. That's when one thing leads to another. We fail one assignment or exam at school and our professional aspirations are dashed. We mess up one thing at work and our career is doomed.

We might try to make light of it. Or someone else will do so in order to protect us. But sometimes when you see smoke, what you see is real, even if it is irrelevant. Of course, there is something that is producing the smoke. And usually it is fire. But when you see smoke, know that it is really smoke and there is a cause for it. And now there is something you have to do about it. No running away. No excuses. Just deal with it—and try not to get burnt along the way.

APRIL

Reliving the Exodus

APRIL 1

The Exodus from Egypt occurs in every human,
in every era, in every year, every day.
Rabbi Nachman of Breslov

Various events color the months and seasons of the Jewish calendar. As we anticipate spring and the renewal that comes along with it, we are also mindful of the Exodus to freedom that our ancestors experienced in ancient Egypt. As particular as is the message of the Exodus from Egypt for the Jewish people, it clearly has a far more universal message. That is why so many people resonate with it, even those with no relationship to the collective story of the Jewish people. It transcends Jewish boundaries and speaks to all people, no matter where they live, no matter their religious, cultural, or national background. We experience this Exodus regularly as we are freed from all that threatens to enslave us.

But Reb Nachman's message is teaching us something additional. The Exodus is bound by neither place nor time. We can experience it every day and everywhere. The message of freedom knows no limits. And it is important to relive the Exodus regularly so that we can appreciate the journey of freedom and what it represents, especially since not all are privileged to bask in its warm and comforting glow.

Today, as you do something, anything, that you are free to do or you are free to refrain from doing, remember the blessing that is freedom. Guard it. Protect it. And never take it for granted.

Holding One's Heart

APRIL 2

A person's prayer is not acceptable unless one's heart is in one's hands.
RABBI AMMI

How does one place one's heart in one's hands? This seems to be a prerequisite for efficacious prayer, according to the Talmudic sage Rabbi Ammi. Perhaps he is teaching us that prayer should not be an intellectual exercise or the rote recital of liturgy, however poetic it may be. Rather, prayer should engage the full self. This includes what is sometimes called the metarational, that which transcends the intellect and is part of the world of the spiritual. Without placing one's emotions in the context of one's prayer, one may not be able to present the self fully before God.

It is ironic, but this may be harder for those who pray regularly. For those for whom prayer is part of their regular spiritual discipline, it is a challenge to make sure their prayer is not routinized and without a depth of emotion. Sometimes the events of the day dictate the level of emotion that enters our prayers. Rabbi Ammi is inviting us to allow such events to become part of our prayers. As we do so, our prayers become more fully part of us, as well.

The Holiness of City Life

APRIL 3

Next year in Jerusalem.
SAID AT THE END OF THE PASSOVER SEDER
AND AT THE END OF YOM KIPPUR

I have placed this text in this section of the book because of its nearness to the celebration of Passover, an event that draws us together more often than most other Jewish holidays. But it could easily be placed in the fall near Yom Kippur or even at the end of the secular year in December. I actually think it could be placed any time during the year, since it is an attitude that transcends any specific date on the calendar. What motivates us to say it? What motivated the Rabbis to make it a fixed part of our liturgy?

Although the modern State of Israel is replete with political challenges and there are implications for taking any position along the political spectrum, the mere utterance of the name of the city of Jerusalem, for me, connotes an uplift of spirit and a time of special happiness. For the Rabbis, that time is encapsulated in the time of the messiah. But whenever we say, "Next year in Jerusalem," wherever we may be, even in the holy city itself, we are offering an unspoken blessing that next year may be better than this year, that next year may take us just a little closer to messianic time—a time when the entire world is of Jerusalem.

Wrapping Ourselves in God

APRIL 4

*Praised are You, Adonai our God, Sovereign of the universe,
who makes us holy with mitzvot and
instructs us to wrap ourselves in the* tzitzit.
BLESSING SAID UPON PUTTING ON THE *TALLIT*

It seems odd that the blessing for putting on the *tallit* doesn't mention the *tallit* at all. Rather, it is a blessing for putting on *tzitzit* (the fringes on the four corners of the *tallit*). That is because the main reason for the *tallit* as a garment is for attaching the four *tzitziyot* (plural of *tzitzit*). Thus, the Hebrew actually tells us to "wear" the *tzitzit*. While we find comfort in wrapping ourselves in the *tallit*, the *tzitziyot* are there to remind us of our responsibility to follow God's direction in our lives. That is why there is a way to count 613 threads and knots in the *tzitzit*, the traditional number of divine commandments.

So wrap yourself in the *tallit*. Feel God's presence. Take a look at the *tzitziyot*. Touch them gently as a reminder of the role of these sacred instructions in your life. Then go out and become a channel through which God's blessings can flow into the world.

Binding Our Prayers

APRIL 5

*Praised are You, Adonai our God,
Sovereign of the universe, who makes us holy with
mitzvot and instructs us to put on* t'fillin.
BLESSING SAID UPON PLACING THE *T'FILLIN* ON THE ARM

Since the putting on of *t'fillin* involves several steps, there are several blessings that are connected with this ritual. Following a meditation that helps to ready us to perform this sacred act, we say the blessing above as we place the first *t'fillin* on the arm.

For many people, the act of wrapping leather with a prayer box around the arm is awkward and strange. It becomes more so as we then place similar straps and a prayer box on the head and then wrap the one from the arm around the hand and finger. For me, it is the fact that it is beyond the usual and commonplace that makes it a unique ritual act. It is why my prayers in the morning (when *t'fillin* are worn—except on Shabbat and holidays) have a different feel than during the rest of the day. They help me to focus my spiritual strength as I confront the day ahead. It is the text from the prophet Hosea, said as the strap from the arm *t'fillin* is wrapped around the finger, that says it all: "I will betroth you to Myself for ever; I will betroth you to Myself in righteousness, and in justice, and in loving-kindness, and in compassion. And I will betroth you to Myself in faithfulness; and you shall know Adonai" (Hosea 2:21–22). These are the words I utter each day as I attempt to regularly renew my acquaintance with God.

Sacred Dialogue

APRIL 6

Set a fence around your words.
BABYLONIAN TALMUD, *NIDDAH* 3B

While most people think of this teaching in terms of the words they speak in conversation, it is a lesson to be learned with regard to the words of blessing that we utter, as well. But why should we build a fence around the words of blessing that we speak? From what should they be protected? And what is to be prevented from escaping? We should set a fence around our words of blessing to ensure that they are not compromised by the banal, secular world that sometimes threatens to engulf them. It is easy to forget the power of such words or their purpose. The words of blessing are part of a sacred dialogue between the individual and God.

As you prepare to speak your words of blessing, whether they come from a prepared liturgical text, the prayer poetry of others, or directly from your heart, remember that they have a sacred goal and should emerge from a sacred source, as well—and not from the secular world that surrounds you.

The Promise of Torah

APRIL 7

It is a tree of life to those who hold it fast,
and all who cling to it find happiness.
PROVERBS 3:18

This verse from Proverbs is also used at the end of the section of the morning prayer service during which the Torah is read. This is the climax of the service for me, as I imagine it is for many people. When the liturgy works and has successfully brought me to the mountaintop, or at least to its foothills, then I am overwhelmed—so much so that my wife will frequently say to me at this point, "You're yelling." I can't help it. I have just experienced revelation—or as close to it as I feel like I am going to get in the context of a formal worship service. And now it is time to return the Torah to the cabinet (*aron hakodesh*) where it is housed. I feel overwhelmed.

I am also immediately wistful about the time I just experienced and the desert experience for which I long to return. I am certain that the Rabbis who arranged our liturgy understood that feeling. That is why they included another text immediately following the one cited above: "Bring us back to you, Adonai. Let us return. Bring back the days of old" (Lamentations 5:21). We are anxious to return to that spiritual time in the desert when our relationship with the Divine was fresh, when we were filled with awe and anticipation every step along the way, when our journey brought us closer to the land of promise and to ourselves.

Freedom from Responsibility

APRIL 8

Children all carry their own blessing into the world.
YIDDISH FOLK SAYING

Those of us who are parents may have to be reminded of the blessings that children carry. Sometimes after we experience the wonder of their birth, the affection of their youth, and the awe of their learning, we are confronted with the reality of their struggle to be free, to be independent—just as we struggled free of our parents' embrace as they tried hard to hold us within it. It is not surprising that our own children yearn to the do the same.

As children, even as adult children, we bring our own blessing into the world, and we are blessed for each good act that we perform. Perhaps the blessing emerges from doing the act itself—but only when we are motivated to do it, to actually *bring* that blessing into the world. We benefit. Others benefit. And the world benefits, as well.

The Memory of the Exodus

APRIL 9

Let all who are hungry come and eat.
SAID TOWARD THE BEGINNING OF THE PASSOVER SEDER

Early in our Passover Seders, we open the doors to our homes and offer an invitation to those outside. While few of us have homes around which people might congregate outside of our doors, the sentiment is important to capture. Of course, some may consider this act perfunctory and simply open the door and then sit back down. Others will open the door, so to speak, for days and weeks before the Seder; that is why there are so many people who come from diverse backgrounds sitting around the table. As far as I am concerned, this is how it should always be.

Nevertheless, this invitation is not just about food. It is also about those who have a spiritual hunger that the Passover Seder can potentially satisfy. For me, the Passover Seder is not about simulating the Exodus journey. It is about stimulating our memory of it. It is 1250 BCE and you are there. So along with the trip we made through the desert was the constant encounter and companionship of the Divine. Now that indeed is worth remembering.

Real Love

APRIL 10

I am my beloved's and my beloved is mine.
SONG OF SONGS 6:3

This phrase has become so commonplace that people often forget its source. Others don't even realize it is biblical in origin. Many people have it engraved on their wedding rings. Among our favorites, we have several pieces of art that prominently display this text. For me, the words can never be said too many times.

According to Jewish tradition, each book from the Bible that was written as a *megillah* (a single scroll rather than the double scrolls of the Torah) is assigned to a major festival to be read aloud and in public. For Passover, the particular text that is assigned is the Song of Songs. Perhaps the Rabbis made this choice because spring reawakens love among people and a longing for one another. Passover is a spring festival and emerges from that origin as part of ancient folk religion. According to the Rabbis, this clearly erotic love poem is really an allegory that reflects the loving relationship between God and the Jewish people. So Song of Songs reflects the love we have for one another, the love we have for God, and the love that God expresses for us, as well.

Regardless of our particular understanding of the text and its origin, when we come to know that we are desired and loved, we also feel particularly blessed.

Leaving Jacob Behind

APRIL 11

You will no longer be called Jacob, instead [your name
will be] Israel, because you have striven with
God and with humans and prevailed.
GENESIS 32:29

This powerful text emerges from the midst of the Genesis narratives, the stories of the matriarchs and patriarchs of the Jewish people. In this episode, Jacob rests for the night—just prior to his long anticipated encounter with his brother Esau, whom he had deceived when they were young men still living in their parents' home. Jacob falls asleep and wrestles through the night. Some say it was his conscience with which he fought. Others say it was the dark side of himself. In either case, he arose as a changed person. His change was so drastic that he was given another name: Israel.

While the scene that is described in the book of Genesis is rather dramatic, our own encounters are no less life changing and transformative. Part of what made Jacob's story so important is that he paid attention to the life lesson that he was being taught. We are not always quite as attentive to what transpires in our own lives when we struggle with other people or even with God. When we pay attention, we can emerge, as did Jacob, with the blessing of a new name and a new sense of self. We too can become Israel.

Becoming Torah

APRIL 12

The giving of Torah at Sinai and the recognition of the one God are renewed each time a Jew hears the divine voice piercing through the words of the text. When we are touched and transformed by the word, we know that there is a divine, operative force at the heart of the world which not only demands that we fulfill the best in ourselves but also sustains us when we fall short.

RABBI NORMAN J. COHEN

This is a powerful lesson about the inherent spiritual power in the engagement with sacred literature. When we study such text, we can encounter God. When we wrestle with the texts of our tradition, we can stand at the foot of Sinai once again. We need not wait for revelation. Nor need we wait for the public reading of the Torah. The opportunity for Sinai is always in front of us. We need only open the pages of a book and enter its pages.

But this is not a simple, superficial read. This is an encounter with the sacred. In each word we utter, with each page we touch, we have the opportunity to affirm our relationship with the Divine.

But there is more. Unlike a summer pleasure read, which is for pure enjoyment perhaps, this kind of text work makes demands on us. We don't simply access the Divine for our own benefit. Rather, the encounter with sacred literature places a responsibility on us. It requires us to open ourselves up to the text and its message and then to become a better person as a result. The sacred text is a mirror. In its image, we see our reflected self—bettered as a result of our encounter with it.

Finding Refuge

APRIL 13

You are my God, my living God.
To You I flee in time of grief,
and You are my miracle and my refuge,
who answers the day I shall call.

FROM *ADON OLAM*, HYMN THAT CONCLUDES
THE DAILY MORNING LITURGY

The hymn *Adon Olam*, including this stanza, is generally taken for granted in most synagogues. The morning prayer service, often quite lengthy, especially on Shabbat, is over. People are beginning to scurry about, in a hurry either for the reception that follows the service, to go home, or to mingle with friends. The entire hymn, as this stanza, is quite powerful. It helps to tell us the reason we are gathered for prayer in the first place. In addition, if we carefully read each verse, we see that it summarizes Jewish theology in one fell swoop.

Adon Olam tells us in any melody possible—since it probably has been sung to more melodies than any other selection of Jewish liturgy—that we can approach God at any time. No matter the reason, we can turn to God with our prayers, as we have just done. And when we are ready to utter them, God is always ready to receive them. Good times and bad, God is always present in our lives, ready to support us each step along the way.

Perfect Faith

APRIL 14

I believe with perfect faith in the coming of the messiah. And although the messiah tarries, nevertheless, I will wait, every day, that the messiah may come.
FROM MAIMONIDES' THIRTEEN PRINCIPLES OF FAITH

This is both a theological statement and a prayer that is often expressed during the most difficult of times. It is probably why it was chosen as the text sung by many Jews as they were marched into the gas chambers of Europe during World War II. Even amidst the horrors of the Holocaust—"although the messiah tarries"—they believed nonetheless.

This statement of belief also became a vision for the Jewish people that drove them forward. It has been a goal toward which they have continued to strive throughout their history. While some peoples' history is the recording of events over time, Jewish history has a direction and purpose—moving toward the messianic era. When we participate in Jewish history, we also participate in its mission and hold in our hands the potential to reach its goal. What we do and how we do it help determine how quickly such a time may come. "Although the messiah tarries," let's not be responsible for making him (or her) late.

Full of Song

APRIL 15

Were our mouths as full of song as the sea ...
FROM THE *NISHMAT KOL CHAI* PRAYER,
PART OF THE MORNING LITURGY ON SHABBAT

This text continues with various other images: "Were our mouths as full of song as the sea, and our tongues as full of joyous song as its multitude of waves, and our lips as full of praise as the breadth of the heavens, and our eyes as brilliant as the sun and the moon, and our hands as outspread as the eagles of the sky, and our feet as swift as hinds, we would not be able to thank you enough." Regardless of the specific image, the notion is the same. Even if we were endowed far more extensively than we have been, we would still be incapable of praising God sufficiently. This forms the beginning of the main section of the morning service. Its purpose is to help ready us for prayer. We may not be capable of expressing ourselves adequately. But we are going to try nonetheless. We are going to take all that God has endowed us with—however limited we may be—and express our appreciation for what we have been given. Rather than petition God for something else or complain about the various qualities that we have not been given, we will use those gifts to express our appreciation and offer praise for the Creator who is responsible for who we are. Now it is up to us to take those gifts and determine what we are to become.

Silence and Stillness

APRIL 16

Be still and know that I am God.
PSALM 46:11

This has always been a difficult text for me. I am rarely quiet or still—even though I work on being both. I guess it is not in my nature, which is probably why the teaching of the psalmist is even more important for me. I am noisy and loud. People hear me coming on steps or walking into a room. When I was teaching regularly at Hebrew Union College, my colleague and friend Rabbi Leonard Kravitz, teaching in the next classroom, would often come and gently close my door—even before the class started. He knew that by the end of the class, the sound of my voice would increase as I became more passionately engaged in what I was teaching.

So the thought of silence and stillness, however attractive, is also very frightening. What do I do with all that time and space if I have to sit still and be silent? But that is the point. If I can discipline myself to be still and silent, then I can make room for the divine presence to enter and hear its voice. Just like Elijah the prophet taught, God can be found in the "still small voice" (1 Kings 19:12). In the silence, I might come to know God.

The World Is God

APRIL 17

*To withdraw from the world is to withdraw from
God, for the world is God manifest in time and space.*
RABBI RAMI SHAPIRO

While there have been some notable exceptions, Judaism does not teach asceticism as a spiritual practice. While a temporary retreat is fine, and might even be recommended, it is important to engage the world directly. It is one of the reasons why there is a requirement for synagogue sanctuaries to have at least one clear glass window or pane of glass, so that when we pray, we are not separated from the outside world. It might be also the reason why we find the Jewish community more prevalent in large cities than in smaller ones!

But God is fully present in time and in space. It is in this nexus that we can best encounter God.

To be a Jew is to engage the world fully—with all of its imperfections. For to engage the world is to commune with God and enter into conversation with the sacred and holy that we bring into our midst.

Finding Strength in Failure

APRIL 18

Errors are part of the game.
Failure is common to us all.
And one in three is greatness.
RABBI MICHAEL FESHBACH

I admit it. I am not a big sports fan. I enjoy the various games but seldom follow any specific teams. However, since my kids enjoy hockey and baseball, in particular, and do have their favorites, I pay attention a little more than I might otherwise. I also recognize that there are many things about life that we can learn from sports. Rabbi Feshbach, obviously a baseball fan, clearly thinks the same way. That is why he offers this lesson on life from the game of baseball. It is one of the few contexts in which failure (called errors) is built into the game and the person who misses the ball (as a batter) two out of three times is considered excellent at his game.

If we can accept such standards in baseball, why is it that we are so much more demanding of others and of ourselves in life? And why are we afraid to admit that we can err, that we can miss the ball when we are up at bat in life, and still be good people?

So the next time you see someone playing baseball, whether child, professional, or weekend athlete, remember the lesson that the player continues to teach us. And remember: Baseball is simply practice for life. The real game is the one we live each day for which there is only one umpire.

Earthly Delights

APRIL 19

Praised are You, Adonai our God, Sovereign of the universe, who creates joy and gladness, groom and bride, mirth, glad song, pleasure, delight, love, brotherhood, peace, and companionship.
FROM THE SIXTH WEDDING BLESSING

While this blessing is specifically designed for the Jewish wedding ceremony, its list of items expresses the ideals for relationship between individuals and a wish for each of us for life. We look for these things in life and value them: mirth, glad song, pleasure, delight, love, brotherhood, peace, and companionship. Thus, they become ideals toward which we all strive.

There are plenty of things to sadden us. All we have to do is turn on the news or read the morning newspaper. But there are also things in life—an overabundance of them—for which to rejoice, for which to be happy. And that is the sentiment of this blessing. For in the relationship of two people is also the potential to create whole worlds, worlds that may shelter us from the pain and suffering that take place, even if it is only in the context of a relationship.

And this relationship, like most others, should reflect the relationship that we are trying to nurture with God, one that is also filled with mirth and joyous song.

Forcing Evil from Our Lives

APRIL 20

Do not let the inclination to do evil dominate us.
FROM A PRAYER THAT IS SOMETIMES ATTACHED
TO THE MORNING BLESSINGS

While this is directed to God, it is really a statement of where prayer should lead us. Not because of what God should do, but because of the message that emerges from prayer and what we should be doing with our lives. According to the Rabbis, we all have the inclination to do evil. But that isn't so bad. It is normal. It is what leads us to find a life partner and build a home. (We also have the inclination to do good.) That is why the text says that our inclination to do evil—which has its positive aspects too—should not "dominate" us.

This may also be why the Rabbis think that the bigger the individual, the larger is the individual's inclination to do evil. Thus, there is a greater possibility for the inclination to do evil in the greater—rather than the lesser—person. There are many opportunities to do good in this life, but there are times when the inclination to do evil threatens to eclipse all of the good. The greater person walks in the center.

Finding the Path

APRIL 21

Give me direction on life's roads.
PSALM 16:11

This is one of the great psalms from the book of Psalms. It is also one of the psalms in what Rabbi Nachman of Breslov called a *tikkun k'lali,* "a general remedy." Reb Nachman taught that if this group of psalms (16, 32, 41, 42, 59, 77, 90, 105, 137, and 150) were read in this order, the individual could actually be delivered from sin. But the individual must also make a commitment to not return to a previous life of sinning.

When facing major decisions—or even minor ones—some people simply pray to God and ask for direction. Some people pray for the answer to a specific question. Others ask for more general insight. But all these approaches have one thing in common: dialogue with the Divine brings clarity to our own thinking. Maybe that is why this text is part of Reb Nachman's general remedy. It is a blessing for all that ails you.

Happiness

APRIL 22

Happy is the one who attends to the needy.
PSALM 41:1

What does it take to be happy? According to this selection from the book of Psalms, all it takes is to care for the impoverished and those who are needy. This is not direction to just give charity. Rather, the text—and the psalmist who wrote it—

imply that we have to discover what are specific needs of the needy and then satisfy them. This means that we have to take a real interest in people. We can't simply give out charity—while this is important—and then be done with it. There is much more that needs to be done to warrant the attention of the psalmist.

Why would this text be included in the book of Psalms, said to be sung by the Levites at the steps of the ancient Temple? This is the message that they wanted the people to hear whenever they entered the precincts of the Temple. It was as if they were singing, "You may come here looking to expiate your sins. You may come here looking for a relationship with the Divine. But the answer to both is in the people who surround you, also here seeking the same thing. If you care for one another, then we can all be redeemed."

Annual Redemption

APRIL 23

Praised are You, Adonai our God, Sovereign of the universe,
who has withheld nothing from the world,
and who has created lovely creatures and
beautiful trees for people to enjoy.

BLESSING ON SEEING TREES BLOSSOMING
FOR THE FIRST TIME OF THE YEAR

One of the beautiful things about spring is the blossoming of trees and flowers. It is also what causes those who experience seasonal allergies to suffer even more. But an acknowledgment of the beauty in the world is an acknowledgment of the Source of that beauty, as well. It also helps us to affirm the dependability of that beauty whenever it reveals itself, but particularly because we know that it will reveal itself each spring.

It is hard to not believe in God when you see the trees blossom and the flowers in bloom, even if your personal world seems not to exude such beauty or magnificence. But that is specifically why the tradition requires that such blessings be said. No matter how you feel, no matter the life you are currently experiencing, the world is filled with beauty—and it is filled with God. Spring is proof of both.

Sacred Space

APRIL 24

Praised are You, Adonai our God, Sovereign of the universe, who restores the borders of the widow [Zion].
ON SEEING RESTORED SYNAGOGUES

This is an unusual blessing and one that is seldom said unless traveling, particularly in Europe, where so many synagogues were destroyed during World War II. Sometimes it is said after the rebuilding of a local synagogue in North America that has been affected by a natural disaster or even by a fire.

This blessing includes a reference to being widowed and to Zion. The text surfaces the images of the destruction of the ancient Temple in Jerusalem, which was first destroyed by the Babylonians in 586 BCE and then by the Romans in 70 CE. This is most poignantly described in the biblical book of Lamentations, in which Jerusalem is painfully pictured as a widow who has lost both spouse (God) and children (the people of Israel).

Whenever you see a restored synagogue, it is important to take note of it. Offer this blessing. It is an expression of hope and commitment for the future. For in the walls of that synagogue is Torah studied. And the study of Torah holds the key to life itself.

Silent Prayer

April 25

*My God, guard my tongue from evil
and my lips from speaking guile.*
FROM THE PRAYER SAID PRIVATELY
AT THE CONCLUSION OF THE *AMIDAH*

This text is read privately following the recitation of what is called the "silent *Amidah*," named as such because it is said by the individual privately (silently or quietly) before being said in public by the person leading the congregation in prayer. It acknowledges that sometimes we need help in doing what is right—refraining from speaking ill of others or spreading gossip about another person. Thus, we ask God for such help.

The author of this prayer rejects the commonly held notion that "if you don't have something nice to say about someone, don't say anything at all." The author of this prayer would probably simply say, "Don't say anything about anyone ever." We may assume that it is OK to say something nice about people, but we can never know how things will be interpreted or if they wanted something to be held privately. This text acknowledges the difficulty of such a posture and sticks with "don't say anything unkind about anyone." It is a nice place to start.

Redemption

APRIL 26

*Praised are You, Adonai our God, Sovereign of the universe,
who bestows favor on those who do not deserve it,
just as you have bestowed favor on me.*

BIRKAT GOMEL, SAID UPON RECOVERING FROM ILLNESS OR
RETURNING FROM A LONG JOURNEY

While some people react negatively to the fact that this blessing is also to be said by the mother following the delivery of a child, it is with the understanding that while we take delivery for granted, life is precious and its beginning can indeed be dangerous. Since this blessing is said publicly in the midst of an assembly, the congregational response is for continued well-being: "May the One who has shown you every kindness continue to deal kindly with you."

It is a shame that such blessings are not regularly employed by people. This is especially true because many people don't find their way into prayer communities. But there are times in our lives when we want to express thanks for our well-being, especially in the community that we call home. And there are times in our lives during which the public expression of gratitude can be transformative. We acknowledge that we have been through a difficult or even life-threatening experience and have emerged from it. We carry this lesson forward in our lives so that we might continue to learn from it and so that we may teach others.

Guidance Forever

APRIL 27

You shall speak of them when you are sitting in your home, when you go on a journey, when you lie down, and when you rise up.

DEUTERONOMY 6:7

This biblical text is also repeated in the paragraph immediately following the two essential lines of the *Sh'ma* prayer around which the remainder of what is called the *"Sh'ma and Its Blessings"* is constructed. While the *Sh'ma* may be called a prayer, it is perhaps the closest that Judaism comes to a creedal statement—the belief in one God. Some will argue that this core belief is what has held the Jewish community together throughout its history. That is why historian Ellis Rivkin calls this the Unity Principle.

Nevertheless, what is crucial about this selection from Deuteronomy is that while it seems like instruction for parents regarding how to teach their children, it is really an expression of Jewish values: The Torah should always be present in your life, whatever you do, wherever you go. The Torah is not something that you call upon when it is convenient for you to do so. Rather, the Torah is what will guide you and your children throughout your lives.

Wholly Separate

APRIL 28

*Remember the Sabbath—keep in mind from Sunday on,
and hold for it anything good that may come your way.*
ELEAZAR BEN HANANIA IM *MEKHILTA* TO EXODUS 20:8

This seems like a simple direction. Yet many miss its importance and choose not to follow its guidance. The observance of Shabbat, as far as I am concerned, however it is observed, is critical to the establishment of a Jewish spiritual life. That is why the Hebrew text uses the term *kadosh* for "holiness," because it means wholly separate, distinct.

Memory plays an important role in the observance of Shabbat. I try to remember Shabbat each day of the week. In the days that precede Shabbat, I anticipate it with longing. And in the days that follow Shabbat, I try to carry its lessons with me throughout the week and into the workaday world. It is important not to rush through each day, not to focus on work at the expense of all else.

I luxuriate in my Shabbat each week, separating myself from the stresses that the workday weekday world places upon me. As the Rabbis teach, Shabbat is indeed both an echo of Eden and a glimpse into the world-to-come.

Light and Joy

APRIL 29

*Give us light and joy, gladness and honor, as in the
happiest of Israel's past.*
FROM THE BEGINNING OF THE *HAVDALAH* RITUAL,
RECITED AT THE END OF SHABBAT

Both the text and the context of this ritual provide us with spiritual insight. This statement is said at the beginning of the

Havdalah ritual by those assembled, after it has been introduced by the one leading the ritual. Here it is Saturday night. Shabbat is almost behind us. Darkness envelops the sky. On the one hand, we want to return to the daily lives that have been suspended for the twenty-five hours of Shabbat. On the other hand, we are reticent to let go of the mystical wonderment of Shabbat. So we let go, but only if we are blessed, much like Jacob asked for blessing after wrestling with the angel, with four elements: light and joy, gladness and honor. These elements seem to represent the high points of the history of the Jewish people and are gained through the embracing of Shabbat.

Marking Time

April 30

Praised are You, Adonai our God, Sovereign of the universe, who makes us holy with mitzvot and instructs us to count the Omer.
BLESSING FOR COUNTING THE OMER

This blessing is said each evening from the second night of Pesach until Shavuot. It uses the traditional formula for blessing and, like so many others, includes the instruction for doing the specific ritual that will spiritually elevate the individual who performs it. But what is special about this ritual act, even though it was originally tied to the barley harvest, is that it is a way of marking time until the experience of revelation and the giving of Torah at Mount Sinai. Unlike so many calendars that we have on our walls on which we count down toward a special occasion, this countdown prescribes a special posture during the period. While it has taken on a sense of mourning because of the ritual practices such as no haircuts or weddings, what it really does is allow us to focus our entire attention on what takes place at the end of the period, what we try to achieve each day of our lives: the Sinai experience and communion with the Almighty.

MAY

The Insight of the Generations

MAY 1

*What is painful to one generation
is insight for the next.*
ELI EVANS

This statement frames the Jewish state of mind during this time of year. Just as a group of holidays are bunched together in the fall and our emotions are intensively pulled in various directions in a short period of time, reflective of our personal lives, the spring is filled with holidays that pull us in other directions, mostly reflective of our collective lives as a people. But what marks this period of time more than anything else is the tension between the depth of pain felt on Yom Hashoah (Holocaust Remembrance Day) and Yom Hazikaron (Israel Memorial Day) and the ecstatic exhilaration of Yom Ha'atzmaut (Israel Independence Day) and Shavuot (which marks the giving of Torah on Mount Sinai). Many of us lived through the actual events that the first three of these holidays commemorate, and the fourth we attempt to relive each time we read Torah in public. For all of us, these holidays have become part of the historical memory of the Jewish people. But in each case, they have the potential to offer us insight for today and for the future, as Eli Evans suggests.

While the collective pain of the Jewish people is felt most keenly during this time of year, such pain becomes suffering only when we do not allow it to provide us insight for living—and for planning the future. The spiritual goal is not to shut out the pain and separate ourselves from it. Rather, we are to embrace the pain, call it our own, and then grow to live beyond it.

Light as a Symbol of the Divine

MAY 2

The reflection of the light of the sun on the moon is like the reflection of Israel's destiny in both this world and the world-to-come.
BACHYA IBN PAKUDA

Light is a symbol of the Divine. It is a symbol of knowledge. And it is a symbol of the future, one that is filled with the possibility of messiah. While the Jewish people has been called the people of the night, since it has been forced to escape at night at various times in its history, Ibn Pakuda is suggesting that it also should be called the people of the light. The prophet Isaiah said it differently and charged the Jewish people with the responsibility of being *l'or goyim*, "a light unto the nations" (Isaiah 42:6).

But this responsibility is not one that is merely collective, one that can be assigned to the people as a whole. In order to be the responsibility of the people, each of us has to do our part. This is the blessing of being part of the Jewish people. So today, contribute to being a light by bringing that light into the life of others. But don't forget to start with yourself. The light comes from the Divine, but it shines in you.

The Dance of Love

MAY 3

Hark! Here comes my love.
You skip over the mountains.
You leap over the hills.
My love is like a gazelle or a fawn.
There you are, standing behind our wall,
looking through the windows and peering through the lattice.
SONG OF SONGS 2:8–9

The public reading of the Song of Songs is assigned by the Rabbis to the holiday of Passover, but it clearly informs the liturgical calendar for the entire season. Spring is the time for renewal and for love—the love between individuals and the love between people and God. And when you are in love, you see the presence of that person everywhere and feel blessed by it. And while the images of this ancient text may be a little awkward and antiquated, the feelings remain the same.

The same is true of our relationship with God. The language that we use to express our feelings may not feel quite right. They may even come from other traditions or cultures. But the feelings are the same. When we are at one with the Divine, we feel so much in love.

Spiritual Showering

May 4

The next time you have an urge to be spiritual,
take a cold shower. Then dry off and do something
kind for someone else.
Rabbi Rami Shapiro

These are the words of my colleague, written under his Hebrew name Yerachmiel ben Yisrael. His spiritual insight and wisdom is down-to-earth and lacks any pretentiousness. For him, spirituality can be boiled down to one basic lesson: do something kind for someone else. In that simple act do we find the sacred and reach the Divine. It reminds me of the teaching of the famous Rabbi Hillel, who wrote that Judaism can be distilled to one notion: "What is hateful to you, don't do to others. All the rest is commentary. Go and learn it" (Babylonian Talmud, *Shabbat* 31a).

For some people, spirituality demands the engagement of sacred text and intricate ritual. And for others, spirituality implies simple acts of kindness. Both are necessary to change the world. In such acts of transformation, we improve a broken world and ourselves.

Restoring Sight

May 5

Praised are You, Adonai our God, Sovereign of the universe,
who gives sight to the blind.
From the morning blessings

Originally, the group of blessings known as "morning blessings" were said upon arising. There was even a specific choreography designed to follow a typical morning routine—opening the eyes, sitting up, swinging around and putting your feet on the floor, and so on. Then these blessings became part of the fixed liturgy and moved into the synagogue (or remained at home if that is where the individual's morning prayers were recited).

As a result, this text really has two meanings. First, it is a specific reference to how we feel upon awaking in the morning. When we awake after sleeping all night, we feel as if we had been blind and now can see. Thus, we are grateful to God for the gift of sight, which we experience anew each morning. These words of blessing help us to recognize this realization as a blessing indeed. Second, we acknowledge God as the one who helps us to really see the world as it is, overflowing with inherent potential for blessing. Irrespective of whether or not we have vision, we are given the gift of sight—to raise to the sacred all that we experience in the world around us.

Memory

MAY 6

Merciful One, bless the soldiers of the Israel Defense Forces and protect them.

ONE OF THE PETITIONS SAID DURING
BIRKAT HAMAZON (GRACE AFTER MEALS)

This is one of many petitions contained in the so-called Grace after Meals. It asks for God to protect those who put their lives in danger on our behalf. It is particularly appropriate that it be recited during this time of year when Yom Hazikaron (Israel Memorial Day) is commemorated. While Yom Hazikaron was originally planned to honor the memory of those in the armed service, it has since been expanded unfortunately to include those who died as a result of acts of terror.

In our home, we also ask for God's protection over those who serve in the American armed forces. It is important to take a moment out of each day to reflect on those who give their lives here and elsewhere on our behalf. May their memory be a blessing to us all.

Dawn

MAY 7

Merciful One, bless the State of Israel,
the dawn of our redemption.
ONE OF THE PETITIONS SAID DURING
BIRKAT HAMAZON (GRACE AFTER MEALS)

This too is one of many petitions included in the Grace after Meals. For so many of us, Israel is already a blessing. It is important to regularly maintain our focus on Israel, particularly as the center of our spiritual lives. And it is particularly relevant to our celebration this month of Yom Ha'atzmaut, Israel Independence Day. For those who survived the Holocaust, the establishment of the modern State of Israel was specifically redemptive. For the rest of us, Israel represents an endless variety of indescribable feelings.

And so we ask God, as the Source for such redemption, to continue to bless us with Israel and provide it with divine protection. The dawn of our redemption refers to the messianic era. Although we may realize that messianic time is still a long way off, in the presence of Israel it often feels like it is already here.

Heavenly Jerusalem

MAY 8

Rejoice with Jerusalem in joy
all you who mourn over her.
ISAIAH 66:10

This text from Isaiah is particularly appropriate this month as we celebrate Yom Yerushalayim (Jerusalem Day), which commemorates the unification of the city during the Six-Day War in 1967. But it is an unusual text. And while the prophet Isaiah was speaking about the destruction of the ancient city of Jerusalem, we understand its contradiction today. Those who mourned over Jerusalem throughout Jewish history did so because of an unparalleled love for the city and all it represents. So we continue to mourn for the destruction it suffered in the past, even as we rejoice in its accomplishments and beauty today.

I take the opportunity to go to Israel whenever I can, even if it is to just breathe its air for a short time. In Jerusalem, I am renewed. It is in Jerusalem where I can be rooted in the ground and soar to its heavens. It is in Jerusalem where I can feel most blessed.

Giving Advice

MAY 9

It is easier to give advice to others than to oneself.
RABBI NACHMAN OF BRESLOV

We are often so busy finding fault in others that we seldom take the time to find fault in ourselves. Similarly, we are so focused on providing advice to others—whether invited or unsolicited—that we forget that such advice is usually relevant to our lives, as well. So before you rush to tell someone else what to do, take a look at your own life and determine whether you are in fact inclined to do it as well. And if not, then stop hurrying and find something else to do.

We often don't like to do the hard things—and taking our own advice is usually pretty hard to do. It is much easier to dole out words of wisdom to others. Perhaps the first word of advice should be: listen to what you are saying. There might be something important to be heard. And there may even be words of blessing hidden in the message.

Finding Strength

MAY 10

If you are lax on a day of trouble,
your own strength will be small.
PROVERBS 24:10

It is not uncommon to find it difficult to interpret the guidance provided by the author of Proverbs. The author is suggesting that our strength is tested and held in reserve for days that challenge us. (For some of us, that may be quite often.) Then we are able to muster the necessary strength on those other—more regular—days to face the rigor of everyday living. But if we are not able to call on that strength on the difficult days of life, then there will be nothing for us to do the rest of the time.

Some may think that the author of Proverbs has it backwards. Shouldn't we need our strength for the really hard days? But it is those days that prepare us for the rest—and for the best—of days. And these are the days out of which life is made. That is the blessing that lies dormant in the dark side of life. Our job is to bring it out into the light.

Doing What Is Right

MAY 11

Everyone will do what is right in one's eyes.
DEUTERONOMY 12:8

While God is indeed the Source for good in the world, we have to set forth the moral compass for what we do. This selection from Deuteronomy is suggesting that we are, in fact, the best arbiter of what is moral judgment—but we have to be prepared to exercise it. We know what is right and can distinguish it from what is wrong. And the exercise of moral judgment is an obligation that we must undertake.

So what motivates us to act, to do what is right? What motivates us to take action when we see what is wrong? It is this inner sense of what is right with which we are all blessed. And it is this inner sense that is nurtured by our relationship with the Divine.

Tomorrow's Joy

MAY 12

On the day of prosperity, affliction is forgotten. On the day of affliction, prosperity is remembered no more.
BEN SIRA 11:25

The human memory is a peculiar instrument. It sometimes works in strange, unpredictable ways. It might actually be good for us to forget those days of pain when we are enjoying the best that life has to offer. That is certainly what some women say after they have experienced the pangs of childbirth only to be overwhelmed by the joy and blessing of a child.

But if we forget those days in which we are overwhelmed by pain and a sense of doom, we may be deluding ourselves. As a result, we may fall even harder when things are not quite right, when the days of our lives are dark and dismal. And we all have such days. It is part of the rhythm of life and the price we pay for all the blessings we enjoy.

So enjoy what today has to offer even as you recall the pain of the past. Tomorrow is a day potentially filled with joy—because in it is contained all the future has to offer us.

Finding Elijah

MAY 13

Don't be too quick to get angry
for anger rests in the bosom of fools.
ECCLESIASTES 7:9

It is easy to get angry at so many things. It seems like the less important things are, the angrier we get about them. It makes no sense at all. And that is what this text from the wisdom teacher named Kohelet is teaching us. He joins us in asking this basic question: Is it worth it? But he goes one step further. Kohelet argues that anger is a reflection of who we are—and those who anger quickly are fools.

There are times to be angry to be sure: when we see injustices perpetrated in the world, when those who are in the right are wrongly accused of misdeeds, when those who are innocent suffer the punishment intended for those who are guilty. But these are reasoned responses. They are not the knee-jerk reactions out of which too many interactions seem to be made. So the next time you feel anger rising up within you, take a cue from the lesson you learned in kindergarten. Count to ten, and then take a look around for the prophet Elijah. He may be waiting to bless us. He may also be waiting for your reaction so that you can join him in ushering in a more perfect world.

Dreaming

MAY 14

A person's every act begins with a dream
and ends with one.
THEODOR HERZL

As the founder of modern political Zionism, Theodor Herzl understood what it was to be a dreamer. He imagined a Jewish state when few others thought it even possible. But the dream of a Jewish people in its own land fueled his adult life. His life teaches us a few things. First, to realize a dream, you must be willing to dream. Some people are so attached to their current situation that they are unable to let go and grow beyond it. Second, you must have a dream. Like Herzl, this dream has the potential to energize you, to motivate you, to move you forward on your life's journey. Then you must be willing to work toward the realization of the dream.

Simple steps. But clearly not a simple process to take them. So here is what I recommend. Reach back into your childhood dreams. What was it that you wanted to be? What was it that you wanted to achieve? If they don't make sense any longer, let them go. Otherwise reclaim them or start dreaming anew. Then take the first step toward reaching that dream. Don't wait until tomorrow. Take that first step today, now, before the moment passes. Dreams have the potential to bring blessing in their wake.

Reaching Higher than the Self

MAY 15

The higher I get, the higher I want to be.
LADINO FOLK SAYING

Some may read this as a statement about the drug culture or a comment on the 1960s. But this is really a statement about aspirations and soaring heavenward. The higher I am able to reach spiritually, the closer I seem to God; the higher I want to be, the closer to God I desire to be. It is not that in the realm of the spiritual there seems to be limited satisfaction. Rather, a connection with the holy motivates us to want to reach higher (to heaven) and deeper (inside ourselves) at the same time.

But life is not about just the high moments. This is perhaps why so many are disappointed by their lives. They think that it should always be about the highs and continue their search for them. But the highs really come from the everyday, the routine, the regular and not so lofty. That is where we might find the holiness that sends us higher.

Reciprocal Holiness

MAY 16

Blessed shall you be when you enter,
and blessed shall you be when you depart.
DEUTERONOMY 28:6

While this is a text—and a blessing—taken from the Torah, it is used quite frequently in other settings as well. In its original context, it is one of many blessings that the Torah tells us an individual receives as a result of following God's instructions. By uttering it, we access holiness in two ways. First, we are able to enter into a relationship with another person that establishes an important level of mutual respect. Why else would you offer a blessing for others as they enter your home or synagogue? In doing so it raises any physical space to a sacred level—as it does the relationship between the person making the blessing and the one receiving it. Second, it offers a hope that the time together may be blessed and thereby establishes the parameters for a continuing relationship.

Imagine if this was the feeling that we had for all relationships and the standards that we set for all dialogue and interaction. Then we would truly be able to reach the idealized version of relationship that the twentieth-century Jewish philosopher Martin Buber called "I-Thou." This "I-Thou" relationship is a goal that we strive toward and is modeled after the relationship of the individual with the Divine. May all of our relationships achieve such a level of reciprocal holiness and reach such a sacred place.

Releasing Our Burdens

MAY 17

Worry weighs the mind down.
A nice word makes it happy.
PROVERBS 12:25

The wisdom of the author of Proverbs is instructional. The author understands that some things we learn should be shared with others. The author understands the challenges of life and all its perils. He understands that we can navigate the challenges of life with the guidance of others. And he wants to shape a life worth living—a life of blessing—and encourages us to do the same.

In this particular quip, the wisdom is simple and straightforward as is his tendency. The book of Proverbs says it straight: Don't worry about things that are out of our control. They weigh us down. They become burdens under whose weight we cannot move. Saying something nice to someone else somehow lessens the burden of our worry. That is how his strategy for living works. If we can't do something about the worrying, we can do something to sweeten another person's day.

Responding to Blessing

MAY 18

*A person embezzles from God when
making use of this earth without uttering a blessing.*
TOSEFTA TO BERAKHOT 4:1

Embezzlement. Sounds more like the kind of headline one might find in a daily newspaper. Embezzlement is the act of dishonestly appropriating goods, usually money, by a person to whom they have been entrusted. Some consider it a white collar crime, since it doesn't usually threaten the physical well-being of another. Nevertheless, this is a rather strong statement to find in a book of sacred writ. But the sentiment expressed by the Rabbis is quite clear. We have indeed been entrusted with the responsibility of being caretakers of the earth and all its inhabitants. When we make use of the produce of earth and all of its natural resources, much of which we too often take for granted, we are obligated to acknowledge their Source with gratitude. If we don't take the opportunity to do so, it is as if we have stolen, taken something that doesn't belong to us and used it for our own benefit.

But there is more. According to this statement from the *Tosefta*, the Rabbis want us to know that we should feel motivated to express our thanks and not do so simply because of a feeling of obligation. Our expression of blessing should come as a natural response to our interaction with our surroundings. As we feel blessed, we should respond accordingly.

Standing Tall

MAY 19

In the place of the great, don't stand.
PROVERBS 25:6

This seems like peculiar advice, even from the pen of the author of Proverbs. But if we dig deeper into the text, a plea for humility is revealed. If you try to stand in the same place as someone who is determined to be great—or even just perceived to be great—then it may be arrogance on your part. In addition, it means that you are seeking to displace the person from where he or she is already standing.

However, it doesn't mean that you shouldn't strive toward greatness. But such striving should emerge from the good that you are seeking to accomplish rather than the recognition for your work that you might potentially receive. Real greatness comes from the blessing of essential goodness.

The Posture of Welcome

MAY 20

Be the first to greet everyone.
PIRKEI AVOT 4:15

This is really what creating a welcoming community is all about. It doesn't take programs or initiatives. It simply takes one person after another deciding that being welcoming and friendly is important. So don't wait for someone else to say hello to the stranger. Rush out and do so yourself.

There are many places in our tradition that we see this in practice and thereby learn from it. The classical source is, of course, the story of Abraham rushing to greet those who have come to visit him. It wasn't enough that he left all four flaps of his tent open. When he saw someone approaching from afar, he ran to greet them. Another context is far more subtle. As the Torah scroll is carried around the synagogue prior to its being read—as well as afterward—people wait to be able to touch it or kiss it. But we are never supposed to wait for the Torah to come to us. We are always supposed to take at least one step toward it. In that one step forward, entire attitudes can change. So follow the wisdom of *Pirkei Avot* and make the difference in a person's life by just saying hello. It is how the blessing of all relationships begins.

Finding Happiness

MAY 21

The best way to gain happiness is not to look for it.
SIR MOSES MONTEFIORE

The pursuit of happiness is ironically a relatively modern enterprise. It follows on living a life of luxury and freedom, which is also relatively new for large segments of the population, especially for the Jewish community. If we live our lives fully and are content with the blessings of the everyday, we may indeed find happiness hidden beneath. But notice that Montefiore didn't say "find happiness," he said "gain happiness." It is as if there is some sort of accrual process. So if you do things as a way of accruing happiness (as if the total of doing X a specified number of times will yield happiness), then you will never accumulate enough to get there. Do them for their own sake. Do what you like to do—because you enjoy it.

It seems that Montefiore's advice holds true in so many areas of life with the possible exception of the most basic and most profound. If we seek a life of blessing, we can indeed find it.

Seeking Knowledge

MAY 22

A discerning mind seeks knowledge,
but the mouth of fools feeds on folly.
PROVERBS 15:14

Sometimes the first phrase of this text is translated as "a discerning heart" rather than as "a discerning mind." Perhaps this is a result of the dispute among the ancients regarding in which organ knowledge (rather than emotion) is seated. But I think that the author of Proverbs believed that discernment in the mind and heart are related, even if this is not a text about feelings. For the author of this text, and the entirety of Proverbs, the difference between the intelligent person and the fool rests in their attitude toward knowledge. The intelligent person wants to gain more; the fool does not care at all.

Knowledge takes time to acquire. For some people, they find a life of the spirit through the mind. For the author, the acquisition of knowledge is the primary way to fill a life with blessing.

The Priestly Blessing

MAY 23

May Adonai bless you and keep you.
May Adonai cause divine light to shine upon you
and be gracious to you.
May Adonai pay attention to you
and give you peace.
NUMBERS 6:24–26

This text from the Bible is generally called the Priestly Blessing or Priestly Benediction. What is powerful about this text is that it empowers people to bless other people by calling on the power of the Divine. They become a channel through which divine blessing can flow into the world.

As the descendants of the priests offer this blessing upon those assembled in the synagogue for worship, they hold their hands in a particular way (the source of Leonard Nimoy/Mr. Spock's Vulcan sign on *Star Trek*). Some see it as a "V," but that is because they are looking at it upside down. According to my colleague Rabbi Eliot Malomet, it is an attempt by the priests to imprint the name of God on the people, spelling out the letters as they appear in the so-called unpronounceable name of God. It is a spiritual tattoo of sorts, where the ink is invisible to most others but quite clear to the one who receives it.

Receiving Torah

MAY 24

Praised are You, Adonai our God, Sovereign of the universe,
who gave us the Torah of truth
and planted within us life eternal.
Praised are You, Adonai, who gives the Torah.
BLESSING RECITED AFTER READING FROM THE TORAH

This blessing is recited each time the Torah is read aloud, in public. Whether it is recited by rote or stumbled over by the person given the honor to do so (and yes, it is indeed an honor), we seldom take the time to reflect on the import of the blessing and its powerful message to us. While the person who recites the blessing is generally not the person who has read the Torah (and instead the former assigns a surrogacy to the latter to do so), the message is the same for all. Torah and what it represents is the source for eternal life in Judaism. Moreover, as this blessing suggests, while Torah was given in the past, ("who gave us the Torah of truth"), the giving of Torah is ongoing ("who gives the Torah"). Each time we hear its words, we have the potential to receive its message—and its blessing.

The Torah is constantly being given to us. We have only to be willing to receive it.

Becoming One

MAY 25

They shall become one flesh.
GENESIS 2:24

How do you determine whether the sexual act about to be performed is appropriate for you—either because of what you are doing or because of the person with whom you are doing it? Rabbi Laura Geller suggests that you ask yourself one simple question: "Can I say a blessing before I perform this act?" But don't just answer the question. Go ahead and recite the blessing.

This confirms the notion that there is indeed a blessing for everything in Judaism. And such a blessing raises sexuality to the sacred level that it deserves when two people—in love—are brought close to one another, in a way that is accomplished through no other means.

Parenting

MAY 26

May God make you like Ephraim and Manasseh.
May God make you like Sarah, Rebecca, Rachel, and Leah.

TRADITIONAL BLESSINGS SAID BY
PARENTS OVER CHILDREN ON SHABBAT AND HOLIDAYS

The first statement is said for boys, and the second statement is said for girls. Then both blessings are concluded by the Priestly Blessing. (See May 23 entry.) I have been saying these blessings for over twenty-five years, each week, first over my sons and later my daughters-in-law, as well. These are powerfully transformative moments for all of us—as these adults line up as children to be blessed. What is it about the power of blessing that draws us together? And why these words?

The blessing for boys mimics the context of blessing offered by Jacob over his grandchildren, Joseph's children, when he took them as his own. The Bible puts it this way: "On that day, Jacob blessed them. He said, 'In time to come, Israel [the Jewish people] will use you as a blessing. They will say: May

God make you like Ephraim and Manasseh'" (Genesis 48:20). According to Jewish tradition, these two brothers lived together in harmony, without rancor, without any measure of rivalry. Thus, it is the prayer of parents that the world may be blessed as a result of the good words of their children.

The blessing for girls calls upon the merit accrued by the mothers of Israel. Each woman contributed uniquely to Jewish history and had her own unique quality. But they also shared something in common. They were able to selflessly live in such a way as to enable others to realize their potential and their gifts as members of the Jewish people. In so doing, they realized their potential as leaders as well.

Together, these blessings form the foundation for our future—what we wish for ourselves and what we wish for our children. May the world be a better place in which to live because we have been blessed by their presence in it.

A Holy Nation

MAY 27

In Judaism, holiness is not the same as perfection.
The Israelites wandering in the desert are called holy,
am kadosh, goy kadosh, *not because of their actions,*
but because of their aspirations.
Each of us is commanded to be holy,
not because we can be perfect,
but because we can perform holy acts
and increase holiness in the world.
RABBI MELANIE ARON

This is the kind of message that should be posted in lots of places to remind us of what we need to do during most of our working moments. Place it on your desk, on your refrigerator, even on the bathroom mirror. Perhaps it can even be used as a *kavvanah* (sacred mantra) that frames our day or that we reflect on in preparation for more formal moments of prayer. Rabbi Aron teaches us that we aren't holy because of who we are. Rather, we can become holy because of where we want to be. Holiness then becomes an ever-motivating goal rather than a state of being. Holiness is a dynamic force and never static. And it certainly does not reflect anything intrinsic about an object or individual. The nature of holiness, then, is always in flux. As we pursue the various activities represented by it, it moves along with us.

This is the way it works, according to Rabbi Aron's words. We can bring holiness into the world by what we attempt to do and thereby become holy as a result of being engaged in the process, as well.

The Gift of Morning

MAY 28

Adonai, in the morning, You will hear my voice;
in the morning, I will offer my prayer to You,
and will look forward.
PSALM 5:4

This is the framework in which daily prayers are offered each morning. We begin the day with such prayers because we are thankful for the gift of life each morning. We are grateful for the opportunity that each new day offers us. We look forward to the day ahead, not knowing what it holds for us but feeling confident because it will be built on the foundation of prayer that we establish each day.

Because of the relationship with God that is presumed in this text from Psalms, the writer assumes that God will hear the voice of the one who is praying, but there is no assumption that God will necessarily respond to those prayers. While that can never be guaranteed, we do know that it takes a lot more for that to happen than the simple utterance of prayer. But we do so nonetheless each day because that is the best place to start—in dialogue with the Divine.

Standing at Prayer

MAY 29

The Holy One of Blessing knows what is in my heart.
I will give God the letters, and
God will put the words together [in prayer].
FROM A CHASIDIC STORY

When there seems to be no fixed words of blessing to be said that emerge from Jewish tradition, reach into your heart and just speak the truth. Don't be afraid if the words seem angry or harsh, or if they are not colored by poetry or clever turns of phrase. You may want to use the traditional formula of blessing to initiate the dialogue with the Divine ("Praised are You, Adonai our God ... "), or you may find a different phrase to be more to your liking (such as "Praised is the Source of life in the universe ... ") and more reflective of how you feel.

Sometimes silence can speak words of blessing, as can the silent scream taught to us by Rabbi Nachman of Breslov (open your mouth and scream as loud as you can without emitting a sound).

Whether with fully articulated words, phrases, and fragments of speech, or silence, pray with all of your being and all the presence you can muster. Wherever you stand in prayer, you will be standing before the Holy One of Blessing.

The Lesson of Memory

MAY 30

We are all people of memory and prayer.
EZER WEIZMAN

These words were spoken—in Hebrew—on January 16, 1996, by Ezer Weizman, then president of Israel, addressing both houses of parliament in Germany. He went on to say, "We are people of words and hope. We have neither established empires nor built castles and palaces. We have only placed words on top of each other."

These are poignant words to be included during a month of memory, both for the Jewish people and for the United States on its Memorial Day. The Jewish people is not merely a people with a history. It is a people with memory. And memory is a blessing. It is that memory that has sustained us throughout our wanderings. It is that memory that has driven us and motivated us and goaded us to dream of a more perfect time and a more perfect world.

Memory, like prayer, is made up of words. But when those words are placed together, they form a powerful spiritual structure that provides us with meaning.

Blessings Ahead

MAY 31

May the Holy One bless the new month for us and for all the people and the house of Israel with life and peace, joy and gladness, deliverance and consolation.
FROM THE BLESSING ANNOUNCING THE NEW MONTH

The new month in the Hebrew calendar is a mini-holiday and cause for celebration. Thus, it is formally announced in the synagogue on the Shabbat before it takes place. The new month, which is designated by the appearance of the new moon, occurs either on the first of the month or the last (of the preceding month). After a month, it is time to reflect on what has taken place and to get ready for the days ahead.

So we ask God's blessings for us and for others. We ask for a month of life and peace, joy and gladness, salvation and consolation. The first items seem to make sense and fit together. It is the last item that gives us pause. From what do we need consolation? Is it perhaps the disappointments that we inevitably sustained? After all, each month of our lives will include success and failure. Or perhaps it is in anticipation of what we might encounter in the month ahead. And we are asking God to provide us a measure of consolation—for whatever we might encounter, especially if it brings sadness along with it. Maybe we are asking God for the strength to be among those who console others at their time of need. Then there will always be someone there to help us, as well.

JUNE

Meditating

JUNE 1

Isaac went out to meditate in the field....
GENESIS 24:63

This is taken from the narrative in Genesis when Isaac meets Rebecca. It is also used as textual proof for the fixed afternoon prayer service in Jewish ritual. Of the three daily services, the *Minchah* (afternoon) service is probably the most difficult to remember and the most difficult to make part of one's daily routine. This is rather ironic, since it is also the shortest of the fixed worship services. The liturgy is rather uncomplicated and generally unchanging (except for the additions for holidays and Shabbat and what are called "liturgical embellishments," simple word constructs and phrases that reference a particular period of time). *Minchah* challenges the notion that things that are difficult are generally long and confusing. Even for those of us whose religious life does not yet include the regular rhythm of three fixed prayer services a day, there is much here to be learned for our spiritual lives.

Add to this difficulty that the time for *Minchah* comes sometime after lunch and you may still be full from that little extra you had, especially if it follows Friday night and Saturday. You've had a big meal, maybe even Sunday brunch, and you're tired. But here in *Minchah*, the body and the soul come together. Both are blessed. Both get renewed through the process.

Prayer Rhythm

JUNE 2

All my bones will say, "Adonai, who is like You?"
PSALM 35:10

This seems like an odd notion. How can "bones" (some translated as "limbs") speak? And yet, it is from this psalm text that emerges the idea that one should pray, one should express oneself to God, with the entire body. Words of prayer are insufficient. Every aspect of one's body should be engaged in the worship of the Divine. It is why large segments of the Jewish community, particularly traditional Jews, *shuckle* (sway back and forth) in prayer.

Some may find such movement distracting, and it certainly is not required. Others may find that it helps them to concentrate on prayer, to center themselves and focus on what they are doing. I find that it helps me to separate myself from my surroundings in an intentionally disorienting way. Much like tapping the foot in response to music, it is a way to help me maintain the rhythm of my prayers. There I find blessing—in the midst of such rhythm. And there I can find myself.

Self-Motivation

JUNE 3

A person who is commanded to do something and does it is greater than a person who isn't commanded to do something and does it.
BABYLONIAN TALMUD, *BAVA KAMMA* 38A

This is another example of how spirituality can be somewhat counterintuitive. After all, one might think self-motivation would be a value in the religious context. What could the Rabbis of the Talmud have had in mind when shaping this notion? While some people may not resonate with the idea of "command," and I certainly prefer "instruct," both assume a relationship. One is commanded/instructed, and the other is commander/instructor. Thus, the one who responds to the command is doing so in the context of a relationship with God. The other may end up exhibiting the same behavior, but it is without the benefit of a divine relationship. Thus, it is not grounded in the sacred and, as a result, will not help the individual to soar heavenward.

Because I personally do not feel commanded, I voluntarily place myself in the context of such a relationship with the Divine so that I can indeed be responsive to such commands. I seek such a covenantal relationship—and it informs all that I do. That is why I make the personal choice to live a life of blessing.

Gaining an Extra Soul

JUNE 4

Before Shabbat comes,
the Holy Blessed One gives each person an extra soul,
and when Shabbat is over, it is taken back.
BABYLONIAN TALMUD, *BEITZAH* 16A

I eagerly look forward to Shabbat and its observance each week. Perhaps it is because of the exhausting week that undoubtedly precedes it. Or maybe it is because I know what to expect of Shabbat—and its observance. I see it all as privilege, not prohibition. Blessing rather than burden. Of its many benefits is indeed this extra soul, which helps to restore me.

In some homes, Sunday afternoon is devoted to cleaning up from the day before, especially since we do not even remove the tablecloth on Shabbat. It remains on the table as a symbol of our entire day of observance and celebration. And if your house is like most, lots of little tasks accumulate during the hours of Shabbat, even simple daily chores that are left aside during Shabbat, or the things we just didn't quite get to as we rushed to get ready on Friday afternoon. That is why when we enter into the regular week, after a day of Shabbat, we do so with full force. And we are able to do so because we are renewed from a day of relaxation and contemplation. Many of us may be off from work on Sunday, particularly those who live in North America, but it feels like a workday nonetheless. Errands. Grocery shopping. Carpools. Nevertheless, because Sunday is not a workday, it provides us with the opportunity to reflect on what we have gained from the past Shabbat experience, what we can take into the days ahead, and how we might prepare better for the Shabbat to come.

Extinguishing Transgressions

JUNE 5

Transgression extinguishes the light radiated by mitzvot but does not distinguish the light of Torah.
BABYLONIAN TALMUD, *SOTAH* 21A

The light of the Divine shines in many places but particularly in the context of the study of sacred texts. Unlike other forms of light, divine light casts no shadow and it can never be extinguished. In the midst of such study, in such penetrating light, we are able to see ourselves more clearly.

But when we sin, when we transgress, when we do something that is wrong, the light that emanates from the mitzvah, a benefit from performing the act itself, is diminished.

Because the light of Torah is not extinguished, it provides us with the ability to discern the road ahead, the path that needs to be taken. That is the real blessing of sacred study.

Savoring Food

JUNE 6

Praised are You, Adonai our God, Sovereign of the universe, at whose word all things come into being.
GENERAL BLESSING FOR FOOD

This is the blessing to be used "when in doubt" or if food doesn't fit into any category of traditional foods. It recognizes God as the Source of all. While we usually think of prayer and ritual—or even the study of sacred texts—as vehicles to be used to bring us into relationship with the Divine, this blessing clearly demonstrates how food can bring us closer to God. Just by uttering this simple phrase, we acknowledge God's role in the world and in our lives.

So if you are about to eat something, especially if you are not sure which blessing might apply or you are not sure of the nature of the food you are about to eat (for example, did it come from a tree or grow on the ground?), don't rush through the blessing in order to get to the food. Savor its words, just as you might the food you are about to eat. Both have the potential to nourish and sustain you.

The Feminine Side of God

JUNE 7

Let us bless the Divine Presence, Spirit of the world ...
FEMININE FORMULA FOR BLESSING

There are many who take the introductory words of most blessings for granted. We allow them to roll off the tongue routinely without giving them much thought. We rush through them as if they are one long, continuous word, just to get to the heart of the matter: the reference point for the particular blessing and act that follows. But these words of introduction are important. They establish the parameters of a relationship. They shape our understanding of the Divine by identifying key attributes.

These words of blessing are used by feminists, in particular, to acknowledge the presence of God in our midst. This presence, known as *Shekhinah*, represents the feminine attributes of God. So this introduction to blessing is used just as is the standard formula for blessing (Praised are You, Adonai our God ...) to bring people into dialogue with the Divine. May they all lead us to a life of blessing.

The Blessing of Bread

JUNE 8

*Blessed is the Merciful One, Sovereign of the universe,
Master of this bread.*

BABYLONIAN TALMUD, *BERAKHOT* 40B

This one line of text is actually offered as a quickie substitute for the lengthy *Birkat Hamazon* (Grace after Meals). Understanding bread as a central substance of our food and representative of an entire meal, it acknowledges and thanks God for providing it to us. Some use the Aramaic original of this text as a *kavvanah*, a sacred mantra, following the meal—any meal—so that we might focus our attention on our gratitude and become centered.

In her understanding of the text, Rabbi Shefa Gold adds this line to the *kavvanah*: "You are the Source of Life for all that is and Your blessings flow through me." This acknowledges God as the source of life and the food we have eaten, while expressing gratitude. But the food didn't just appear on our table. So this is a reminder that we all have a sacred obligation as the channel through which blessings can flow into this world.

Up All Night

JUNE 9

You upright, having heard hymns of praise,
May you be in that blessed fellowship.
You will deserve to sit among that circle
If you obey God's words of majesty.
For God, in the heights at Beginning and End,
Bent forward in love to give us the Torah.

FROM THE *AKDAMUT* POEM, READ ON SHAVUOT

By providing a motivation for its listeners to cling to the Torah, this unusual poem reflects the salient elements of the holiday of Shavuot. While it was originally designed as a statement against the mock "debates" forced upon the European Jewish communities by invading Crusaders in the eleventh century, it provides us with insight for contemporary faith, as well. The poem presents us with a vision of what is possible in a messianic era and what will be required for us to be able to take part in it while, at the same time, being responsible for ushering it in.

Out of love and compassion, God gave us the Torah. It provides direction for our lives if we follow its guidance and continue on the path established by it for us. On the holiday of Shavuot, after staying up all night in anticipation, we can relive the blessing of its revelation once again.

Improving One's Life

JUNE 10

*The prime purpose of a person's life is to constantly improve to break one's bad traits.
Otherwise, what is life for?*

VILNA GAON, *EVEN SH'LEIMAH* 1:2

The rabbinic authority known as the Vilna Gaon exerted a great deal of influence on the Jewish community of his time. He stood in opposition to Chasidism and favored an intellectual approach to Judaism. This notion of his, as articulated above, suggests that we should always be traveling on a path of self-improvement. This is how our life should be defined. He acknowledges that we all have bad habits, but he does not name them as sins. Perhaps the sin or transgression comes in not trying to improve on our behaviors. For the Vilna Gaon, the blessing of life comes in the opportunity to improve.

Some of us may feel frustrated and disillusioned and say, "What's the point?" But the Vilna Gaon comes to remind us that the potential to improve, to grow, is the point. And it is this notion that motivates us to move forward. We are placed on this earth as human beings, but he sees this as the blessing of humans becoming.

The Holy City of Jerusalem

JUNE 11

Let Jerusalem, the holy city, be renewed in our time.
We praise You, Adonai. In compassion
You rebuild Jerusalem.

FROM *BIRKAT HAMAZON*, GRACE AFTER MEALS

This notion emerges frequently in our liturgy. A yearning for Jerusalem pervades holiday celebrations and life-cycle events. It is amazing that this impassioned longing has not abated—even since the independence of the State of Israel in 1948 or the reunification of Jerusalem since 1967. The idea of a restored Jerusalem is built in the messianic hope of Judaism and, as a result, actually represents the coming of the messianic era.

This is also one of four blessings around which the Grace after Meals is constructed. So for those who recite Grace after Meals regularly, as we are instructed to do, Jerusalem becomes a central focus of our spiritual lives.

Some people may find it difficult to understand the relationship between an expression of gratitude for the food we have eaten and the desire to rebuild Jerusalem. We may require food to live, but a love for Jerusalem sustains our souls.

Fulfilling One Commandment

JUNE 12

If I fulfill only one mitzvah in and through the love of
God, it is as though I have fulfilled them all.

BAAL SHEM TOV

The Rabbis of the Mishnah suggest that the study of Torah is the most important of all those mitzvot (sacred commandments) whose fulfillment is not determined by a particular amount of time. In other words, how many times you study or how much you study is not specified. The notion is that the study of Torah is important because it leads to the fulfillment of other mitzvot. But Baal Shem Tov, the founder of what has come to be known as Chasidism, is suggesting something far more spiritual. He is focused on the relationship between God and the individual. For it is that relationship and the love that binds it that sustain all mitzvot and our ability to fulfill them. It is the attempt to fulfill only one mitvah fully motivated by a love of God and a desire to get closer to the Divine that allows us to complete any other.

Since rituals, in particular, are designed to foster a relationship between the individual and the Divine, if we are able complete one ritual fully, then we will have achieved the goal of them all. And we receive the blessing of coming closer to God as a result.

Transforming Darkness

JUNE 13

The Holy One created light out of darkness.
LEVITICUS RABBAH 31:8

This is a lesson that seems to come right out of the story of creation. But it is also an important spiritual insight that has direct application to our daily lives. As much as we would like things to be constantly flowing in a positive direction, it doesn't always happen. There is disappointment, illness, and loss. These diminish the light in the world and are directly responsible for its darkness. It is only as a result of that darkness that we are able to discern the light. And light is a blessing. The text above takes this notion even further. Its author argues that God actually creates the light out of the darkness.

This is a challenge for all of us. How do we take the darkness in our lives, with the support of the Holy One of Blessing, and transform it into light? Admittedly, it isn't easy, but it is possible. Without light, there is no shadow. And without God, there can be no light.

Sweet Melodies of Prayer

JUNE 14

Melodies I weave, songs I sweetly sing
Yearning for Your presence to You I long to cling.
ANIM Z'MIROT, FROM THE MORNING SERVICE

These are the introductory verses to an unusual liturgical poem that is included in the morning liturgy. It was written by Yehuda Hechasid, a twelfth-century kabbalist. In it is a complete theology of Judaism. But its message is not didactic. Rather, it endeavors to teach us what the mystics call *d'vekut*, an attachment to God, and to which we should all strive. After all, that is the entire purpose of liturgy and prayer—to bring us into an intimate relationship with God, to be as close as is possible without giving up our individual sense of self.

While the prayer poem is included early in the prayer book, it is most often sung near the close of the worship service. If the individual is flush from the prayer experience, then such attachment is possible. These are the sweet melodies that we sing throughout the day that remind us of the presence of God and of our relationship to the Divine.

The Rewards of Prayer

JUNE 15

*For the ordinary worshiper, the rewards of a lifetime of faithful
praying come at predicable times, scattered throughout the
years, when all at once the liturgy glows with fire.*
HERMAN WOUK

Herman Wouk captured a treasure trove of emotions in his
mostly fictional writing. But his passion for Judaism and understanding of a spiritual life are encapsulated in this one statement. Some of us attempt to pray, even routinely, then give it up
because we are not able to reach the mountaintop each time we
immerse ourselves in prayer. We may attend formal services at
a synagogue and come away disappointed. But a regimen of
prayer provides us with a foundation so that as we build upon
it we come closer to ecstasy each time. And when we are able
to reach the peak of the Sinai experience, we have readied ourselves for it—and are swept away by its spiritual force.

These moments may be fleeting. They may come only once
or twice in a lifetime. But for those of us who have experienced
its profound depth, I promise you: it is well worth the wait. So
pray hard. And be patient. Rapture awaits.

Saying Little

JUNE 16

*Better to say a little with intention
than a lot without intention.*
TUR, ORACH CHAYIM 1

While the Hebrew word *kavvanah* is usually translated as
"intention," as in the intention or inclination with which one

prays, it really means a great deal more. Generally, we read the *Tur* as suggesting that we "say what we mean and mean what we say," as the American English idiom has it. The equivalent Yiddish folk saying is "Better a little and right than a lot and bad."

This is an especially difficult lesson for wordsmiths and others—who spend their days shaping meaning from words—to learn. For all that we invest in words, the *Tur* teaches us that the words are of less significance than what motivates us to articulate them in the first place. So select your words carefully, and limit them as well—so that all know that when you speak, you fully intend to do so.

Avoiding Evil

June 17

*The inclination to do evil
attacks humans daily with renewed vigor.*
BABYLONIAN TALMUD, SUKKAH 52

This is not a statement about the shortcomings of humans. Rather, it emerges from the Rabbinic notion of what constitutes each of us and the various internal forces that drive us to do things or refrain from doing things. Our desire to do good holds in balance our desire to do evil. And our desire to do evil keeps our desire for doing good from overwhelming us. But the desire to do evil is not evil in the common sense of the word. Rather, it represents those drives that become evil if they are not held in balance by our desire to do good. For example, the desire to procreate may be good, but it can become evil when it deteriorates into lust.

So we begin our day with a plea to God: do not let the inclination to do evil dominate us. It is not that we ask God to remove such an inclination entirely. That would throw our entire life out of kilter. Thus, this is a request for balance and centeredness in our lives. Only in such a place can we find tranquility and blessing.

Forgiving Sins

JUNE 18

Happy is the one whose sins are forgiven,
whose transgressions are wiped away.
PSALM 32:1

What does it take to be happy in this world? The psalmist gives us a specific formula. The psalmist doesn't say those who don't sin are happy—for there is a recognition that humans sin. Rather, the psalmist seems to be emphasizing the relief that one feels when one can let go of one's sins because they have been forgiven. While some people think that this notion has to wait until the fall and Yom Kippur, the Day of Atonement, the psalmist comes to teach us that this can happen at any time. That is the blessing of forgiveness. But what does come from our understanding of Yom Kippur is that sins that have been committed against another human being can only be wiped away by God once they have been resolved with the one against whom they were committed.

We all make mistakes and do things that we shouldn't have done. Often that realization comes to us too late, after the act has been committed. Know that if you have done something wrong, it does not have to stay with you your entire life. The potential for forgiveness and the happiness that accompanies it is present following every misguided action that you take.

Conquering the Enemy

JUNE 19

Rescue me from my enemies, my God,
From those who rise up against me, strengthen me.
PSALM 59:2

While written by the psalmist, this is a plea—a prayer—to God that all of us have spoken in our own lives at various times. Perhaps the words are not the same, and may even be more earthy in tone, but the sentiment is the same. We ask for help outside of ourselves, help that allows us to deal with all those who wish us harm, no matter the kind of harm wished upon us. Usually we think of enemies as those who threaten the sovereignty of a nation. We seldom think of them as neighbors, as competitors, as those who live in our community. But these are people who try to make our lives miserable in one way or another. And so it is not surprising that we would want them out of our lives or, at least, want to limit their ability to do us harm. We do not ask God to destroy such people. That would be wrong. Rather, we ask God for the strength to help us to confront them and to keep us from harm's way. And when someone has succeeded in doing us wrong, just work hard. A demonstration of personal success is all the revenge that is needed.

Sunshine

JUNE 20

Praised are You, Adonai our God, Sovereign of the universe,
Source of creation.
BLESSING OF THE SUN

While we might look for a more extensive or complicated blessing to express our appreciation for all that the sun provides us, this is a simple blessing that acknowledges the sun and its power, as well as the Source of its creation—and our own. This blessing, along with a group of psalms, is said on the morning following the vernal equinox, which marks the "turning" of the sun across the equator. According to Jewish tradition, this is the position of the sun at Creation. This blessing is recited after the morning prayer service when the sun is about ninety degrees above the eastern horizon on the first Wednesday of the month of Nisan (late March, early April).

For some people, this kind of a blessing seems rather esoteric and not worth much attention. It is better left for the zealots and the religiously right, they say. For others, it is a rare opportunity to offer an expression of gratitude that must be seized, for it reflects how seriously we can take a disciplined spiritual life. Whenever the occasion to offer a blessing presents itself, we should rush forward and raise ourselves to the sacred task. We too will be uplifted as a result.

The Human Fabric

JUNE 21

Praised are You, Adonai our God, Sovereign of the universe, who has made the human in Your image, after Your likeness and has prepared for each human a perpetual fabric out of the essential self. Praised are You, Adonai, Creator of the human species.

FOURTH WEDDING BLESSING

This is the fourth of seven blessings offered at a wedding ceremony. In some weddings, all seven blessings are spoken by the same person. In other ceremonies, people close to the wedding couple are invited to recite one of each of the blessings. This blessing is quite unusual. It contains the familiar formula for blessing. So it acknowledges God as the Source of all life in the universe. And through the invitation to dialogue with the Divine, it also invites in the presence of God. Thus, it helps to create the sacred space necessary for a wedding to take place. The blessing also reflects the belief that we are all created in the image of God. The wedding ceremony recognizes that we try to emulate God through many acts, particularly the act of pro-creation. Finally, the blessing reminds all those assembled that each individual is unique. Each individual is shaped from an essential fabric distinct to each particular person.

So in the midst of a ceremony that brings together the entire community, all those gathered to celebrate the love of two people, is a lesson in traditional Jewish theology. Listen and learn well.

Rising above Responsibility

JUNE 22

Praised be the One who has freed me from the responsibility for this child's action.

KNOWN AS THE *BARUKH SHEPTARANI* BLESSING, SAID BY PARENTS WHEN THEIR CHILD BECOMES BAR OR BAT MITZVAH

This is a rather controversial blessing. Perhaps the discomfort that some people have with it emerges from a misunderstanding of the text, especially when taken out of context. When recited by parents, this blessing acknowledges that their child has taken an important step forward and reached adulthood—from the perspective of the Jewish religion. According to Jewish law, parents are responsible for the action of their children prior to their thirteenth birthday (twelfth for girls). This means that they are also responsible for any penalties that such actions incur. So the blessing is not an expression of "Thank God, I am finished with this child." Rather, it is more like

"Thank God. This child is growing and developing according to the way things are supposed to be." For all parents, this is an overwhelmingly emotional transition. It reminds us that our children are no longer children. Their independence is inevitable. And this makes us realize and accept that their dependence on us (beyond financial and other forms of material support, which is less significant from the perspective of Jewish tradition) is quickly diminishing.

This is also yet another reminder of our own finitude and our struggle with our limited years on this earth. It is expressed as a blessing because we pray that the values that we have attempted to instill in our children, the things that are most important to us, will be continued. We thank God for the privilege and the blessing of letting go of our children.

The Blessing of Freedom

JUNE 23

*Do not oppress a stranger. You know how it feels to
be a stranger, because you were strangers in Egypt.*
EXODUS 23:9

This idea permeates much of the Jewish perspective on how we treat others, whether visitors to our home or strangers in the street. We know what it was like to be treated as strangers and oppressed in Egypt. We were enslaved as a result. We felt constricted. We lived in narrow places (the folk etymology for the name of the land of Egypt). And while this idea is repeated throughout the Torah, it isn't clear whether its frequent appearance is due solely to its import and the desire of the Torah to emphasize it as a value or because our ancestors—like us—frequently forgot to express this value in our actions.

It is a blessing to be free. We realize its depth because of the experience of our ancestors. But the Bible is not speaking only of political freedom. It is a freedom that extends far beyond the confines of political sovereignty. It is the freedom that motivated the Jewish people in all of its years of wandering. And it was this lesson of being a stranger that informed its choices along the way. May the notion of being a stranger and all that emerges from it continue to burn a fire in your soul so that you may help others to enjoy its blessing.

Immersing Ourselves

JUNE 24

Praised are You, Adonai our God, Sovereign of the universe, who has made us holy with mitzvot and instructed us to immerse in the mikvah.

BLESSING RECITED UPON USING THE *MIKVAH*, WHEN REQUIRED

This is the blessing said when immersing in the *mikvah*, the ritual bath. But it is only recited when a required immersion takes place. What is special about immersion in the *mikvah*, whether required or a (highly recommended) voluntary spiritual experience, is that it is one of the few rituals that are truly full-body experiences. Immersing in water can be transformational. It can offer healing, as well, especially when using the bath prior to or following a major event in one's life, a transition that is positive or negative. Rabbi Nachman of Breslov used to say that when the messiah comes it will feel like immersion in the *mikvah*. He also said that the water used in the *mikvah* comes from paradise itself. Thus, the two waters (from a source of natural running water and rain water) that are brought together (where they "kiss," as the tradition calls it) merge Eden of the past with the potential inherent in the future. Perhaps this is one of the reasons why each visit to the *mikvah* involves more than one immersion.

When the immersion is not required, some people like to use a *kavvanah* (sacred mantra) to focus their thoughts. These words are suggested by Rabbi Sheldon Zimmerman: "In Your oneness, I feel healing. In the promise of Your love, I am soothed. In Your wholeness I too can become whole again."

Avoiding the Evil Eye

JUNE 25

Don't give it a kenanhora.
YIDDISH FOLK SAYING

While this might sound like a strange blessing, it is one that I have heard since childhood—repeated frequently by my grandmother and mother, among others—whenever someone shared good news about anyone, especially those whom they loved.

The word *kenanhora* itself is a collapsed form in Yiddish. (This is what the linguists call it.) But it is a reference to the "evil eye" and a wish that mentioning the good should not be an invitation for the evil eye to be cast and thereby transform the good into the bad. So, as emerges in folk religion, it becomes an inverse blessing of sorts, a wish for well-being from one person to another.

Such blessings, especially when they arise out of the honesty of folk religion and thereby are woven into the Jewish fabric, are no less significant than those penned by the Rabbis. They are as deeply embedded in my soul as are the other prayers of my heart. May they find the same place in yours.

Living a Life of Blessing

JUNE 26

Be a blessing.
GENESIS 12:2

While this was originally spoken to Abraham, it really transcends the specific textual reference. Rather than talking about the words we speak, the Torah text refers to what we do and how we act. When I think about this instruction, which I consider to be rather sacred, the following text always comes to mind: "In a place where people do not act like human beings, strive to be one" (*Pirkei Avot* 2:6). While this text is usually translated as " ... where there are no men," I have never thought that the Rabbis were being gender specific in their teaching—particularly here, but in most places. And while the literal Yiddish translation for "man" is mensch, it really refers to a great deal more. Thus, "strive to be a human being" and "strive to be a mensch" basically mean the same thing. Strive to exhibit the best of the God-given traits that you can muster. Be gracious to the other. Be kind to the other. Treat everyone fairly. When no one else is doing so, stand up and be the exception.

In her own way, my grandmother used to say this to me as I left the house each morning when I was a young child. She never said, "Have a good day at school" or "Be good." She would always say, "Be a mensch." That is all I needed to hear. My actions became her blessing for me.

Never Being Alone

JUNE 27

*Though I walk through the valley of shadows,
I fear no evil, for You are with me....*
PSALM 23:4

While part of this translation may be a little unfamiliar, it does reflect the Hebrew more literally. It is also much more reflective of the way in which we sometimes walk through our lives. There are many shadows in it. Some are a result of illness and tragedy. Others come from death itself and a reminder of our own limitations and mortality. But the psalmist who penned these words understood our feelings precisely. The love of family and friends provides us immeasurable support during times of discouragement. But the thing that gets us through sometimes—the only thing—is our faith in God. To have such faith is a blessing.

We recognize that life is not always what we want it to be. We know that we will lose our loved ones through illness and death. Some of our dreams will be shattered. But evil will not reach us. It can never consume us, as long as we acknowledge that God is with us.

For All Who Have Taught Us

JUNE 28

*For our teachers and their students and the students of
the students, we ask for peace and loving-kindness....
And for all those who study Torah, here and
everywhere, may they be blessed with all they need....*
KADDISH D'RABBANAN BY DEBBIE FRIEDMAN

While these words have been stylized by a contemporary Jewish folk singer, they express the sentiment of the original blessing. These words are recited following the study of sacred literature. By reciting these words, in the context of community, we acknowledge our relationship with those teachers and students who have come before us, as well as those who are currently studying in places near and far from us. Whether in the past or present, we are all engaged in the same pursuit. While such study can be an independent pursuit, it is also framed within the context of prayer—for the study of sacred texts is the touchstone of Jewish spirituality.

Such study provides us with a common language of discourse. It creates a bond among those who study—across time and across the miles. Such study is not static. We develop a dynamic relationship with the text as our understanding is layered upon what all those others who have studied the same text have learned from it. The space in which we study becomes sacred, for all those who have taught these texts are present as we give voice to their words.

Overflowing Happiness

JUNE 29

Come let us be joyful and let our happiness overflow.
"HAVA NAGILA," FOLK SONG

Even for those who do not know the words of this song, "Hava Nagila" probably represents the most well-known of all Jewish folk songs. The words are seldom sung on their own. Usually the words are accompanied by circle dances, sometimes called *simkhah* (literally, "happiness") dancing, and usually following some wonderful occasion like a wedding or a bar/bat mitzvah. This is the time in which nothing else seems to matter. It is pure joy, the kind that nothing—and no one—can spoil. To experience such joy is a blessing.

"Hava Nagila" is just the beginning. Good *simkhah* dancing never ends. It is one continuous song. One continuous dance. Even when the music stops, the dancing continues. Over and over until you are totally consumed by the dancing.

So next time you hear the words or melody of "Hava Nagila," even if you are not a good dancer or don't like to dance, don't just sit there. Get up and dance. The joy of the community depends on it.

Words of the Heart

JUNE 30

Words spoken from the heart enter the heart.
MOSES IBN EZRA, *SHIRAT YISRAEL*

This saying of Ibn Ezra has entered into the folk lexicon of the Jewish people. This notion gets repeated frequently without any reference to the source, almost as if it had become an anonymous folk saying. Nevertheless, the words ring true to all of us, whether we are speaking about words of blessing or just conversation between people. Honest words, words that reflect our deepest feelings, words that emerge from the heart, are really heard by others. They elicit a response. They are neither ignored nor overlooked.

Words are more than a random assembly of letters. They can be powerful spiritual tools. They can bring us closer to God, to ourselves, and to others. So when you speak, consider your words carefully. Each word contains the power to heal. Choose them wisely. May all your words rise and find their place to become a blessing.

JULY

Rest and Renewal

JULY 1

Observe the Sabbath day and keep it holy,
as Adonai your God instructed you.
DEUTERONOMY 5:12

The commandment to rest on Shabbat is indeed a blessing. Unless you have shut out the world on Shabbat, it is hard to fully understand—or appreciate—the depth of its spiritual power. No computers, phones, or TV. No business, shopping, or travel. Only the chance to reflect on the week that has passed and renew oneself for the week ahead.

Blu Greenberg said it this way: "Six days shall you be a workaholic; on the seventh day, shall you join in the serene company of human beings. Six days shall you take orders from your boss; on the seventh day, shall you be master/mistress of your own life. Six days shall you toil in the market; on the seventh day, shall you detach from money matters. Six days shall you create, drive, create, invent, push, drive; on the seventh day, shall you reflect. Six days shall you be the perfect success; on the seventh day, shall you remember that not everything is in your power. Six days shall you be a miserable failure; on the seventh day, shall you be on top of the world. Six days shall you enjoy the blessings of work; on the seventh day, shall you understand that being is as important as doing."*

The best part about Shabbat: whenever you are overwhelmed by work or the stress of daily living, Shabbat is always less than a week away. And that indeed is a blessing.

Students and Learning

JULY 2

Without disciples, there can be no sages.
GENESIS RABBAH 42:4

The Rabbis of the midrash who penned these words were doing more than just stating the obvious. It is true that without students, there can be no teachers. Without students, there is nothing to teach and no one to be taught. But the statement from Genesis Rabbah wants to convey something more. Students become disciples when they take what they learn from their teachers and share it with others—and when they apply what they learn. In so doing, especially when their fellow students join them and do the same, they elevate the status of their teachers and what they have learned. These teachers become sages in the eyes of the tradition. This is the blessing of becoming teacher to student and student to teacher.

But the ability to be a teacher is not limited to those Rabbis in the past whose names appear in sacred literature. Each time we learn something from someone else, we raise them—and

*Blu Greenberg, *How to Run a Traditional Jewish Household* (Northvale, N.J.: Jason Aronson, 1989), pp. 26–27.

their teachings—up. And when we share what we have learned with others, we are raised up, as well. All of us have the capacity to become teachers. It is one of the reasons why teachers are held in such high esteem in Judaism. When groups of people are engaged in such learning, the entire community is moved heavenward.

Starting the Mitzvah Process

JULY 3

If one begins a mitzvah, one is likely to conclude it.
TANCHUMA, EIKEV 6

This is the power of doing mitzvot. Unlike other acts whose completion is uncertain until they are, in fact, completed, mitzvot seem to contain a spiritual energy that propels the doer to the end. At the same time, the doer is brought to greater depths. As a result, the doer feels compelled—motivated—to complete the act. This notion from the *Tanchuma*, a collection of midrashim that dates to the ninth century, gives rise to this Rabbinic expression: "One who utters the letter *alef* will likely utter the letter *bet.*"

But completion doesn't mean an automatic "spiritual high." The spiritual life requires discipline. And with that discipline comes a life of blessing. Such discipline doesn't come so easily for most people. And it takes time to get on the spiritual path in the first place. Often people are anxious to reach a spiritual high immediately. Maybe what the *Tanchuma* is therefore saying is not that when we start a mitzvah, we are likely to conclude it. Rather, the Rabbis of the *Tanchuma* are suggesting that if we begin on the path of mitzvot, it is likely that we will continue on the spiritual path that supports it. That is its conclusion.

Liberty

JULY 4

*Proclaim liberty throughout the land
unto all the inhabitants thereof.*
LEVITICUS 25:10

Liberty is not a state of being. It requires that we take certain steps if this value is to be fully realized. That is why this text from Leviticus—which is emblazoned on the Liberty Bell housed in Independence Hall in Philadelphia—demands action from us. We have a responsibility to liberty. According to this teaching, we are first obligated to share this notion with others. It is not a value that we keep to ourselves for a limited number of people to enjoy.

This is also why it is a perfect text on which to reflect on the Fourth of July. It is an important idea for Jews, and it is an important idea for all Americans. Thus, it becomes particularly important for American Jews. So this year, amidst the barbecues, fireworks, and parades, take a moment to think about the blessing of liberty and remind others of it as well.

Navigating the Distance

JULY 5

*Not all that is close is near,
and not all that is distant is far.*
NUMBERS RABBAH

This reads like an odd statement. If things are near, then they are close. And if things are distant, then they are far away. How can things be near and far at the same time? But like so many spiritual notions, this text from the midrash appears to be counterintuitive. When something is close to us, it doesn't mean that it may always be so near to our heart and mind. And it may not be easy to access or grasp.

Similarly, just because things are far away doesn't mean that they are also harder to grasp. They may seem like difficult notions and yet they are actually easy to understand. Things that are far away may motivate us to reach further and deeper and thereby bring things closer. As a result, this will cause us to grow and expand.

Getting Used to the Truth

July 6

*A person who gets used to telling lies
will be enticed to falsehood.*
ZOHAR 1:192B

The first lie that one tells may come with difficulty. But after it is told, telling lies seems to be a lot easier. That's because telling lies actually causes us to lose control of the truth. We become unable to use truth to discern falsehoods. As a result, we then become seduced by falsehoods. Such lies provide us with a deceptively more pleasant lens through which to view the world. Falsehoods allow us to construct whatever reality we prefer. And that is often nicer than the truth.

But truth carries within it an intrinsic spiritual power that is divine in origin. Consequently, the telling of truth can bring us closer to its Source. That also means that telling lies pushes us far away from the Divine. And if we are far away, then we cannot seek out a life of blessing.

So tell the truth and discover the blessings that lie underneath.

Running to Pray

JULY 7

*It is a mitzvah to run to the synagogue
and to any other activity involving a mitzvah.*
RABBI SCHNEUR ZALMAN OF LIADI, THE ALTER REBBE

This has been said in various ways in our tradition, but the message remains the same, irrespective of the author. We should run to the synagogue. We should run to do any sacred task, but we should leave it slowly. Otherwise, as the Alter Rebbe goes on to say, it would appear to others that the task has become a burden for us and we are rushing to rid ourselves of it. My own teacher Rabbi Jakob Petuchowski used to say that he could tell how engaged people were with worship services by how quickly they left afterward.

The notion of rushing to do a mitzvah of any kind dates back to Abraham. We are told in the book of Genesis that Abraham arose early in the morning for the *Akedah*, the binding of Isaac. Abraham's act of getting up early has also given rise to the tradition of the *hashkamah minyan* (early morning prayer service). We want to initiate a dialogue with God as soon as we are able to do so. So get up early. Run for the sake of your soul.

Blessing Community

July 8

May the one who blessed our ancestors ...
bless this holy congregation.

BLESSING SAID FOLLOWING THE READING OF THE TORAH
ON BEHALF OF THE ENTIRE CONGREGATION

Following the public reading of the Torah, which is designed to simulate—or reenact—the revelation of the Torah at Sinai, words of blessing are offered on behalf of the entire congregation. The tasks of each member, no matter how small, are recognized. It is part of the realization of what makes community and an affirmation of how blessed each person is to be part of it. Each of us has to participate in it, and each is responsible for its upkeep and continuation. The text of this blessing speaks not only of lofty ideals but also asks for God's blessing for those who simply "enter to pray, those who give the lamps for lighting and wine for *Kiddush* and *Havdalah*, bread to the wayfarers, and charity to the poor and all who occupy themselves with the needs of the congregation." In order to receive, we have to also be willing to give.

While each individual has his or her own spiritual practices and there are times even in the midst of community prayer designed to separate the self out for private prayer, Judaism, in general, is designed for community. In the midst of community, we celebrate and we mourn, we lift up and are lifted. In community, we are blessed and offer blessing to others.

Discovering the Blessing

JULY 9

How goodly are your tents, O Jacob,
your places of dwelling, O Israel!
NUMBERS 24:5

This is the blessing spoken by the prophet Bilaam in the Bible when he was asked by the king, Balak, to curse the people of Israel. This phrase has been introduced into the fixed liturgy of the morning service—and set to various melodies that have become *kavvanot* (sacred mantras). The words have become so important that they are to be said upon entering a synagogue in the morning for prayer. Since you may not be immediately moved to make such a statement when you enter the synagogue—there are many things to distract you—it is helpful to make it part of your practice to do so. It may seem contrived at first, but soon the words will emerge from your heart on their own, and you will soon begin to understand why Bilaam found no other words.

It seems to me that if we can rediscover what Bilaam saw—and share it with others—then more would be motivated to repeat the words of this ancient prophet, *Mah tovu ohalekha Yaakov*, "How goodly are your tents, O Jacob."

Obliging the Truth

JULY 10

It is forbidden to tell a falsehood,
but it is not always obligatory to tell the truth.
JEWISH FOLK SAYING

This is a hard one. We are taught to tell the truth and to avoid falsehood. Even the Ten Commandments have something to say about lying: "You should not swear by My name falsely, so that you profane the name of your God: I am Adonai" (Leviticus 19:12). Lying is serious business, especially when God is called to witness the lie—or when you invite the power of the Divine as part of the oath you take.

But the saying quoted above is not a purely theological statement. It is colored by the interactions between people. Sometimes, truth can hurt. Sometimes, truth is used intentionally to hurt. So while we should avoid lies (it is all right to say that's a pretty outfit even if you don't really like it or think that it is), people sometimes think that telling the truth is the same as telling people whatever is on their mind. Feelings sometimes trump the truth.

There is no need to lie. But there is also no need to tell all that you know. But always remember: truth paves the path for blessing.

Praying Outside the Heart

JULY 11

One should not pray the Sh'moneh Esreh
in the heart alone.

RABBI SCHNEUR ZALMAN OF LIADI, THE ALTER REBBE

While this is a particular reference to the central prayer in Jewish liturgy known as the *Sh'moneh Esreh* (literally, "eighteen," for the original eighteen benedictions included in it)— also called the *Amidah* or "Standing Prayer," since it is said while standing—the Alter Rebbe's teaching offers general advice about prayer. His point is that it is important for the individual at prayer to actually hear the words of prayer being said. That is why the liturgy refers to the individual reciting of the *Sh'moneh Esreh* prayer rather than its silent recitation—as some people say—since it is to be said quietly but not silently to oneself. The heart yearns to hear what the person is trying to say.

Schneur Zalman warns us, however, that individuals at prayer should make sure that their voice cannot be heard by someone else standing four cubits—the length of four forearms—away. He argues that those who recite this prayer too loudly have meager faith—acting as if God would not or could not hear a whispered prayer.

The Words of Blessing

JULY 12

Speech is the pen of the heart.
AARON BEN ZVI HAKOHEN

There are many ways for us to communicate what we feel to others. And the most common is probably through speech. But speech is not always the most exacting way to express what is in our heart. Sometimes we cannot find the right words to express what it is that we want to say. So we look for other things, as well, perhaps a nod, a touch, a smile. Often these enhance what it is that we are trying to say. And sometimes they actually replace the words. However inadequate, the words that we speak are the most enduring, Aaron ben Zvi Hakohen seems to say.

Consider carefully the words that you use. While it may seem like words are spoken and then they disappear, words, in fact, endure for a long time after they leave your mouth.

Blessings too are made of words. They shape the communication we intend with God. Consider these words carefully. Unlike the communication between humans, the words you share with God have an infinite life to them.

Our Role as Partners

JULY 13

Where a Jew finds illness, she is commanded to heal.
Where a Jew finds hunger, he is commanded to feed.
Where a Jew finds suffering,
we are commanded to identify with the sufferer and
to alleviate their pain.

RABBI BRADLEY SHAVIT ARTSON

Rabbi Artson has the responsibility of the Jewish community in mind when penning these words. But they are also the responsibility of individual human beings, for when we act, we act as partners with God. The big difference perhaps is that these are not voluntary acts. We have no choice, as Rabbi Artson conceives our responsibility for these as directives from God. By responding to them, we affirm our role as partners in the covenantal relationship.

There is something more in these statements that demands our attention. Why are these the three responsibilities that are isolated among the many that could have been chosen? Perhaps it is because in doing so we are able to emulate the acts of God and thereby serve as channels for bringing divine goodness into the world. This is the blessing of being human with souls that soar to heaven, with feet planted firmly on the ground.

Making an Offering of Self

JULY 14

You shall season your every offering of meal with salt;
you shall not omit from your meal offering the salt
of your covenant with God;
with all your offerings, you must offer salt.
LEVITICUS 2:13

This text, from the book of Leviticus, may seem peculiar. After all, why does the Torah emphasize the use of salt on the sacrificial offerings of grain? And even so, what does it have to do with us? This is the source of the custom of placing salt on bread on Shabbat and festivals after saying the blessing and before eating. People may find it odd when you salt the bread on your table, but this simple act actually elevates your dining table to the status of an altar. And all who participate are elevated as well.

Salt is one of the simple substances of life. Thus, its application teaches us that Jewish spirituality does not have to be complicated. Words of blessing do not have to be difficult They can be quite simple—as long as they are done with integrity and with a fullness of heart and mind. For once the altar has been established in your home, your actions need now reflect its sacredness. And those sitting around the table have the responsibility of maintaining its level of sanctity. So go, salt your bread and raise up your soul.

Going beyond Possessions

JULY 15

Do not covet....
EXODUS 20:14

The last of the ten commandments seems out of place with the rest. They all seem more serious and much more in keeping with the sacredness of the Torah. But the issue of coveting—and our refraining from it—is at the very foundation of daily life. We see something and we want it. We are driven to own it. And we will do whatever it takes to get it. But because our drive to possess is flawed, our taking hold of the possession will give us momentary pleasure at best. For owning—and coveting—is responsible for the undermining of a value-filled life. Like Ecclesiastes of the Bible ("I increased my possessions. I built houses and planted vineyards for myself" [Ecclesiastes 2:4]), we think that our own happiness—and what others think of us—will be determined by how much we own and what we possess. But nothing is further from the truth. Our physical possessions are temporary. We are merely temporary stewards. But the values that we hold dear and share with others—particularly our children—last for an eternity.

So coveting, although saved for the last of the ten commandments, is considered by some the most important of them all. If you are able to observe the last one, then you will be able to observe the nine that precede it as well. And that truly will bring you a life of blessing.

Receiving Torah Each Day

JULY 16

Every day, let the Torah be beloved to you,
as if you received it from Mount Sinai today.
TANCHUMA

It may sound corny, but I like to say that "a day without Torah is like a day without sunshine." The giving of Torah was not a one-time event. The echo from Sinai is continuously heard. It is one of the reasons that the Rabbis placed the study of Torah into the fixed liturgy of the morning service. They understood its power and its impact on our individual daily lives. And beginning each morning with Torah study helps us to navigate the rest of our day.

For those of us who love the regular study of Torah, it is sometimes hard to explain to others why it is so. But that is the way love is. We can feel it. We can demonstrate it. But we can't really explain it. And the Torah is like God's love letter to the Jewish people. We caress it. We treat it gingerly. We read it over and over again to make sure we capture every nuance of meaning from it. And that is how we keep our love—and the blessing of Torah—alive.

The Wells of Miriam

JULY 17

One who wants to see the well of Miriam should go
up to the top of Mount Carmel and there see the likes
of a sieve in the sea; and that is the well of Miriam.
BABYLONIAN TALMUD, SHABBAT 38A

Of all the things in the Torah and in the folk history of the Jewish people that have captivated me, I think that Miriam's well certainly ranks among the most significant. The well provided water for the Jewish people throughout their desert wanderings. It followed the people wherever they journeyed—until Miriam's death.

It was this well that inspired Elijah the prophet when he sought to embarrass the prophets of Baal on Mount Carmel (1 Kings 18:21). Because Elijah is to announce the coming of the messiah, according to Jewish tradition, the well is also connected to the future and to messianism. So if you are in Israel and climb up Mount Carmel and look out into the sea, then you will be able to see Miriam's well. And if you are not in Israel, then you can close your eyes and see her well there too—and be satisfied as a result. May Miriam's life, and the nourishing waters with which she provided sustenance to the Jewish people, be remembered for blessing.

Looking at God

July 18

When you look at the world,
you are looking at God and God is looking at you.
BAAL SHEM TOV

For many people, part of the spiritual quest is being able to find glimpses of God. Some may seek God in prayer and in the study of sacred texts. Others may seek God in their relationships with others, particularly those whom they love. But Baal Shem Tov is offering us a simpler lesson about everyday life. We can see God in the world. That is something that we may see as an extension of the feelings we have about experiencing God in nature: mountains and streams and oceans and lakes. But we can also see God in the less majestic aspects of nature as well: a blade of grass, a strewn pebble, a child's breath. We can also see in the world our relationship with God—in every interaction we have.

There is a well-known story told of Rabbi Abraham Joshua Heschel. In response to a child's query about seeing God, Heschel told the young boy that he could find God by looking into the mirror at home. He ran quickly home. The first mirror was occupied by his father, who was shaving. So he couldn't get in front of the mirror. The second mirror was occupied by his sister putting on her makeup for the day—so he couldn't get in front of that mirror either. Finally, he found a free mirror in the house. And when he looked at it, all he saw was a reflection of himself. That is when he learned Heschel's lesson about God. Perhaps had he known of Baal Shem Tov at the time, he would have learned the Besht's lesson cited here as well.

Rendering Fair Decisions

JULY 19

Every judge who renders a fair decision is like a
partner of the Holy One in the act of creation.
BABYLONIAN TALMUD, *SHABBAT* 119B

While this teaching is directed at judges, those who are in a position of authority to render legal decisions and judgments, it is a lesson that can be applied to all of us. For we make judgments all day long of one kind or another. We may judge the work of a colleague or a friend. It might even be of a carpenter or plumber who is fixing something in our home. Or of the waitstaff at a local restaurant. And we often do so without thinking, without realizing the importance of such evaluations. We make a judgment on the spot and then move on with our lives. But we don't realize that our decision may significantly impact the lives of other people. In that judgment is contained the power to offer blessing to others, as well.

Perhaps such judgments are not as noteworthy or important as those rendered by legal authorities. But in each case, if we are to take this teaching of the Rabbis of the Talmud to heart, we are partners in the ongoing creation of the world. For each time we make a judgment of any sort, we participate in the shaping of the life of another. May they be blessed by our words.

The World Is Full of God

JULY 20

There is nothing in the world empty of God.
ZOHAR

Nothing? Nothing! It may be easy to see God in things of beauty. It is a lot harder when things don't seem so beautiful on the surface. But if God is the Creator of all, if God is part of all that there is, then God has to be present in everything. Everything! Start your day with this notion as a *kavvanah* (sacred mantra). And as you go about your daily routine, repeat it over and over in your mind. As you encounter things during your day—people and objects—remember that there is nothing in which God is not part. Such a notion will elevate others in your mind—and it will elevate you, as well.

If God is present in everything, it means that all people and things have the potential for blessing. It also means that God is always near. God can never be far away. All we have to do is call out—and the answer appears, for it is always very near.

Body Beautiful

JULY 21

In my flesh, I see God.
JOB 19:26

This is a generation of people focused incessantly on body image. We go to fitness centers more to look good than to feel good. There are diets galore. And a new procedure to make us look younger is advertised almost every day—or it certainly seems that way. Whatever we look like, short or tall, skinny or not, we are all made in the image of God, slightly lower than the angels, claims our tradition. So take a look at each part of your body. Don't be embarrassed by it. For in your body, you can see God.

So how does this notion impact our relationship with others? Well, if we look at our own bodies and see God, then when we look at anyone else, we can see God in their body, as well. And that means that we have to treat others as vessels of God. Sometimes it is easy to look at another's body and see God. At others times, it may be tough. So work at it. Your body, whatever its shape or form, has been given to you as a blessing from God. Enjoy all the beauty that God has to give.

A Soulful Body

JULY 22

In whatever you do, you should consider your body as the Holy of Holies. Think of it as a part of the manifestation of the Almighty on High. If you do, you will keep the evil impulse at bay.
RABBI LEVI YITZCHAK OF BERDITCHEV

Rabbi Levi Yitzchak has always been a hero of mine, ever since as a child I heard stories about his actions. He refused to accept everything that happened in the world. He held God responsible and often confronted God publicly in the midst of the community he served in Berditchev. He had what the tradition calls *chutzpah k'lappei malah*. This is a hard notion to translate, but it really refers to courage (some may say arrogance or moxie) in the presence of God. Rabbi Levi Yitzchak always stood his ground in front of God and spoke his mind to the Deity, knowing full well the potential consequences. He refused to utter words of blessing unless and until God was prepared to bless the people, as well.

Here he offers a simple lesson, especially to those who spend their time focused on a life of the mind, at the expense of the body. The body is not only important as a vessel to house the soul; for Jews, the body and soul are one unit. It is the reason why they are united in traditional understandings of the afterlife. Body and soul together serve God. So take care of your body now. You will need it much, much later.

Giving and Taking

JULY 23

When God created human beings, God created them capable of giving and taking.
RABBI ELIYAHU E. DESSLER

While we often think of the covenant as reflective of our relationship with God, Rabbi Dessler teaches us that such dynamism is intentionally built into the relationship that human beings have with one another. We give and we take. Both actions are necessary for a relationship to be complete. While some may think that giving is better than taking, one action is no less worthy than the other, one no more meritorious than the other, at least according to this statement by

Rabbi Dessler. In order for someone to be able to give, the other person must be willing—and able—to take.

Since our creation was intentional, "giving" can't be considered more virtuous than "taking." For in the action of taking is the notion that we take in God's bounty in the world—which was placed there for our benefit. But because both actions are necessary, we also have to make sure that we give and give back. The blessing is found in the dynamism between the two poles—giving and taking. And we benefit from both.

Serving God with Body and Soul

JULY 24

You may be free from sin, but if your body is not strong, your soul will be too weak to serve God properly. Maintain your health and preserve your strength.
BAAL SHEM TOV

My junior high school physical education teacher had never heard of Baal Shem Tov. Of that I am fairly certain. But he used to warn me often, "Your good grades don't mean a thing if your body is not in good physical shape." And that was before he directed me to run a mile in the unrelenting Florida sun— and that was before class even formally started. He may have forgotten what he taught me, but I never have. It is one of those lessons that drives me on the treadmill even when it is easier to avoid it, that pushes me to work harder at the gym.

I understand that I do it for him, I do it for myself, and I do it as part of my obligation to the Divine. And I will continue to do so. May my body be powerful enough to ward off sin, and may my soul be sufficiently strong so that I may continue to follow the path of the Divine. May I be strengthened even as I make myself strong to lead a life of blessing.

Respecting Parents

JULY 25

My child, attend to your father's discipline;
don't let your mother's teaching slip away.
PROVERBS 1:8

Maybe it was the old age of my parents that first made me pay attention to this text more than I did when I was younger. The message seems to be true: as we get older, our parents seem to know much more. A more literal translation of the verse uses the term *musar* (ethical piety) rather than "discipline" and *Torah* rather than "teaching." While my translation is not coincidental, neither was the particular choice of words by the author of Proverbs (which Jewish tradition claims was King Solomon).

There are certain things that I learned from my father and other kinds of things that I learned from my mother. And it is sometimes hard to distinguish one from the other. I also realize—if I am honest—that there are things that I learned by what my parents didn't do. But I am the product of their teaching nonetheless. This is the blessing of being a child. Now the obligation continues. That is the blessing of being a parent. Whether to your own children or those whom you choose to parent, the obligation is the same. Teach them what you know. Let them benefit from your experience. And model the ethical values that you consider precious.

The Wisdom of Others

JULY 26

*If they tell you there is wisdom among the nations,
believe them.*
LAMENTATIONS RABBAH 2, 9:13

This is an unusual statement. It is an acknowledgment in Jewish sacred literature that knowledge and understanding are not restricted to Jewish sacred texts or text teachers. Thus, it gives us permission to study Torah wherever we find it and from whomever teaches it—and there find blessing. This is a rather bold assertion for a tradition that some people consider parochial and insular. It also reflects a profound understanding of the individual and the quest for knowledge and enlightenment. If we are going to seek it elsewhere, we might as well have permission to do so in order for us to return and apply that knowledge and understanding within our own communities.

So if you find wisdom in other places, do not be afraid to imbibe it, to mix it with what you already know. Eat from the tree of knowledge wherever it has borne its fruits.

Asking for Wisdom

JULY 27

*One should ask for wisdom above all other virtues,
for it contains everything else.*
SONG OF SONGS RABBAH 1:1, 9

It seems odd that one would ask for wisdom from God when wisdom has its source in human experience. Unlike revelation, which comes from a divine source, wisdom is a result of knowledge and perspective gained directly from the experience of living. If this is the case, then why or how would someone make a request—pray for—wisdom from God? But wisdom is not the automatic result of living, no matter how many years, no matter how many accumulated experiences. Wisdom is only gained when we learn from what we experience. And when that learning is shared with others who can benefit from it, then it truly becomes wisdom.

So when we ask God for wisdom, we are not asking for a specified amount of knowledge. Rather we are asking God for discernment, the ability to review what we have experienced and benefit from it, the capacity to understand how to share it with others and then do so. Such ability will lead us to understand all other virtues and to a life that is identified by them.

Keeping Clean

JULY 28

You should bathe your face, hands, and feet every day in honor of your Creator.
BABYLONIAN TALMUD, *SHABBAT* 50B

This is the Jewish spin on the English expression "Cleanliness is next to godliness." But this statement is not really about personal hygiene for its own sake. Rather, this text from the Talmud suggests to us that our bodies are holy vessels, created in the image of the Divine, shaped for our responsibility as partners with the Divine. Thus, we honor the Creator and its image by taking care of our bodies. Washing our face, hands, and feet is symbolic of how we treat our bodies. It is one of the reasons why the Jewish tradition has an articulated blessing for washing our hands when we arise in the morning. But washing is not all we are required to do. There is much more that has to be done. No abuse to the body—to us or to others. No permanent marks or alterations. Our bodies are lent to us to use during our lifetimes. We are merely stewards and caretakers. For at the end of our lives, we return our bodies to the earth from which we are derived.

As you wash your face, hands, and feet today, consider the holy act that you are undertaking. No less than prayer, when you wash with intention, conscious of the body with which you were created and the Creator who formed it, then you elevate the act. The mundane becomes sacred. Through it, your body becomes the holy vessel it was always intended to be.

Perfect Joy and Pleasure

JULY 29

In this world, there is no perfect joy, unmixed with anxiety; no perfect pleasure, unmixed with envy; but in the future, the Holy Blessed One will make our joy and our pleasure perfect.

P'SIKTA D'RAV KAHANA 29

It is hard to experience pure joy. Even the birth of a child is accompanied by pain. We break a glass at a wedding to remind us of the destruction of the ancient city of Jerusalem. Many people in attendance at weddings find such a juxtaposition odd. At the penultimate climax of the wedding, we mourn for Jerusalem and commit ourselves to her sustenance. But Jewish tradition teaches us that we should be reminded of our pains and disappointments—and those of others—even at the times when we are reveling in the joys of life.

This is a teaching about life—for we will experience disappointments. It is normal. But is also a teaching about the future and what might be possible, especially in the messianic future.

Then we will be able to experience unmitigated joy, pleasure that knows no pain. May we all be blessed to inherit such a future.

The Questions of Life

JULY 30

From a question you cannot die.
From a question you can begin to live again.
YIDDISH FOLK SAYING,
ADAPTED BY RABBI HAROLD M. SCHULWEIS

I am always taken aback by the sharp wisdom of Yiddish folk sayings. Perhaps it is because they take me back to my grandparents, who used them in ways that I was generally too young to understand. It is only now in my reflection on them from the perspective of mature adulthood that I am able to really make any sense of them. My grandmother, my *bubbe*, encouraged me to ask questions all the time. For her, it was a sign of intelligence. For her, asking the right question was far more important than knowing the answer.

Questions have a way of taking us forward. Even if someone thinks—or tells us—that the question is silly or stupid, there is no real harm done in asking it. And if asking the question motivates us to seek an answer or builds a relationship between a student (anyone who asks the question) and a teacher (anyone who helps us to find an answer), then it really does have the potential to offer us a way to live again.

When we make a mistake, we are motivated to find out what we did wrong, how we can fix it, and what it will take to avoid the mistake in the future. This works in school, and it works in life. From a mistake we can discover blessing and new life.

Essential Reality

JULY 31

There are worlds more real than this one. Shabbat is more real than Wednesday. Jerusalem is more real than Chicago. The sukkah is more real than a garage. Tzedakah is more real than income tax.

RABBI LAWRENCE KUSHNER

Expressed in his unique spin on words, for Rabbi Kushner reality has more substance to it, more lasting value than what most people might consider real or material. Reality, thus, transcends both time and space and better informs the essence of our being. So Shabbat is not just another day of the week. It eclipses all of the other days. It has intrinsic value. Chicago may be a city in which millions live, a city to which many are loyal and feel at home. But Jerusalem is the center of the universe. We may have to pay our income tax. It may take much more of our income than we would like and far outdistance any other expense item on our budget. But even if we give only a small amount of money as *tzedekah*, these coins are of far-lasting value and importance. They help to adjust the imbalance between the poor and the wealthy.

But this all only becomes real if we make it so. When we make Shabbat truly a different day than Wednesday, then Shabbat becomes real. When Jerusalem becomes the center of our lives, irrespective of where we live or our hometown loyalties, then Jerusalem becomes real. When *tzedakah* drives our concerns about money, far more than April 15 each year, then it too becomes real. When we are able to accomplish these things, when they become values in our lives—and extend to other places too—then we, and the lives we lead, become real too. They actually become a journey along the path of blessing.

AUGUST

The Blessing of Friends

Blessed are they who bless you,
Cursed are they who curse you!
NUMBERS 24:9

These words, as recorded in the Bible, were spoken by a non-Jewish prophet named Bilaam. As much as he tried to curse the Jewish people, at the request of King Balak, an enemy of ancient Israel, he was unable to do so. This text of Bilaam has been turned into a metric of sorts, used to evaluate or weigh the future of a nation. If the Jewish people—and others among its citizenry—are treated well, then the country will succeed and prosper too.

This promise was made by God to the Jewish people through Abraham. As early as the book of Genesis, God promised Abraham, "I will multiply your seed as the stars of heaven, and will give to your offspring all these lands; and by your children shall all the nations of the earth be blessed" (Genesis 26:4).

While both of these statements may be considered bold, even presumptuous, they remain important indicators in Jewish history. These notions reflect the collective body of the Jewish people. But they also speak to us as individuals when we consider our own life history and our relationship with others. May we only know such blessing.

Healing, Binding, Raising Up the Other

AUGUST 2

God known
Not alone
But in relationship.
Not revealed through lonely power
But through our kinship, friendship,
healing, binding, raising up of each other.
RABBI HAROLD M. SCHULWEIS

As he does frequently, Rabbi Schulweis offers us insight into Jewish theology through his sensitive words of poetry. For Schulweis, God is not absolute power. Rather God is relationship. God is covenant. God is partnership. And in the midst of this special bond, we find the Divine in ourselves and in others.

But how does it work? Is it something that we stumble over? Or is it something that we have to fashion on our own? Relationships have to be worked at in order to discover God dwelling in our midst. When we do what Rabbi Schulweis suggests—"healing, binding, raising up of each other"—then we act as channels for the Divine into the world. And that is how blessings flow.

Repentance

AUGUST 3

Repentance only occurs when a person abandons one's sins and evil deeds. Abandonment does not depend on knowledge alone but on will.
Repentance is complete only when one changes the internal balance of his desires.
One no longer sins because one has succeeded in making one's desire to return stronger than the desire to sin.
RABBI ELIYAHU E. DESSLER

Repentance is an ongoing process. It is not relegated to the season of the fall holidays, particularly Yom Kippur. Rather, it is a model for daily living. Thus, it is a process that leads us all year long. Rabbi Dessler helps us to understand the exact nature of repentance, how it works, and when we know that it is effective. He says it quite frankly. Repentance is real when the individual has abandoned his or her sins and evil deeds. He believes that this is doable, that it is not an impossible task. Sins are real and so is the possibility of repentance.

So it is not about what we know—that is, the learned are no less likely to be able to repent just because they know a great deal. Rather, repentance is dependent upon the will of the individual. We have to want to repent and work at it. The desire to sin is normal. It affects all of us. Repentance then is successful when our desires are fully balanced, when the desire to sin is not what drives us and our behaviors. Rather, it is successful when the desire to repent—to return to a life of God, a life of blessing—takes precedence in our soul over the desire to sin.

Strive with all your being to repent, to return. Use whatever strength is necessary to do so. And then let go of your desire to sin—and then it will let go of you.

Acquiring Knowledge

AUGUST 4

If you lack knowledge, what have you acquired?
If you acquire knowledge, what do you lack?
NUMBERS RABBAH 19:3

Knowledge is often used as a measurement for many things. In the Jewish community, knowledge of sacred literature, Jewish tradition, ritual law, are all considered important. Possessors of such knowledge are held in high esteem in Jewish tradition. If this is so, why is the author of this text from the midrash implying that knowledge on its own may not be as significant? Instead, knowledge must be combined with virtue, with a desire to bring God's blessings into the world, into the lives of others.

So in acquiring knowledge, we have acquired a great deal. But we have not acquired all that we need—nor all that is needed from us. In acquiring knowledge, we have only acquired the foundation for the acquisition of more important things—a life of blessing through a life of good deeds.

Minimizing Happiness

AUGUST 5

When the month of Av enters,
we minimize our happiness.
BABYLONIAN TALMUD, TA'ANIT 29A

This seems to be the emotional tone that colors this time of year for the individual who is in sync with the spiritual rhythm of the Jewish calendar. The Hebrew month of Av, also called M'nacheim Av (the Consolation of Av), is colored by the ninth of the month, Tisha B'av, on which date the ancient Temples were destroyed. Other tragedies occurred also on that date throughout history. The text is not teaching us that we should let go of our happiness or that events such as this in our history should eclipse all else. But it is telling us that there are certain times when we have to realize that all is not right with the world, that we have suffered and that such suffering requires reflection.

Maybe it is the perspective of history that allows us to return to that period of time in our history, if only for a day, and gain new insight from it for our daily lives, as well. It was a severe physical loss, but the destruction cannot consume our spirit. Nothing can steal the soul of Judaism. While it may not have been the case for those who experienced the destruction of the Temples and of Jerusalem, we are now able to see how light can indeed emerge from darkness. Joy can emerge from sorrow. For we emerged a stronger, more resolute people as a result. And it is we who inherited that perspective on the world to share its blessing with all those around us.

Anticipating the Sabbath

AUGUST 6

You should keep My Sabbaths. I am Adonai your God.
LEVITICUS 19:3

This text from the Torah is usually taught as one of two versions of the same sacred commandment to observe Shabbat. It becomes translated into the blessing that separates Shabbat from the rest of the week. As someone who looks forward to, anticipates, and enjoys a traditional Shabbat each week, I find this makes a lot of sense. But the emphasis on the word "remember" is what has always intrigued me about this text. How do we remember Shabbat? Why would we remember

Shabbat when we are observing it? Does it just mean remember to observe Shabbat? Or do we remember Shabbat most when we are not observing it? My sense of the verse is that we should remember Shabbat in whatever we choose to do on Friday night and Saturday, wherever we are—even if not engaged in traditional ritual activity. For the act of remembering itself has intrinsic spiritual power.

How does this work? Imagine that you are on vacation, in a city far from the one in which you live. The end of Friday afternoon approaches. What do you do? You remember—if only for a short time, for that short time will eventually grow. You remember that God created the heavens and the earth. You remember that God rested on the seventh day. And you remember that you have the opportunity to do the same.

Drawing on Our Suffering

AUGUST 7

Ultimately we choose whether to draw on our understanding of suffering to be a blessing to others.
RABBI ELIE KAPLAN SPITZ

There are very few—if any—people in this world who make it through life's journey without some measure of pain and suffering—no matter what it looks like to the outsider, the bystander of another's life. And unfortunately, there are those who undeservedly suffer more than others—or so it would appear. But how we respond to suffering, what we do with it, is a choice that is left to the individual. Rabbi Yitzchak of Berditchev once remarked that it wasn't suffering he feared, it was that his suffering would have no meaning, that troubled him.

Rabbi Spitz suggests that it is up to us to determine whether our suffering can be used as a means of blessing for others. We have the capacity to learn from what we experience and share it with others—in an effort to lessen their burden. It may not be our choice as to whether we suffer or not. It is our choice whether we will transform such suffering into a life of blessing for others. The pain is no less great, but the reward knows no limits.

Bursts of Holiness

AUGUST 8

Though not all of life is holy, the holy can come bursting through the everyday at any time.
RABBI LAWRENCE A. HOFFMAN

According to Rabbi Hoffman, the modern tendency, especially in North America, is to separate the everyday from the sacred—as if we live in two different worlds, two different lives. But Judaism never intended for our lives to be so compartmentalized. We may be traveling and suddenly a beautiful mountain appears on the horizon. A blessing should be said, either with the traditional words of blessing or a prayer from the heart, but both are evoked as normal response to such beauty and majesty in the world. We never know when such things can burst through our everyday life. So we have to be prepared for them.

Among the hardest things for people to recognize is that our lives are not filled with mountaintops and majestic visions every day. Rather, it is the everyday that is the majesty of our lives: the familiar friend, the comforts of home, the love of a lifelong partner—and its routine. Too often, we fail to recognize the mundane as the majestic. And so we are reminded that we live in a sacred place—wherever that may be—through the appearance of real mountaintops and their consequent words of blessing.

Accepting the Call for Help

AUGUST 9

We pray that God may accept our call for help. But we also pray that God, who knows that which is hidden, may hear the silent cries of our souls.

RABBI URI OF STRELISK

There are many things that we want to say to God. And there are many things that we want to say and are unable to do so. Some say this was the function of the psalms—to put into words the feelings that emerge from our hearts that we are simply unable to articulate. It is not humility that robs us of our ability to speak. Rather, we just can't find the right words. We are unable to separate out the many emotions that course through our souls, one indistinguishable from the other, so many that they threaten to overwhelm us.

We can't imagine that God may not be willing to respond to our prayers, our yearnings, our cries for help. We just don't want to think it at all possible. So we pray that God may indeed respond to us and answer us. And we pray that God will reach into our silence and help us to discover the voice of our despair.

Looking for the Way Together

AUGUST 10

We know that the way we have been going is not the way. Now let us join hands and look for the way together.

RABBI HAYYIM HALBERSTAM OF ZANS

This bit of advice comes from a well-known Chasidic story. It seems that a man had entered a forest and gotten lost there, unable to find his way back. He ran into another person who had also lost his way. While neither of them knew the route to leave the forest, they reasoned that the way from which both had come was wrong. So they decided that they would find the way out together. It takes some compromise to come to this recognition in life, but it is an important recognition nonetheless. Such a realization requires both individuals to set aside their egos. Both have to admit that they have lost their way and do not have the answers that they need. But by working together, for their mutual benefit, they will be able to find their way. It is the blessing of real friendship.

Like so many Chasidic stories, this is a metaphor for life. Many of us have lost our way. Few have the found *the* path. But if we journey together, we just might discover it. We just might find the path that will lead us out of the forest. It may not be easy to find it together, but we know that we can't do it alone. None of us can do it alone. And if we invite God to join us in our search, then we may be able to see the path that we seek more clearly.

Repentance and Healing

AUGUST 11

If they see with their eyes, hear with their ears, and understand with their hearts, they will repent and be healed.
ISAIAH 6:10

Our senses are constantly being assaulted. Sometimes it is intentional messaging by those who want to sell us a product or convince us of something. At other times, it is just the noise of the city and of daily life. The prophet Isaiah understands our challenge. In order to see, hear, and understand God's message to us, God's direction for our lives, we have to be able to filter out all else that we see and hear that compete to claim our attention. If we aren't able to do so, then we will not be able to discern God's presence in the world or in our lives. And until we do, we can't enter on the path of repentance and healing and blessing.

So we begin the process by opening our eyes to the possibility of God's presence around us, searching for evidence of divine acts in the world. And we refrain from the tendency to explain things away that our Western rationalist education taught us as a first response. We listen clearly so that we might hear God's voice amidst all the noise that interferes with our ability to do so. Then we might all find our way to the path of repentance and be healed.

Community Norms

AUGUST 12

The ultimate moral test of a community is to include those who have been downtrodden and forbidden to speak, to give them a voice and grant them the dignity they deserve, because they are creatures fashioned in the image of God animated by holiness.

RABBI DAVID ELLENSON

This is a powerful statement that can be read in numerous ways. It might be an indictment against those communities—larger and small—who don't care for those on the periphery of the community or see it as their responsibility to look out for them or include them. The statement could be an inspiration to do so. It could also be a moral directive to the individual. After all, a community is only made up of individuals who choose to act—or not act—in a certain way.

If you wonder what the essential work is that you have to do, or if you want to discover the right community for you, use Rabbi Ellenson's words as a personal measure. Work to create holiness by making sure that those who find themselves on the outside of the community are brought in. And be first in line to do this—and offer them the blessing of being welcomed into your midst.

Making Sense of Our Life

AUGUST 13

The most important things in life don't make sense.
RABBI HAROLD KUSHNER

This seems contrary to the way most of us were educated. We were taught to probe things until they make sense. This is the force behind science and the pursuit of knowledge. The rationalists brought this quest—and the tools of science—to their exploration of sacred texts in order to understand their "real" meaning. But there are many things in life that defy such rational analysis and understanding. And Rabbi Kushner tells us that these are the most important things.

Consider, he suggests, whom we choose to marry or where we decide to work. These are not well thought out, analyzed, and scrutinized decisions. Rather, these are decisions that come to us without necessarily making any sense. Perhaps that is what makes them the most important—because they transcend our understanding, bringing blessing in their wake. And in so doing, they elevate us heavenward.

Making Progress

AUGUST 14

There are three things in life: facts, dreams, and faith.
RABBI IRVING "YITZ" GREENBERG

These are the three things that Rabbi Greenberg suggests we use to navigate our world and make progress in our daily lives.

Facts provide us with information. They appear to be the foundation on which the rest of life is built. They offer us stability, things on which we can count and depend. But facts are actually quite limiting. They lure us into a sense of fulfillment and knowledge. We think that the more facts we accumulate, the more we know. Sure, facts are important, but they don't allow us to dream. And they don't provide us with any room for faith. And it is our faith that provides us with the capacity to soar heavenward. Nevertheless, the three are in harmonious tension with one another.

Dreams propel us. They motivate us. They help us to articulate a goal or aspire to do something—even as facts might guide us, providing journey markers along the way.

Faith helps us to stay the course. Faith helps us to understand the value and worthiness of the pursuit. Faith motivates us to speak words of blessing. Faith takes us to an ultimate place, to a more perfect world.

Serving God

AUGUST 15

We know not how we shall serve Adonai
our God until we get there.
EXODUS 10:26

This verse has a specific context in the Bible along the route of our journey from Egyptian slavery to the blessing of entering the Promised Land. But the meaning of the text is not limited to a specific place in the book of Exodus. It transcends even the journey of our people in the desert. It provides us with direction for our entire lives. As it does in other places, the Torah is teaching us that "there" is not a physical destination. Rather, "there" is where we will be—an elevated spiritual state—once we are able to reach the point of serving God. This is one of the counterintuitive notions of Jewish spirituality. It seems circular, but that is indeed the point. Once we get "there," then we will know how to do it, that is, to serve God.

As our ancestors learned in the desert wanderings, moving them from slavery to freedom, it is not an easy journey. Once we arrive at that place, to the point of knowing how to serve God with our lives, then we are brought to yet another new place, to a much higher place. As I like to say, it is easy to find a job—what is most difficult is finding the work we are supposed to be doing in this world.

Finding Yourself

AUGUST 16

*Each individual must first find oneself;
then one must also find oneself in the world about oneself,
one's society, one's community, one's nation.*
RABBI ABRAHAM ISAAC KOOK

This reads like a spiritual work plan for each of us. And that is exactly Rabbi Kook's intention. He is suggesting that we cannot find our place anywhere else until we have found our place in ourselves. It might be that involvement in these other places will lead us back to ourselves or help us to find that path, but as much as we look elsewhere, we can only find the way to ourselves in ourselves. Otherwise, such effort simply brings us to become other people. And that is what too many others attempt to be—which is what brings Rabbi Kook to offer this advice.

So start with yourself rather than the motivation to be like other people or to live their lives.

But this process is not only about ourselves. It is also about the world and its perfection. It is about helping to shape a life—and world—of blessing. As Rabbi Kook teaches, the world also has to find its self-direction, as it brings us to that ultimate purpose: "Eventually the universe must find itself in the fullness that fills in the highest light in the hub of life in the divine light."

Finding Comfort in a Community of Prayers

AUGUST 17

Sudden terror won't frighten you nor the devastation by the wicked should it come.... For God is with us.... Even to your old age I will be the same; when you are gray-headed, still will I sustain you. I have made you, and I will bear you; I will sustain you and renew you.
PROVERBS 3:25; ISAIAH 8:10, 46:4

Following my father's death, I found myself, as expected, reciting the *Kaddish* memorial prayer each day in the syna-gogue. Because of my travels, I would often find myself in a dif-ferent synagogue—while I longed for the support of my home community. Just after each recitation, I found the words above, which appear in the traditional prayer book, to be particularly comforting. This text buoyed my spirit, no matter in which community I read the words of *Kaddish*, no matter that the sea of faces who surrounded me were unfamiliar.

These words are generally not said aloud, but it was as if the entire congregation was whispering them in my ears, and I con-tinued to hear—and feel—them after the final "amen" of the *Kaddish* was spoken. They truly help me whenever I read them. After all, what is the liturgy about if it is not to strengthen us, to lift us up in anticipation of entering the world once again—especially after we have experienced the death of someone we love, someone who is close to us?

And so, when I see people with whom I am not acquainted but who have clearly made their way into the community to say *Kaddish*, I speak these words aloud, hoping they will be lifted up, as I have been.

Eating in Paradise

AUGUST 18

Praised are You, Adonai,
for the land and for our food.
SECOND BLESSING IN *BIRKAT HAMAZON*, "GRACE AFTER MEALS"

Because I, like many people, believe that Israel is at the spiritual center of the universe, it is easy to conclude that this blessing is simply an expression of gratitude for the Land of Israel. And it is included in the Grace after Meals because we are grateful for the produce that the land yields—which nourishes its inhabitants, among whom we can be vicariously counted. But there is a powerful spiritual lesson that undergirds this text of blessing. For the blessing of the land, that is, the Land of Israel, has become a substitute for the Garden of Eden, paradise, from which Adam and Eve were expelled.

In the book of Genesis, we are told that following the expulsion from Eden, Adam and Eve—and humankind that follows—will be forced to eat of the grasses of the land and toil for food (Genesis 3:17–19), something that was not the case in paradise. But with the gift of the land, we are told in Deuteronomy that the animals will eat of the grasses and that we will be able to enjoy the produce of the land (Deuteronomy 11:15). While it is clear to anyone who has visited the Land of Israel that it took—and continues to take—a great deal of hard work for the land to yield its abundance, the blessing is clear, nonetheless. The desert land has indeed blossomed, and we are its beneficiaries. So when you next recite the Grace after Meals, thank God for what you have eaten and the blessing of the land's abundant produce.

Standing Tall

AUGUST 19

You are standing [atem nitzavim] *this day....*
DEUTERONOMY 29:9

We are all standing there (that's what *atem nitzavim* means)—at the foot of the mountain, at Sinai, waiting impatiently, yearning for revelation. We have no idea how long the journey will take or what's in store for us, or even where we are going. All that we know is that we have left the narrow place of Egyptian slavery behind us and that we have been given the promise that is inherent in freedom. And this is the second time we have heard the story of our ancestors, first in Exodus and now, once again, in Deuteronomy, as a reminder before we cross the Jordan into the land of promise.

Nitzavim seems to be the theme statement for this portion, something that we might expect to be carried throughout the Torah or at least through the end of the portion. In case we need some extra help, we are given a list of who the "we" is that is standing there: leaders, tribes, elders and officers, infants, spouses (sorry, the text actually says "wives"), and "those who live among you"—including the one who cuts wood and the one who draws water. Then we are also reminded that there are others included in the covenantal agreement: those who are born and those yet to be born. The Torah in its wisdom provides enough room to accommodate all who would drink from its well, all who would care to live in a community infused by its divinely revealed wisdom (Deuteronomy 29:9–14).

"Those who live among you" (Deuteronomy 29:10). Who are these people? Are they merely itinerant laborers who joined the Israelite camp to service them? Are they the mass multitude that scholars tell us joined the Exodus from Egypt? (It seems that they too had been enslaved and took advantage of the "midnight move" to leave slavery behind.) Or perhaps they were men and women from other peoples whom the Israelites married and brought into their camp?

Being given the privilege of standing at the foot of the mountain each day is a blessing. It seems to me that regardless of their source of origin, the Torah makes one thing quite clear: we have the opportunity to share the experience of Torah with whomever wants to camp among us.

Revering God

AUGUST 20

Does Job revere God for nothing?
JOB 1:9

Job's tragedy reflects the worst that is possible. Perhaps that is why it was included in the Bible, so that we see that what we experience is generally less than the worst possible. Whatever the tragedy we experience, it appears to be the most tragic. And none of us are immune from such experiences.

But whatever the tragedy, contained in it is the possibility, the potential, for holiness, for blessing. In the midst of the tragedy is the potential for finding our path in life once again—when we never thought it possible. That path is in the context of a relationship with God.

This seems to be the simplest message offered to us in the most profound way. It is when we are lowliest, when we have experienced the worst that life has to offer, that we may yet find God. It is in that encounter, no matter the context, that we can find holiness. So I invite you to keep looking along with me.

The Book of Days

AUGUST 21

You open the book of our days, and what is written there proclaims itself, for it bears the signature of every human being.

FROM THE *UN'TANEH TOKEF* PRAYER FOR THE HIGH HOLY DAYS

During the Hebrew month of Elul, which precedes the High Holy Days—and which generally begins in August—we begin our preparations. We start on our path of *t'shuvah*, of repentance, hoping for renewal that comes with such a journey. We do so for a variety of reasons, including that we are taught that there are three things that mitigate the severity of the decree of life or death that symbolizes the holiday period: prayer, repentance, and *tzedakah* (righteous acts of giving charity).

As the lines from the *Un'taneh Tokef* prayer suggest, we don't have to report on the misdeeds that we have done. They will all speak loudly for themselves. But the same thing is true for all that we might do this month to repair what we may have done. They too will call out to God—and to others. So do your deeds quietly, gently, humbly. But not for their reward or their report. Blessing will come into the world as a result—and help pave your path to repentance along the way.

Fearless

AUGUST 22

Adonai is my light and my salvation. Whom shall I fear?
Adonai is the strength of my life. Of whom shall I be afraid?
PSALM 27:1, REPEATED EACH DAY FOR
THE MONTH PRIOR TO AND DURING THE FALL HOLIDAYS

This is the spiritual message of the period that immediately precedes the High Holy Day season. It is actually the message of all of Judaism. The words are easy to say. They are harder to claim as our own. That is why we are instructed to repeat them each day during the month of Elul, the month prior to the High Holy Days, and during the ten-day period including Rosh Hashanah through Yom Kippur. In many communities, they are repeated even longer through Hoshana Rabbah. By saying these words aloud, by allowing ourselves to hear them each day, they are able to enter into our soul and provide support for our spirit. Thus, they become a blessing of sorts.

With such faith, no enemy, however great or small, can bring us to fear. With such faith, the entire world—and our lives—are illuminated with the divine spirit. In such light, there can be no darkness.

Knowledge of the Holy

AUGUST 23

I have not learned wisdom,
but I have the knowledge of all (that is) holy.
PROVERBS 30:3

This verse from Proverbs has always intrigued me. Wisdom comes directly from learning through the experiences of living.

Its source is human. Revelation comes from the Divine. It is revealed to us from God. But the book of Proverbs is indeed a book of wisdom and not a book of revelation—it is not part of the Torah. Perhaps the author is trying to teach us that experiences in life can bring us close to the holy, even if we don't gain wisdom from them. And we can find blessing in them. That is the profound wisdom of this teaching.

So maybe we should not be spending our time trying to gain wisdom. Rather we should be looking for the holy in our lives. There we may be able to find the wisdom that we seek.

Making Blessing

AUGUST 24

[In the act of blessing,] we make a statement of mutual relationship, that we are givers as well as receivers.
RABBI ARTHUR GREEN

The act of blessing. Some people think that blessings always have to be orchestrated or done in groups, especially when assembled for meals or at the synagogue. This is what I sometimes refer to as public acts of Judaism. And so we wait for the "orchestra leader," usually the rabbi, to tell us when it is time to do something or just to make sure that we are all doing it together. But blessings are generally not for crowds. They help form our personal connections with the Divine, especially when done quietly and personally.

So the next time you do something, the next time you eat or drink something, take a moment. Consider the act or the source of food or drink. If you know the traditional words of blessing, then use them. And if you don't, start with your own words of thanksgiving. For the true blessing emerges in the pause you take before you act.

Nourishment

AUGUST 25

Praised are You, Adonai our God, Sovereign of the universe,
who creates variety of sustenance.

BLESSING SAID BEFORE EATING SNACKS

This is known as the *m'zonot* blessing. We are instructed to recite it before eating snacks. There are two ways of knowing that this is the appropriate blessing to be recited. Generally, if none of the other required blessings apply and if the snack is made from a variety of items, then this is the appropriate blessing. And if you have eaten a wonderfully delicious snack, then you are indeed ready to say a blessing—even if it will require a lot of exercise later on.

But the wisdom of the tradition is more clearly apparent in the requirement for such unusual blessings than it is for more traditional foodstuffs. We really take snacks for granted. We gobble them mindlessly—often on the run or while doing other things. We usually eat them for fun rather than for nourishment. Thus, it means that we have the leisure time and funds available to enjoy them. So the blessing implies not only the substance but the context—and its Ultimate Source.

The Process of Peace

AUGUST 26

Peace be both to you, and peace be to your house,
and peace be to all that you possess.

1 SAMUEL 25:6

This is considered by many to be the words of the ultimate house blessing, for there is no blessing as important as peace.

And they are particularly fitting when they are offered by a prophet, for a prophet, according to Jewish tradition, is a spokesperson for God. And the Divine is the source of real peace. This not only refers to a lack of conflict, but it also means a completeness, a wholeness, a sense of tranquility and security. So we ask that blessing for an individual and for the individual's entire household.

The words of the prophet Samuel extend beyond this moment and beyond the physical nature of our homes. The blessing he offers is one of ultimate peace, one that comes as an ideal for which we all work, one that comes at the end of days. So it is both a blessing and a directive. The blessing of peace can come. It will come. But peace is not static. It is a dynamic state of being for which we will all have to work.

Speaking Up

AUGUST 27

For the sake of Zion I will not be silent,
For the sake of Jerusalem I will not be still,
Till her victory emerges resplendent
And her triumph like a flaming torch.
ISAIAH 62:1

While this reads like a poeticized version of a Zionist political stump speech, it refers to what Israel and Jerusalem represent in the world. Some will read this as a political statement. Others will read it as a set of ethical values that Israel is duty-bound to share with the world. For me, these words of the prophet Isaiah combine to make a strong statement about Jewish spirituality.

Isaiah speaks about the ancient city of Jerusalem that has become desolate. This is why the Rabbis chose this text to be part of the weekly Torah readings that follow Tisha B'av in the late summer. The writer will not be comforted. He will no longer be still. So he urges the people to work for the rebuilding of Jerusalem and the reinstatement of its values as those that guide the people.

The first two lines of this poetry have become a *kavvanah* (sacred mantra) for me, no less than the formulaic words of blessing that I commonly recite. I repeat them regularly, for they tell me what I have to do and where is the source of my inspiration. I too will not be silent until these values motivate us—and all peoples.

The Renewal of Paradise

AUGUST 28

Let the loving couple be very happy,
just as You made Your creation happy
in the Garden of Eden, so long ago.
FROM THE FIFTH WEDDING BLESSING

This text from the seven blessings recited at a wedding asks for God to bless the new couple with a life similar to the one that God shaped for Adam and Eve in the Garden of Eden. This blessing is for a life of companionship. It is a life of knowing the other as one—the ultimate goal of Adam and Eve when they came together in the garden. It was only through such knowledge that Adam and Eve could bear the fruit that became humanity.

As each couple starts out in their relationship, no matter its structure or form, they have the potential to create their own paradise together. Eden is not a place, fixed by time or space. Eden transcends such limitations, especially those of physical location. But a couple also risks expulsion from the Garden—as Adam and Eve experienced.

When a couple comes together as one, paradise is renewed, and the Garden is brought forward for others to share in its fruits.

Good Fortune

AUGUST 29

*May we and all Israel have a favorable omen
and good fortune.*

FROM A TRADITIONAL JEWISH FOLK SONG

Usually sung loudly and joyously, this text is a spontaneous expression of blessing that is repeated over and over until it evolves into more of a *niggun* (wordless chant), often in the synagogue following bar or bat mitzvah celebrations or *aufrufen* (premarital blessings). Whenever a happy life-cycle event takes place in the Jewish community, it is considered an affirmation of life and optimism for the future.

In the Jewish community, life-cycle events are not considered private affairs. They are celebrations of community. And while families now provide formal invitations for most events, it is actually considered inappropriate to offer invitations for events such as *b'rit milah* (ritual circumcision). So don't expect one and you won't be disappointed. Just go and enjoy. You will help to transform the event into a community.

Making Miracles

AUGUST 30

For the land that you are about to enter and possess is
not like the land of Egypt from which you have come.
There the grain you sowed had to be watered
by your own labors, like a vegetable garden;
but the land you are about to cross into and possess,
a land of hills and valleys,
soaks up its water from the rains of heaven.
DEUTERONOMY 11:10–11

These are the words that the ancient Israelites heard as they were about to enter the Land of Israel. It is the last line that has always struck me—that the fruits and vegetables of the land are nourished by the "rains of heaven." Such a beautiful image of the land. While we know that hard work transformed the modern State of Israel—it didn't just happen on its own— the image still remains. For the people have truly caused the deserts to bloom. And they understand that it is a blessing to be able to live on the land and work it.

Maybe it is indeed hard work that brings heavenly rains. There is a connection between the work that we undertake and the partnership with the Divine that we can enjoy. It is like the truism that suggests, "We have to make our own miracles."

Work the land and it will yield its produce. Enjoy the fruit of your labors. And be thankful to God for sending the heavenly rains that simultaneously nurture our crops and our souls.

Rising toward Life

AUGUST 31

Thus says the High and Lofty One who inhabits eternity, whose name is holy: "I dwell in a high and holy place with the one who has a contrite spirit, so that I might revive the spirit of the humble and the heart of those who are crushed."

ISAIAH 57:15

There are days and nights in which we feel desperate and disillusioned. We wonder whether God has perhaps forsaken us. We feel low of spirit and broken of heart. We may not know what to do. We may feel alone and isolated. The prophet Isaiah understands what it is to feel such pain. He saw such distress rise among our ancestors. So he comes to remind us, as he did our people before, that when we feel that way, God is actually closer to us rather than farther away. We need only reach out for God's presence in our midst—to find that God has been sitting with us the entire time.

God gave us life at the beginning and gives us life once again. What we do with that life, once revived, is up to us. Arise from your desolation and live a life of blessing. Arise and live your life, for God has restored it to you.

SEPTEMBER

Renewing the Past

Renew our days as in the past.
LAMENTATIONS 5:21

September is a time for beginnings. School starts, as do new jobs. Regardless of the climate in which we live, summer seems to fade into autumn just as soon as we cross over the threshold of Labor Day. Soon the fall holidays will be upon us. And that will lead us back into the grind of daily living. Perhaps what makes beginnings hard no matter the starting point is the fear of where they may lead us—back to where we once were. What would it take to make sure that what you just started doesn't lead you back to where you just ended?

There is intentional wisdom in the coming together of the various beginnings of the fall with the start of the Jewish holiday season. So maybe it isn't so coincidental that Rosh Hashanah and Yom Kippur occur at about the same time that our North American society is focused on the beginning of the year—even though January is still several months away.

The primary message of the fall holidays offers us perspective and grounding for the days ahead. People often look for the message deeply embedded in the liturgy and rituals of the season. But the blessing of beginning again *is* the message. We can let go of the past and start over. Such a notion helps us to take the routine of daily life that has the potential to drag us down and instead raise it heavenward—and we can go along with it for the ride.

The text cited here needs to be reviewed in its entirety, as it is each time the Torah is returned to the ark after it is read: "Return us, O Adonai, to You, and we will return; renew our days as in the past" (Lamentations 5:21). Such renewal is connected to our desire to connect with God. The author of the text is helping us to say: I know that I can count on You to help me make the days as they once were—full of hope and inspiration. May I be able to start again each year, each day, overwhelmed by that sense of blessing in my heart—for it is that which will lift me up.

Hope against Fear

SEPTEMBER 2

And Adonai, Godself, will go before you. God will be with you; God will not fail you or forsake you. Do not fear and do not be distraught.

DEUTERONOMY 31:8

What other words do we need to hear? No matter what happens, no matter where our journey takes us, God will be with us. These were the words spoken by Moses to Joshua as Moses transferred the leadership of the Jewish people to Joshua prior to Moses's death. These words are especially comforting to someone who might be an inexperienced leader, who is afraid of the task ahead. But this text, coming toward the end of the Torah, on Shabbat between Rosh Hashanah and Yom Kippur—called Shabbat Shuvah, the Sabbath of Return—is particularly inspiring. While we are in the liminal state between the holidays, between the metaphor of the book of life and death, we seek the comforting presence of God.

This statement represents an important Jewish ideology. As my colleague Rabbi Eliot Malomet likes to say, Judaism offers us "hope as an antidote to fear." That hope is communicated through the constant presence of God. And Judaism offers us a variety of contexts to feel that presence: sacred study, ritual, the doing of mitzvot, and the support of community. May we always feel the blessing of God's presence in our midst.

Unburdening the Soul

SEPTEMBER 3

A day that is all Shabbat.
MISHNAH TAMID 1:4

Yom shekulo Shabbat: the Hebrew seems to capture the intent of the phrase much better. It is the most that we can wish for in a day, and it is especially helpful to think about following the routine burdens of daily living. It is such an important idea that this rabbinic concept is included in the Grace after Meals prayer during Shabbat. It forces each of us to step back and consider what might be possible in the future just after completing a relaxed and sumptuous meal that is also joyous, surrounded by family and friends.

The notion is emphasized because it suggests that within the observance of Shabbat is a taste of the world-to-come. Just imagine. A day in the future that is entirely Shabbat. No beginning. No end. No work. A perpetual engagement with the sacred that is not burdened by the mundane. Each week, we have an opportunity to luxuriate in its potential, if we would only stop and allow Shabbat to wash over us.

It isn't easy to let go of our workday responsibilities, to step away from the computer and telephone, to detach ourselves from the various daily tasks that burden our soul.

A day that is only Shabbat—for which we are grateful—is ours for the taking. This is a sign of the future world, what we call the messianic age. But we don't have to wait for it until the end of life as we know it, or even wait for its approximation each week as Shabbat approaches. Instead, we can actually transform each day into a potential day of waiting for the messianic age by what we do, how we act and treat others. This is the blessing of daily life. What we do and how we do it will not only give us a taste of that special day, it may actually even bring that day closer.

Embracing Life

SEPTEMBER 4

Reverence for Adonai is the beginning of knowledge.
Only fools scorn wisdom and discipline.
PROVERBS 1:7

This verse has become the motto for the entire biblical book of Proverbs, because it captures the essence of the entire volume. Its specific interpretation depends on the lens of the reader and how one views the world. Unlike revelation, which emanates from the Divine, wisdom emerges from the experience of this world, the everyday. So for one reader, this text from Proverbs might only be a directive about ethical standards of behavior. For another, it is all about self-control. And for a third, the idea that is contained in this Proverbs text refers to ritual observance. Simply put, the writer of this proverb is suggesting that the opportunity for study is a blessing. But it comes through discipline. Learning is a process. And there are no shortcuts to wisdom. Embracing life—with all its challenges, and there are many—is the only way to acquire it.

But if the acquiring of wisdom were only about living, then there would certainly be more wise people in our midst. To be sure, it would make our lives a lot easier. Perhaps it is merely that people don't learn from their own experience or the experience of others. Or maybe they think that such learning has nothing to do with their experience of the Divine. The ability to learn from our experience is directly related to our relationship with the sacred. For it is only in the context of such a relationship that we can garner wisdom from the everyday that otherwise appears to elude us. It is only in divine light that we are able to see it so clearly.

The Answering Heart

SEPTEMBER 5

*Just as face answers face in a reflection in water,
so should one person's heart answer another.*
PROVERBS 27:19

My friend, writer and educator Joel Grishaver places this text at the bottom of each e-mail that he writes. When I read it, especially as part of our ongoing dialogue, it provides a context for our communication and, even more importantly, for our relationship. And I feel blessed by it, for such friendship is indeed a blessing. Whatever we are discussing, it provides the lens that I need to read what he has to say to me. This is particularly helpful if there is criticism or disagreement. By reflecting on these words, I am able to remember the source of his words and the love that supports them.

Rabbi Eugene Borowitz, a leading liberal Jewish theologian, once taught me a similar lesson. He suggested that when we thank someone for doing something, the thanks should be commensurate with the task—how much we appreciated it and what was really done. If the thanks we offer is short, clipped, brief, then the person to whom we are directing our thanks might be led to believe that is what we thought of what he or she had done. On the other hand, when we take the opportunity to express our profound thanks to a person, carefully crafting our words and emotions, then the person on the receiving end begins to understand how much we really appreciate what was done—and often on our behalf.

If this is the case with human interaction, imagine how important our words and actions are to God—as we attempt to communicate what is in our hearts to the Divine.

Being Mighty

SEPTEMBER 6

Who is mighty?
The one who makes an enemy a friend.
AVOT D'RABBI NATHAN 23

It is easy to make enemies, much harder to find friends. In this season of forgiveness, fueled by the Hebrew month of Elul, which takes place toward the end of the summer and just prior to the fall holidays of Rosh Hashanah and Yom Kippur, it is the right time to think about our so-called enemies and how we got to this place in our relationship with them. The sentiment expressed by Rabbi Nathan the Babylonian above does not seem to be about warring countries or even opposing sports teams. Few people, thankfully, are involved in the former, and we voluntarily place ourselves in the latter. Rather, the notion of "enemy" is probably more about those with whom you contend in school or at work, or even your next-door neighbor, the one who competes with you at every turn. So what will it take to turn that person, the one who brings you distress by his or her very presence, into a friend? What will it take to realize that such a relationship can be transformed into a blessing?

We begin by ascertaining what it really takes to make an enemy. Short of someone who threatens the well-being of self, family, or community, no one is really an enemy. Rather they are simply folks trying to find their way in a perilous world, much like you. Perhaps the journey will be less dangerous if you are able to find your way together.

Maybe the only change required begins with you instead of your so-called enemy. Just taking a step forward toward your fellow will actually bring you closer. And in that step is contained a world of possibility. How you fill in the remaining gap is up to you. The willingness to take that step actually brings us closer to the messianic age. And it is entirely in your power to do so. So what are you waiting for? Take a running jump. We will all be better for it.

Fixing the Self

SEPTEMBER 7

If you can fix yourself,
then you have the power to fix others as well.
RABBI NATAN SCHAFER

In an age of liberalism, the idea of being able to fix someone else is not very popular. One of my former teachers, Rabbi Alvin Reines, used to refer to this idea as the rainbow covenant. I like to add that it is a blessing to live within the shadow of the rainbow covenant, which covers us with its wondrous hues and tones. He said that *my* freedom extended to the edge of where another's freedom began. And then it stopped. My neighbor's freedom extended the same distance in my direction.

So who am I to arrogate myself to fixing someone else? Only God has the power to do so—and only when the individual is willing to partner with God on his or her own behalf. But that is exactly the point. You—and I—can become God's channel into the world, partners with the Divine toward perfection. But what Rabbi Schafer is saying, and he knows it firsthand from his experience working many years in the Massachusetts prison system with those whose lives and souls need a lot of fixing, is that no one is capable of fixing anyone else until that person is ready to fix him- or herself. In the humility of what is required for self-repair, the individual is able to see the potential in the other. The ability to help another starts with a willingness to work on yourself.

The irony of the notion of personal repair—and perhaps this is what Rabbi Schafer is suggesting—is that any form of self-repair is an ongoing process. It never really stops. We realize this at this time of year more than any other time, since so much of the Jewish and secular calendar points us toward introspection, all in a forward direction toward the months and year ahead.

Loving the Other

SEPTEMBER 8

Hillel said, "That which is hateful to you, do not do to your fellow. This is the entire Torah. Go and learn it."
BABYLONIAN TALMUD, *SHABBAT* 31A

This is Hillel's oft-quoted response to the potential convert to Judaism who wanted the rabbi to teach him all of Judaism while standing on one foot. Presumably it was the student who was perched in such a way and not the rabbi. Where so many others have failed to do so, Hillel seems to have cleverly captured the essence of Judaism. The so-called Golden Rule is actually a recasting of Hillel's words. But those who focus on the first part of Hillel's statement really miss the cleverness of his response, especially since his final point is often neglected by those who quote him.

It takes real effort ("go and learn it") to be able to consider the behavior toward our neighbors in such a context. It isn't easy to measure the behaviors that would be offensive to our neighbors and then refrain from doing them. We are so used to a quick response—what I often refer to as "going on automatic pilot." We react to words and other behaviors and seldom consider the consequences of our own actions and certainly not their impact on others.

Here is where Hillel's real genius comes in—in discovering the inherent blessing in such study. To learn about the consequences of our actions takes a great deal of empathy. But such empathy doesn't emerge by its own volition. Rather, the kind of empathy that Hillel imagines—and considers ideal—evolves in the context of intimate study of sacred texts. In the midst of such study will you be able to encounter the Divine.

Rising above Suffering

SEPTEMBER 9

Down I went to the base of the mountains.
The bars of the earth would always be over me.
Yet, Adonai, my God, you brought me up from the pit.

JONAH 2:7

These are the words spoken by the reluctant prophet Jonah after he is rescued from the waters into which he was cast to protect the lives of his fellow passengers on the ship. He thought that his life had ended, even before being voluntarily cast into the turbulent waters of the sea. As a result, Jonah thought that he would always be kept from God's presence. Jonah was unaware of the fact that he could never leave the blessing of God's presence, because God's presence was everywhere—even when Jonah tried to evade it. Perhaps this is one of the reasons why the entire book of Jonah is read in the synagogue on the afternoon of Yom Kippur.

Even if we think that what we have done may have caused us to be unable to stay within the protective shelter of God's presence, we learn that we are never really far from it. Listen to what Jonah said only a few verses prior to the text quoted above. His sentiment is quite simple, one that often washes over many of us: "In my need, I called to Adonai from the belly of Sheol and God answered me. I cried out and You heard my voice" (Jonah 2:3).

We may not always receive the response that we seek, but we do want to be assured that God hears us when we cry out. Perhaps that alone will give us the strength that we need. If God could raise the reluctant prophet from his misfortune and suffering, then God can certainly help raise us above ours.

Rebalancing Our Lives

SEPTEMBER 10

Repentance is the mechanism for rebalancing lives that have been distorted by mistakes or by sin.
RABBI DAVID J. WOLPE

Repentance is not a term that flows easily off the tongue of the contemporary individual—man or woman. And yet it is the foundation stone for the entire High Holy Day period. Thus, repentance colors the month of September and the beginning of October for many people. If sin—another unpopular word—is what takes us off the straight path of the good life, then repentance is what gets us back on it. By attempting to undo any wrongdoing that we have done—by repairing what we have broken, particularly in our relationships with others—we can balance our lives once again.

T'shuvah, the Hebrew word for repentance, means "to turn back, to turn around, to return." In the synagogue we get started on this path of return with prayer and reflection. We gain strength for this process by feasting on Rosh Hashanah and ironically by fasting on Yom Kippur. Rosh Hashanah is about life, as is Yom Kippur. But in order to be reborn a better person, we have to first experience a spiritual death on Yom Kippur. It is one of the things that is emphasized in the fast.

But what really counts is what we do the next day—that we are granted the blessing of a next day—for what we do after the holidays becomes the shape of our everyday world. How have our patterns of behavior changed? What are we doing differently as a result? If we are confronted with the same moral challenge, will we now respond differently as a result of the process of repentance, of *t'shuvah* change, that we have just undergone? Wait a couple days and see. The promise of redemption is always worth waiting for.

Words of Hope

SEPTEMBER 11

We are a people of memory and prayer.
We are a people of words and hope. We have neither
established empires nor built castles and palaces.
We have only placed words on top of each other.
We have fashioned ideas; we have built memorials.
We have dreamed towers of yearnings—of Jerusalem
rebuilt, of Jerusalem united, of a peace that will be
swiftly and speedily established in our days.

EZER WEIZMAN

Like too many days that have been seared into our memory because of the horrific events that have occurred on them, September 11 has certainly and unfortunately achieved such prominence in the shared history of American Jews. The Jewish people is not a people of mere history. Rather, as Ezer Weizman, a former president of Israel suggested, we are a people of memory. But not memory alone. We take our experience of earth-shattering events and rather than just marking them in time, we elevate them to sacred status by attaching our prayers and dreams to them. This is what transforms tragedy into blessing. In so doing, we are able to move tragedy into purpose and direction, buoyed by our undying hope and optimism for the future. Such an approach gives meaning to our own lives, as well. Hopefully, we can learn thereby how to shape a better world and how we can be instrumental in doing so because of the lessons derived.

I remember hearing Golda Meir, the former prime minister of Israel, describe this approach in a different way, when speaking about forging a diplomatic relationship between the modern state of Israel and what was then West Germany.

People were amazed at her willingness to develop normative relations between the two countries. Israel certainly had less reason to do so than other countries. Meir was fully prepared to unconditionally forgive but help us to live in a way that we would never forget.

September 11, 2001, for most of us, is still too fresh a memory to transcend. And in the midst of a world transformed by terror, we find it nearly impossible to forgive those who continue to perpetrate such acts on the world. But we can use the recollection of the day to motivate us to press forward for freedom for all those not yet blessed by it. But freedom is not just a statement about the form of politics and government. It has to reflect our spiritual state, as well. No one is indeed free until we are all free—and we work to bring the messianic era upon us.

Subtle Awareness

SEPTEMBER 12

Spiritual interpretation depends on a subtle form of awareness, through which we learn to connect the events of the world to the role God plays in them.
CAROL OCHS AND RABBI KERRY M. OLITZKY

It would be easy to just walk through life and see the events that unfold in front of us as unconnected to one another, to us, or to the Divine. It seems like a lot of work to make the connections, so we refrain from doing so. But not doing so actually makes life harder, more difficult. It would make our days seem like mere markings in time with no reason or direction. A life that is totally random serves little purpose. So our challenge is to see each event in our lives through a spiritual prism, a lens of blessing. This is what helps to elevate the mundane into the sacred, what transforms the routine into the holy.

Too many people frantically search for artificial highs in life as if that is what will give them meaning or, at least, help them to escape what they perceive as a dead end, as if that is "all there is to life." The frantic dash for "fifteen minutes of fame" seems to propel society and our interest in those who have found it. But such fame is fleeting by its very nature.

The counterintuitive nature of spirituality, of establishing a relationship with God, teaches us that life gains its real momentum in the grounding of the everyday. It is the routine of every day that brings us closer to one another and to ourselves, because it is orderly and dependable. The familiarity brings with it comfort. And then when we experience the high points of life that come as a result, these are what can truly elevate us heavenward.

The Holiness of Time

SEPTEMBER 13

Judaism teaches us to be attached to holiness in time,
to be attached to sacred events,
to learn how to consecrate sanctuaries
that emerge from the magnificent stream of a year.
RABBI ABRAHAM JOSHUA HESCHEL

Shabbat comes each week, every seven days. It comes whether we are ready for it or not. Who isn't ready for twenty-five hours of freedom from our workaday world? Although we often boast of Shabbat as *the* gift of the Jewish people to the world, few of us really take the opportunity that it affords us to refresh and renew. We feel so intimately tied to our work that we somehow refuse to let go of it even as we complain how overwhelmed and overburdened we feel from it.

That is where Shabbat can really help. Use it as a way to let go entirely. Rather than *you* controlling the calendar, let the changing time for the start of Shabbat (about eighteen minutes before sunset each week) determine when it is time to stop working. Shut down the computer. Get off of e-mail. Put away the BlackBerry. Just stop working. It will be there for you when you return to it on Saturday night or Sunday or Monday morning. And when you finally get there on Sunday or on Monday, that is when you really experience the blessing of Shabbat.

Rabbi Heschel taught us that things are not holy in Judaism. Only time is holy. You can only find such holiness when you allow Shabbat to wash completely over you—and cleanse you as a result. Go ahead. This week, even if you have never done so before, take the time to do so.

Neighborly Good

SEPTEMBER 14

If you have done your neighbor a slight wrong,
let it be a serious matter in your eyes.
But if you have done your neighbor much good,
let it be a small thing in your eyes.
AVOT D'RABBI NATAN 41

Consider the two statements here by the author of this Rabbinic collection of ethical maxims, the one whom the text calls Rabbi Natan. Imagine what the world would be like— what our lives would be like—if this were the primary ethical principle that guided our lives.

Take seriously all of your actions, but particularly those that negatively impact others. In this case, it doesn't matter whether the actions were intentional or not. The end result is what becomes significant. Of course, it does matter how your actions affected your neighbor. Nevertheless, what is most important here—and what will therefore shape your future behaviors—is how you reacted to them. If you wronged someone, even if that wrong was slight, repair it immediately. Consider it a grave offense and be more careful.

If you do something nice for someone else, even when the benefit to your neighbor is significant as a result, take no pride in it. Instead, let the knowledge that you have improved someone's life—even it is for just a minute—be your blessing. No other acknowledgment or expression is necessary. And once you are finished, rush ahead and do something nice for someone else. You will never know in the midst of which simple action the messianic era may be waiting to burst forth.

Speaking Out

SEPTEMBER 15

We must speak out ... so that we do not change.
RABBI DAVID SAPERSTEIN

Rabbi Saperstein has it right. We do have a moral imperative to speak out against whatever wrongs and injustices we encounter in the world—no matter how large or small, near or far. If we do not speak out, not only do we become complicit through silence, but the act actually changes essentially who we are. So we speak out to make sure that we do not change who we are or the essential blessing of life that we have received, so that we continue in our striving to be among the righteous in the world.

It isn't easy to be responsible for the whole world. Some will say, "Just worry about changing yourself. The rest will follow." And sometimes that is true—when interpersonal relationships are involved. Working on the self may be the first step, but it can't be the only step. Rabbi Saperstein is not talking about changing other people. He is talking about righting the wrongs in the world.

My Chasidic colleagues who are part of the Chabad community have a similar outlook to Rabbi Saperstein's, but they translate his statement in the context of personal spirituality. They travel as emissaries to the most remote places on earth to serve the Jewish people. And they bring with them their unique prism on Jewish life. In the most distant and isolated places, they work to influence others, but they themselves do not change. Some may call this "old school." Others may say it is a way of preparing for the future by anchoring yourself in the past.

Being Ready

September 16

Love draws a veil over wrongdoing.
FROM THE *HINEINI* PRAYER CHANTED BY
THE CANTOR ON THE HIGH HOLY DAYS

The *Hineini* prayer takes its lead from the various times in the Bible when a character responds to a request by God by saying *Hineini,* literally "I am here." But the word means much more. It is a statement that suggests to God—and to others—that I am ready to complete the task assigned to me. I am ready to fulfill my obligation to self, to others, and to God. In the midst of congregational prayer, the cantor plaintively approaches God in front of the holy ark. With a great deal of diffidence and humility, the cantor asks to be worthy of the task at hand—to represent the congregation of Israel as the people face their Maker during the High Holy Days, so that they feel blessed in the relationship between the individual and the Divine as a result. It is an awesome responsibility at a very sacred moment in time.

The phrase quoted above is taken from that prayer. It reflects the hope and faith of the cantor—who speaks on behalf of all those assembled. May the love that God feels for the people eclipse any wrongdoing that might have been perpetrated by those assembled during the past year. Thus, the people won't be punished and instead will be rewarded with yet another year of life.

The phrase has also become a well-known idiom in Yiddish. But in its Yiddish form, it reflects the love between men and women rather than between humans and God. Nevertheless the hope is the same. May the love shared between these two human beings be strong enough that had either done anything wrong during the year past, such wrongdoings may be overlooked by the other. Love makes it possible, and love makes it stronger.

Living with Certainty

SEPTEMBER 17

There is no certainty without a doubt.
RABBINIC SAYING

Most of us would probably like simple answers to the tough questions of life. It seems to be part of our human nature. Some of these answers—once we find them—have the potential to actually change our lives. But such life-transforming answers don't come quickly or easily, nor do they have the kind of absolute certainly that we would prefer. We have to work hard at them. We have to work hard at seeing the blessings in the world around us, even in the small world in which we live and spend our daily lives.

Jewish tradition understands this challenge and actually seems to prefer the constant struggle of faith even when it results in continued doubt over certainty. For some, this notion is unsettling. For others, it is actually affirming, because it forces us to continue to ask questions, to probe more deeply, to refrain from stock answers and "quick fixes." This approach motivates us to constantly and relentlessly pursue the truth wherever we may find it. It also requires our faith in God to be ever responsive to our evolving experience of the mundane.

So don't expect to wake up one day and discover you have found *the* answer, regardless of the question. Instead, be thankful that you have figured out the right questions to answer and have found the path on which to discern them.

Leadership

SEPTEMBER 18

People are led on the way they want to follow.
BABYLONIAN TALMUD, *MAKKOT* 10B

A quick reading of this text will lead us to conclude that the Rabbis of the Talmud who authored this statement are offering us a lesson in political leadership. To make things easier, perhaps leaders should simply determine the direction that people want to go in and lead them there. Had Moses assumed that posture in the desert, he might have ended up leading the ancient Israelites back to Egyptian slavery, rather than to the Promised Land. Certainly Egypt seemed to be the place that they wanted to go—if we interpret superficially all of their complaints, listed in the Bible. But a leader knows where to take people, where they need to go in order to realize themselves. A leader knows how to help people see blessing in their lives and in the world around them even when they don't see it for themselves. This is why Moses continued to lead the ancient Israelites to freedom from slavery through the difficult journey in the desert.

It is hard to find the direction that is right for our lives. Some of us are lucky enough to find it early. Others take many years in order to discover it. This is why the process of finding the right leaders is such a crucial—if arduous—task. The right leader can help us get where we *need* to go, even if it doesn't always seem that it is the direction we *want* to go.

A second reading of the statement yields a more substantial interpretation. People will only take direction from a leader when they are ready to follow. When they are ready to change their lives and get on the right path, when they are ready to see the blessing implicit in the everyday world, a leader can take them on the path to the Divine.

Self-Control

SEPTEMBER 19

Better is the one who is slow to anger
than the one who is mighty. Better is the one who
controls the self than the one who conquers a city.
PROVERBS 16:32

Generally, it is inappropriate to compare people one to the other. But knowing what characteristics contribute to making a good person can be helpful in finding a direction for our own lives. Such an approach provides us with concrete goals toward which to strive. Prior to reading this statement from the book of Proverbs, we might have thought that being mighty is a primary goal. After all, it is important to be strong, to be able to defend ourselves against our enemies, to avoid being victimized. But if such strength is released in explosive violence, against those who are defenseless or in the use of force that emerges from unchecked anger, then it isn't really the kind of might that the writers of Proverbs had in mind at all. To them, such might would be considered bullying or, in the political arena, tyranny.

So this manual for personal leadership—which is one of the explanations for the writing of the book of Proverbs in the first place—tells us that it is more important to control ourselves, more important than anything else, even than conquering an entire city.

Few among us probably have aspirations to conquer entire cities or even a neighborhood, but we may have the desire to take over a business or organization, to defeat a competitor or assume control of an industry. Leadership itself is a blessing, although many take it far too lightly. So before you try to do so, remember the words of Proverbs and control yourself. Avoid demonstrating your strength for its own sake. You will be a better person for it. And you are the only person for that job.

Rejoice and Do Good

SEPTEMBER 20

*I know that there is nothing better than to rejoice
and do good in one's life.*
ECCLESIASTES 3:12

The author of Ecclesiastes, whom Jewish tradition names as King Solomon, experienced a great deal over the course of his lifetime. He was blessed with many things. The aphorisms that are contained in the book resulted from the personal insights he garnered. Some may even consider his words to form a foundation for Jewish ethics, that is, the steps necessary for leading a righteous life. In this statement, he reduces his entire book into two basic ideas: rejoice and do good.

Rejoice, because you are alive. Rejoice, because there is much blessing in life. Rejoice, because of the gifts that have been given you. Rejoice even when it isn't easy to do so, when it seems that your life is hard and not filled with blessing. That's his point. It is easy to rejoice when things are going so well, when there appears to be an abundance of blessing in your life. It is much harder to do so when things appear dismal and you are disillusioned as a result. This is the time you *need* to rejoice. And as Ecclesiastes points out, there are many things over which to rejoice—even the breath of life itself.

But there's more. Following his second bit of advice will lead you further toward rejoicing. Do good in your life. Simple acts of kindness are all that is necessary. No need to save the entire world. Just treat your neighbor kindly. Make sure that the world is a better place for your having lived in it. Then there will be plenty for others to rejoice about, as well.

Compassion

SEPTEMBER 21

I know that You are a compassionate and merciful God, slow to anger, full of steadfast love, renouncing punishment.

JONAH 4:2B

While Jonah's statement about God presumably reflects his reluctance to carry out a mission assigned to him by God, it is really a statement about his faith and belief in God. Some people miss this during the reading of Jonah in the synagogue on Yom Kippur afternoon. Even when Jonah feels least connected to God, he is blessed by having a relationship with the Divine.

The text here may be unique to the book of Jonah, but its phrases and sentiments certainly are not. We read them in various places in the Bible and they have been adapted to various places in the liturgy, particularly when holidays occur on weekdays and the Torah is read.

When we are placed in relationship with the Divine, we are motivated to reflect on God's attributes, as Jonah does—and as other characters in the Bible do as well. Unfortunately, Jonah is upset that the people of Nineveh will repent of their sins and not be punished by God. For the rest of us who read the text, this is good news. If there is hope for the people of Nineveh, then there is hope for each and every one of us, as well.

Starting Over

SEPTEMBER 22

It is never too late to start over again, to feel again, to love again, to hope again.
RABBI HAROLD M. SCHULWEIS

If I had to summarize the message of the fall holiday season, this is certainly the way I would express it. Each year as we get older, we feel the pressure of time more swiftly upon us. While the passage of time is incremental, somehow it feels like we suddenly become adults, suddenly become middle-aged, suddenly become older adults. How do the years accumulate so quickly while we are struggling to meet the demands of daily living? We reflect back on the past twelve months and the preceding years and ask ourselves the question that seems to haunt us: How did I get here?

Rather than focusing on what transpired, what we could have done differently, what we should have done differently, Rabbi Schulweis offers us a different message, one that is more helpful for the future. He suggests that regardless of our current age or station in life, it doesn't matter where we have been. It only matters where we are going. He tells us to start over, to feel, to love, and to hope. This is the key to seeing blessing in the world around us.

With the onset of the New Year, anything seems possible, including starting over. The fall holiday calendar supports our efforts as Yom Kippur takes us through a spiritual death so that we might experience a rebirth at its conclusion. All year, perhaps, we have isolated ourselves from our own feelings. Such a rebirth is possible when we let ourselves begin to feel again. Sukkot assists us in doing so as it brings us back in touch with the natural world that surrounds us. In order to start over, we have to let our feelings rise to the surface and embrace them. Such an approach will lead to love. And through love comes hope.

Lifting Our Hearts

SEPTEMBER 23

In the twilight of the vanishing year,
I lift my heart to You, O God.
WILSHIRE BOULEVARD TEMPLE (LOS ANGELES),
HIGH HOLY DAY PRAYER BOOK

There is an implicit tension in the High Holy Days: simultaneous celebration and a fear of finitude. While Rosh Hashanah is flush with optimism for the new year, Yom Kippur is entrenched in the vicissitudes of the year just past. It seems somewhat counterintuitive that we would celebrate the New Year first and then take a look back at the year that has just concluded in anticipation of Yom Kippur. One would normally expect it to be the other way around. Perhaps it is the optimism that is implicit in Rosh Hashanah and the year ahead that gives us the courage to approach the spiritual nakedness required during Yom Kippur. Probing such spiritual depth is only possible when we are prepared to fully engage the Divine, as the prayer book quoted here suggests, to "lift my heart to You, O God." And that depth potentially emerges from a soul-filled celebration of Rosh Hashanah.

I consider Rosh Hashanah and Yom Kippur, which are taken by most to be two separate holidays, as the beginning and end of the same holiday. And together they represent the denouement of the holiday season that begins weeks prior during the Hebrew month of Elul. During Elul, individuals take an introspective look as part of the process of preparing to enter the New Year. The Hebrew calls it *cheshbon hanefesh*, "an accounting of the soul." And then after the process concludes, when you lift your heart to God, the *new* year becomes possible. And then you can feel blessed by it.

Finding Balance in Our Lives

SEPTEMBER 24

Everyone should regard oneself throughout the years as exactly balanced between acquittal and guilt.
MOSES MAIMONIDES, *MISHNEH TORAH*,
SEFER MADA, *HILKHOT T'SHUVAH* 3:4

It is usually surprising to learn that Maimonides and other medieval philosophers believed that the desired path to follow in life is in the middle, away from the extremes, evenly balanced in the center. It is what they called the golden mean. No matter what behaviors were concentrated in the extremes, the middle was the best place to be. It is the place where the individual can find tranquility and well-being. Getting situated in this central place is particularly important during this time of year as we forge a path to follow as part of the renewal process of Rosh Hashanah and Yom Kippur.

The notion of a golden mean assumes that most people do not spend their time in one extreme or another. In the case of moral virtue, as referenced by Maimonides here, few of us are completely guilty or fully innocent. Rather, most of us spend our lives navigating the space somewhere in between. Nevertheless, it is finding the center and living in it that is the most desired, where we feel particularly blessed. And it is divine compassion—and our own hard work at personal spiritual renewal—that prevents us from wandering too far away from the center.

The rhythm of the High Holy Days helps us to locate that center and stay close to it. Now all we have to do is stay in sync with it.

Self-Examination

SEPTEMBER 25

To live the unexamined life is not really living.
RABBI IRVING "YITZ" GREENBERG

This notion might be considered Rabbi Greenberg's take on— or maybe the Torah version of—the words of the ancient Greek philosopher Socrates, who said, "The unexamined life is not worth living." This fall season of Jewish holidays is all about examining one's life. We move from the celebratory Rosh Hashanah and the introspective Yom Kippur to the personal harvest of our work during Sukkot. Through the holidays we are reborn each year. We leave the old self behind and start anew. And if you don't keep getting reborn, you die. And here is the ironic part. If you are the same as you were last year, claims Rabbi Greenberg, then you died a little in between.

Some people wait for a life crisis—or maybe middle age—to take a good hard look at themselves, what they have accomplished, what they have done with the personal gifts and talents that God has provided us individually. For some of those who have followed the regular pattern of self-examination, their crises unravel, and they do as well.

That's why the process of self-examination doesn't end with the fall and its compact Jewish holiday season. The rest of the Jewish holidays that unfold over the course of the year help us to stay on the path of personal examination. It is a perpetual process, one that never really ends. And it is this process that fosters personal growth no matter our age or station in life. The work is not easy, to be sure. It is difficult, sometimes even painful. But the benefits are enormous—we get to keep on living and enjoying the blessing of being alive.

Fasting Easily

SEPTEMBER 26

What a wise person can accomplish by spiritually eating and drinking on Erev Yom Kippur, a fool cannot achieve by fasting on Yom Kippur.
RABBI ISRAEL SALANTER

Ironically, much of our attention on the High Holy Days is turned to food, even on Yom Kippur, when the point of fasting is so that we can focus on the more spiritual aspects of repentance and renewal. We are concerned with the meal prior to the fast, the fast itself, and then the break-the-fast following the day of fasting. We wish one another an easy fast in anticipation of Yom Kippur, and we ask people how their fast is going when we encounter them in the middle of the day.

Rabbi Israel (Lipkin) Salanter, the nineteenth-century Lithuanian spiritual leader behind the ethical piety movement (called *musar*), has something important to say about the whole idea of eating and fasting. He argues that the preparation for Yom Kippur is as important as the night itself. This is why he suggests that eating on Erev Yom Kippur, the night that precedes Kol Nidre, can be as spiritually nourishing as the fasting that we do on the actual day of Yom Kippur. In other words, it is not the fast itself that is transformative—which is why it has no impact on the fool. Rather, it is the intention with which we approach the religious or ritual act that is potentially transformative.

When it is time to eat, eat heartily and with the recognition of food's power to sustain. But always remember its Source— as the Source of all blessing. When it is time to drink, do so with a full heart. But always remember the Source. And when it is time to fast, turn yourself inward. And remember *your* Source.

The Truly Righteous

SEPTEMBER 27

*There is no person on earth so righteous
who does good and never sins.*
ECCLESIASTES 7:20

While most of us would consider ourselves basically good people, there are probably few among us who would call ourselves fully righteous. This seems to be a category reserved for others, particularly those who may have come before us and are relegated to history. It seems that the past is always filled with better people than the current generation, no matter the time period.

Similarly, we wouldn't consider ourselves evil. Sure, we err. We make mistakes. We sin—even if we don't warm to the term so readily—or we gravitate toward the Hebrew understanding of sin, which is closer to the term used for an arrow missing its mark rather than what we understand in English as sin. So we navigate our world bolstered by a sense of being good enough, admitting to the occasional moral mistake or ethical error.

Ecclesiastes' text, which comes from the perspective of a lifetime of experience, provides us with an important lesson and a measure of comfort. While we should continue to try to better ourselves, we shouldn't beat ourselves up when we fail or fail to measure up to perfection. For none of us are fully righteous or fully sinful. We are simply human beings, or better said, we are blessed to be humans becoming.

Trusting God

SEPTEMBER 28

Those who trust in Adonai
shall exchange strength for weariness.
ISAIAH 40:31

No matter how you look at it, life can be wearying. Large or small, the challenges are plenty. On a personal plane: Growing up. Raising a family. Making a living. Or on a global scale: The economy. Peace in the Middle East. The Iraq War. These are tiring endeavors, especially as we try to sort them all out and personally engage them. But the biblical prophet Isaiah has a remedy for us. In this remedy is direction for our lives, as well. And Isaiah's words are much more than the so-called simple truths that we learned in kindergarten. Isaiah's teaching is straightforward. Trust in God and you will gain strength. In exchange for your weariness, you will be strengthened. Sounds like a simple formula. But how exactly does it work?

We present our tired selves to God, and in return, we are given renewed strength. We give ourselves over to God at night, and in the morning we are reborn, ready to face the day once restored. The Rabbis say that we are actually reborn each day. That is an amazing blessing by itself. Then each week, we are given the opportunity to gain a second soul to replenish what has been depleted in the first. But there is more to this exchange than just showing up. It will be necessary to take hold of what has been given to those who came before us and make it our own. Once it is fully ours we are able to give it to others. And here is where the real strength comes from. The more we give it to others, the more we gain from it ourselves.

Renewing the Old

SEPTEMBER 29

The old has become new and
the new has become holy.
RABBI ABRAHAM ISAAC KOOK

Just as the end of Shabbat on Saturday evening, which we mark as *Havdalah*, is really a mixture of sacred and secular time and is therefore somewhat unsettling and simultaneously captivating, so is this time of year, which combines elements of the year past and the year ahead. This is why Rabbi Kook's insight is so important. As the first chief rabbi of the modern State of Israel, he clearly understood what it meant to take something that was old and transform it into something new.

Starting over, starting a new year, does not mean that we discard our entire past. That would be impossible to do—even if it were the preferred approach, which it is not. With each successive day of living we are the sum total of the days and years that are consigned to our past. So the challenge this time of year is how to take the many things that have gotten old and whose memories have continued to envelop us and then to raise them to holy levels.

When we take the past and use it to plot our future, then it becomes new. By embracing our past and transforming it, we are able to make it holy and feel blessed by it.

Choosing Life

SEPTEMBER 30

Choose life that you may live.
DEUTERONOMY 30:19

It all sounds so simple, straightforward, and logical. But it is in the choice and our desire to live that we are given the ability to grasp hold of life and live it fully. This text comes from the last book of the Torah, toward the conclusion of the desert journey of the ancient Israelites and the end of Moses's speeches to the people. It is the essence of what he wants to teach the people. If they are to remember nothing else of what he taught, it should be this singular notion. We could even say that it is the foundation text for Jewish living. It is focused on life and not death. Judaism is more about the here and now and not about the hereafter. While Judaism contains an ever-present vision for the future—and the messianic future—there is an abiding recognition that the present always comes first.

This is the message that the Israelites carried with them into the Promised Land. By keeping the message prominent in their thinking, it actually helped to transform the land into one of promise. Similarly, it has the potential to transform our lives as well.

To end this month, here's the perhaps counterintuitive message of spirituality that emerges from this text: Rather than a repetition of the expression "Plan for tomorrow," I would say, "Plan for today." It is the best that we have. This is our blessing. And we each have the ability to make it better by what we do. So, "choose life that you may live."

OCTOBER

Words of Courage

OCTOBER 1

Behold, God is my salvation.
I will trust and not be afraid, for Adonai is my
strength and song. God has become my salvation.
ISAIAH 12:2, CITED IN THE INTRODUCTORY BLESSING
FOR *HAVDALAH*

Havdalah is perhaps the most mysterious time of the week. It is a mix of light and darkness, as the stars strain to illumine a darkened sky. We light a candle to mix the time of Shabbat with the week ahead, as well as to bring light into a quickly darkening world. We are sad to let go of Shabbat, but we are anxious to reclaim the routines of daily living. There is much work yet for us to do. The tasks that we left behind in order to welcome Shabbat seek us out once again. So we desperately try to capture Shabbat moments and carry them into the week that follows. Some people even rub the *Havdalah* spices into their clothing as a reminder of their Shabbat experience. Some dip their fingers in the *Havdalah* wine and rub it on their eyelids.

During Shabbat we find ways to separate ourselves from the workaday world and enjoy an intimate relationship with all that is holy. After this separateness, it may take some courage to reenter the week—and the challenges of the world. According to midrash, Adam was terrified when the sun set and darkness threatened to envelop him following the first Shabbat. Frightened, he thought to himself, "This darkness will get me." So God inspired Adam to take two stone flints and rub them together. On one of the stones was marked *afelah* (darkness), and on the other was written the word *mavet* (death). The friction produced a spark, and from the spark Adam made a flame. The fire warmed him, providing him with comfort throughout the night. And in the morning, the sun rose—as it has for each day since. Adam understood that this is the way the world works (Babylonian Talmud, *Pesachim* 54a; Genesis Rabbah 11:2). Light and hope emerge from darkness and fear. It is the reason we say a blessing over fire at the end of Shabbat—the time when it was first created. As a result, we are not afraid to enter into the week ahead. So the *Havdalah* ritual is introduced with these words of courage. They provide us with a foundation for the week ahead.

Doing Twice as Much at Half Speed

OCTOBER 2

Try to do as much work in half a day
as you would normally do in a full day.
This serves several purposes: It alleviates guilt at
leaving work early, it emphasizes the difference between
the work week and the Shabbat, and it exhausts the
body and the mind so that you will welcome, even yearn
for, the release and the relaxation that Shabbat offers.

RICHARD SIEGEL

Richard Siegel offers us an interesting perspective on the workday, around which most of us organize our daily lives.

Work is what we are intended to do in the world. Even so, our work can be all-consuming. So his suggestion provides us with a rather unique way of approaching it. This is particularly interesting, because Judaism constructs each day in anticipation of Shabbat. We work so that we can get closer to Shabbat. And the nature of our work can actually bring us closer to the essential nature of Shabbat.

It is easier to find a job than it is to discover the real work we are supposed to be doing in the world. It often takes time, and we might move from job to job until we find it. If our job and our work coincide, we should consider ourselves lucky—and very blessed. Often we find our work outside of the limited parameters of our job.

Work each day. Give it your best. And know that Shabbat is always only a few days away.

Hearing the Call

OCTOBER 3

Praised are You, Adonai our God, Sovereign of the universe,
who has made us holy with mitzvot and
instructed us to hear the sound of the shofar.

SHOFAR BLESSING

Many of us are captivated by the shofar call each year and find its inspiration unparalleled. The sounding of the shofar is designed to be a wake-up call. It is supposed to motivate us so that we might shake off our own complacency. This is why we blow it each day for a month in anticipation of the High Holy Days and why we use it during the holidays themselves. Each day we need to be reminded until we remember it ourselves. This is perhaps also why the mitzvah of the shofar is not in its blowing. Rather, it is in its hearing. As we acknowledge its sounding, we accept the responsibility of responding to its alarm.

So what do we do? Rabbi Zalman Schacter-Shalomi says this is a good time for doing *t'shuvah*. Seek out someone you have offended during the week (particularly a member of the family you may have hurt). Apologize. Then do something that demonstrates the sincerity of your apology. You will find blessing in both the act and the action.

Sacrifices

OCTOBER 4

What Abraham learned on the mountain is that
God doesn't want us to sacrifice a part of ourselves
in order to serve God.
God wants us to pay attention,
to be present, to bring the fullness of our selves
into our relationship with God.
RABBI LAURA GELLER

Rabbi Geller comments on the Torah reading known as the *Akedah*, the Binding of Isaac, read each year on Rosh Hashanah. There are many different perspectives on this episode in the life of our ancestors. Many of us are troubled by the willingness of Abraham to sacrifice his son Isaac just because God instructed him to do so. And even though the sacrifice was averted, the instruction was still very real—as was the intended response.

Abraham was wrong in his response, as far as I am concerned, and so was God for asking Abraham to do so in the first place. Nevertheless, according to Rabbi Geller, real learning took place—the kind of learning that transcended the specific incident, the kind from which we can all learn.

What was that learning? In order to have a real relationship with the Divine, we have to be willing to bring our fullness of self into the relationship. Otherwise, such a relationship between God and self is not possible. And without such a relationship, how will we reap its blessing?

Revealing Our Name

OCTOBER 5

And Jacob asked him [the angel] and said,
"Please tell me your name." And the angel said,
"Why do you want to know my name?"
And the angel blessed him [Jacob] there.
GENESIS 32:30

It is very late at night. Darkness covers the sweeping expanse of the heavens. The only light comes from the stars, which have already been out for a long time. Jacob is exhausted from his journey. He has been traveling for a long time and probably should have stopped hours ago, but he pushed onward—anxious to see his brother after so many years of painful separation. At the same time, Jacob fears his reunion with Esau. After all these years, Jacob has come to realize what he has done to his brother. He hopes that just as Jacob has grown beyond his childhood pranks, perhaps Esau has grown beyond his resentment of them.

The desert sun that overwhelmed Jacob with its intensity during the day has set. Now the cold of the desert night threatens him. Even amidst his entourage Jacob still feels alone. He stops to rest and immediately falls asleep. And while he sleeps, a stranger (maybe an angel sent from God to bring him a message) engages him in a struggle that lasts through the night. Just before dawn, the stranger tries to wrestle himself free, injuring Jacob as a means of getting free. But Jacob refuses to let the stranger-angel leave until he receives a blessing. Just as the blessing Jacob stole from Esau cost him a relationship with his brother, this blessing (like many others) comes with a price. The stranger escapes and Jacob—with his injured thigh—hobbles away with his victory and his blessing: Israel, a new name and a new perspective.

It is not clear with whom Jacob is actually wrestling in this well-known and oft-cited text from Genesis. Maybe he is wrestling with an angel. But what is most significant about this passage is Jacob's unwillingness to desist, to stop wrestling, until he is blessed. Why was such a blessing so important to him?

Maybe Jacob was dreaming. Maybe his was a supernatural experience limited to expression in the Torah. Or maybe that night, Jacob finally confronted the dark side of himself, the side that lay hidden for many years. Perhaps the journey to reunite with his brother forced him to wrestle with this dark side until he could victoriously emerge as Israel (a name understood as "one who struggles with the Divine"). Like Jacob, we all have dark sides of the self. We may not always be proud of them, but some of us have figured out a way to live with them, since they are part of who we are and what we have become. They are not completely "other." If we snuff them out altogether, we run the risk of dulling the bright side as well. Jacob's encounter helps us to understand that we must engage our dark sides so that they do not eclipse the light. In his struggle with the dark side, Jacob came to know God and through the process he came to know himself. If we are prepared to engage the other side of ourselves, we can do the same. That is where we may find the blessing.

Moving toward Messianic Time

OCTOBER 6

*Our lives can be made better and the world can move
closer to a messianic time of healing and redemption,
if only we realize that our sacrifices should not merely
involve the giving up of food on a fast day,
but rather the giving of self to the other
in our lives every hour of every day that we live.*

RABBI NORMAN J. COHEN

While the Jewish religion has numerous fast days, most Jews relate to fasting only one day a year—on Yom Kippur. And this fasting colors the fall season considerably, which is why Rabbi Cohen's message is so important. Abstaining from eating should be a symbol for us. It is not all of what we do. And it is certainly not a sufficient act on its own. Rather, fasting should motivate in us a willingness to give up a part of ourselves to help form a relationship with others. A real sacrifice includes a sacrifice of self, of ego, and of self-centeredness.

It will take each of us to make sacrifices to bring the messianic era into reality. This is not easy in a world where the acquisition of "stuff" is too often used to prove our individual worth and value. The more we have, the more important we are, so goes this logic. But Rabbi Cohen is teaching us that as we give up a piece of ourselves, we can bring the messiah faster. This is the blessing of less being more.

Praying with a Broken Heart

OCTOBER 7

Who ever said that one must pray with a whole heart?
Perhaps it is preferable to pray with a broken heart.
RABBI URI OF STRELISK

I feel like Rabbi Uri is speaking directly to me. I know that my prayers feel more complete when I approach prayer feeling incomplete. And I often feel such a sense of incompleteness—particularly after a difficult day. Perhaps it is when a relationship that I have been trying to nurture deteriorates, or when that undifferentiated feeling that all is not right in my world bubbles up from the depths of my soul. And then I enter into prayer, and as a result, I feel more complete. This is the peculiar nature of spirituality that sometimes seems to defy rational logic. But it is not the prayer itself. Rather, prayer is the dialogue that helps frame my relationship with the Divine. And it is because of that relationship—in the midst of that relationship—that I am able to feel more complete.

I pray to God for insight and understanding but it is because of my prayers that I feel the power of blessing. We bring ourselves to God, no matter the shape we are in. At night, we give over our broken souls, our tired, distressed souls. God returns them to us in the morning, and we feel somehow renewed as a result—ready to confront the day once again. And just in case we need extra support—and most of us do—we get an extra soul, some redoubling of support, on Shabbat, to prepare us for the week ahead and all that our daily life has in store for us.

Full-bodied Prayer

OCTOBER 8

*Praised are You, Adonai our God, Sovereign of the universe,
who has made us holy with mitzvot
and instructed us concerning immersion.*

BLESSING SAID UPON USING THE *MIKVAH*, THE RITUAL BATH

Those who have not used a *mikvah*—a ritual bath—may find it hard to feel a connection to this blessing. Like most blessings, contained in it is the instruction to do what the blessing is all about. But the key to understanding the blessing is the promise that is made explicit—in the performance of the particular ritual act is the potential to find holiness. This is what is meant by the phrase "who has made us holy with mitzvot." These ritual acts and other mitzvot that are instructed—and framed by such a formulaic blessing—provide us with a list of opportunities to find holiness.

The *mikvah* is a full-body experience. The use of the *mikvah* is primarily for women. Men are instructed to use it on fewer occasions. Regardless of who uses it, it can be a transformational experience. Mimicking the birthing experience, we actually can emerge from the *mikvah* renewed, restored, and reborn.

Expressing Gratitude

OCTOBER 9

*We have eaten, and we drank. And to the Holy One of
Blessing we expressed gratitude that God gave us and
will give us bread to eat, and clothes to wear,
and years to live.*

FROM THE LADINO *YA COMIMOS* PRAYER

Written in one of the folk languages of the Jewish people, this Ladino prayer poem is recited after *Birkat Hamazon*, Grace after Meals. It confirms for me the notion that sometimes the simplest words are among the most profound. When we are hungry, we may be motivated to say a blessing—*Hamotzi* before we eat. We are anxious to rush into our food. Perhaps that is one of the reasons the blessing before we eat is so short. But when we have concluded our meals, we feel satiated. Consequently, we may not feel the same sense of obligation—especially since *Birkat Hamazon* is a relatively long set of blessings. So this statement offers us perspective, direction, and spiritual guidance.

We have eaten. And we have offered our words of thanksgiving to God, the Source of our food and the Source of all life. But beyond this table and the food we have eaten, we will continue to look to God for sustenance, clothing (and shelter), and life itself. What more needs to be said?

Prayers for Goodness and Blessing

OCTOBER 10

*May it be Your will, Adonai our God
and God of our ancestors, to renew our lives in
the coming month. Grant us a long life, a peaceful
life with goodness and blessing, sustenance and
physical vitality, a life informed by purity and piety,
a life free from shame and reproach, a life of
abundance and honor, a life embracing piety and
love of Torah, a life in which our heart's desires
for goodness will be fulfilled.*

FROM PRAYERS USHERING IN THE NEW MONTH

I always feel a rush of anticipation when approaching a new month. This prayer is placed in this book toward the middle of the month of October to remind us that the beginning of the

Hebrew months don't usually coincide with the secular months. Moreover, while anticipation is the sentiment expressed at the beginning of the month, it is really what we feel at the beginning of each year—and at the beginning of each day.

There is so much for us to do, so much that we want to accomplish. And yet we also feel the burdens of this world and of our daily life. So we ask for God to shower us with blessings. And while all beginnings are difficult, we anticipate each beginning with both trepidation and renewed optimism, for ourselves and for the world. What else could one wish for than to be showered with the blessings that are described in this particular prayer?

Digging Deeply

OCTOBER 11

You shall do according to the law that they will teach
you, and the judgment they will instruct you.
You shall not turn away from the thing
that they say to you, to the right nor to the left.
DEUTERONOMY 17:10–11

While the text quoted above is taught in Moses's name in the book of Deuteronomy, and it is designated for a specific time on the journey of the Israelites—just before they enter the Promised Land—it is really a lesson for all time and all places. Moses tells us that each generation will include those entrusted with the task of *interpreting and applying* the laws of the Torah. But the responsibility of engaging sacred text is one that we all share.

The text from Deuteronomy seems to imply that there is no flexibility in the law. That is what is meant by not turning "to the right or to the left." But the Torah text and the law it yields are not static at all. They are dynamic. And it is this dynamism that has the potential to capture the spirit of each generation.

For me, the important lesson in this teaching is that we should not turn away from it. We need to keep ourselves focused on the Torah and what it teaches, for in it we can find spiritual direction for our lives. But unless we are prepared to fully engage the text, struggle with it, wrestle with it, we will not find the blessing of its spiritual yield. So dig deeply into the text and dig even more deeply into the self.

Guiding Our Steps

OCTOBER 12

Praised are You, Adonai our God, Sovereign of the universe, who guides the steps of humanity.

FROM THE MORNING BLESSINGS

Each morning I repeat these words as part of my morning prayers. It is one of a series of blessings that shape my general outlook and provide me with direction for the day. Each blessing in the series helps focus me, whether I say it aloud or simply respond "amen" to the words articulated by those who surround me in my community. As I wipe the slumber from my eyes, this particular blessing helps to remind me that I am not alone in my world, that I am never alone. Whatever my relationship to others, God is there to guide me—and others as well.

There are those who may think that such guidance is unnecessary, especially those who feel like they are masters of their own universe, whatever their profession. But those who are indeed advanced in their achievements understand that such guidance is indeed always necessary—and particularly welcome.

Whether in Hebrew or in English or in any other language with which you feel the most comfortable, repeat the words slowly. The first ones help you to establish a relationship with God. Then the next phrase will help form your outlook for the day and what you seek for yourself and for others—guidance and direction, a righteous path on which to walk.

Facing Judgment

October 13

God will bring to judgment every act, whether good or bad, even that which is hidden.
ECCLESIASTES 12:14

These are the words of Kohelet, who according to our understanding of the text was a powerful, rich, and influential individual. Thus, he had gained great perspective on the world. Jewish tradition assigns King Solomon as the author. Perhaps it is better said that he was a Solomon—in other words, his influence, insight, and understanding were equal to that of King Solomon. In any case this verse reflects a rather traditional attitude toward reward and punishment, something that is not reflected in most of the book of Ecclesiastes: those who sin are punished; those who do good are rewarded a life of blessing. But we have to dig more deeply into the text in order to determine the author's essential teaching.

Kohelet is committed to an ethical balance in the world, something that most of us seek, even if our experience does not always promise such results. But what is most important is his notion of what is hidden. Kohelet argues that even those acts that seem to be hidden will be revealed, particularly those that are bad or sinful or evil. In a religious world where God is accepted as the divine authority, nothing can really be hidden.

The biblical Adam learned this in the Garden of Eden. The prophet Jonah learned it as he tried to flee his responsibility. Both came to learn of God's presence and God's knowledge of what seems to be hidden.

How can Kohelet's words be easily summarized in a directive for our daily living? Never do something in private that you don't want to become public.

Guardian Angels

OCTOBER 14

I am sending you an angel in front of you
to guard you as you go
and guide you to the place I have prepared.
VERSE FOLLOWING THE *T'FILLAT HADERECH*,
THE TRAVELER'S PRAYER

Those of us who travel a great deal—whether for business or pleasure—understand the risks in doing so. This is why we are sometimes called "road warriors." It is not easy, and it seems to be getting more difficult each year. I am not sure whether it is that we get older or that traveling itself gets more difficult. But there are ways to ease the burden of traveling. One way is the recitation of the traveler's prayer. By uttering such words of blessing, we recognize that as we travel, especially when we are distant from our family and those we love and who support us, we can rely on God for such nurture and support. Moreover, God makes a promise to us, as is stated above.

Few of us travel without a destination in mind. But sometimes we are open to the experience of the road and make decisions when we get where we are going. This verse teaches us that we find our destination when God causes us to see. But we always have to be open to the direction that God is providing us, whether we are traveling or just going about our daily routine. May we all be privileged to open our eyes so that we may be given the blessing to see the place that God wants to show us.

Correcting the Defect of Sin

OCTOBER 15

T'shuvah *redresses the defect [of sin] and restores the world and life to their original character.*
RABBI ABRAHAM ISAAC KOOK

T'shuvah, the act of repentance and renewal, may be the path we take during certain times of the year, but it should be a journey that we undertake the entire year. Rabbi Kook's notion is quite interesting. It suggests that our acts of *t'shuvah* benefit more than just the self. The spiritual benefits of our *t'shuvah* are far-reaching. Moreover our turning, our *t'shuvah*, actually brings us back to the way God intended us to be at the beginning, before we did what we did. Because our misdeeds, whether intended or not, whether major or minor, change the direction that God had intended for the world. So it is our responsibility to set the world back on course. And we can do so through our *t'shuvah*.

This is a powerfully spiritual notion. When we undertake our obligation to do *t'shuvah,* and, in fact, do so, we become the person we once were. We return to a state of being that I like to call "informed innocence." Our spiritual state is more than it was as a young child, because it is informed by the experience—and wisdom—that possibly comes with adulthood. Thus, the process of *t'shuvah*—of sinning and then repairing the brokenness that we created—brings us to the possibility of a better place than before the sinning. That is the blessing of *t'shuvah*.

The Good Old Days

OCTOBER 16

Bring us back to you, Adonai. Let us return.
Bring back the days of old.
LAMENTATIONS 5:21

The end of this verse is often translated as "Renew our days as of old," and may be more familiar to you in this form. This text has always spoken powerfully to me. It is used in the liturgy when the Torah is placed back in the holy ark and we have to move on with the worship service. We become wistful as the ark is closed, wistful of the time in the desert—which is represented by the service of the reading of the Torah—a time when we stood at the mountain of Sinai, listening carefully for the divine words and the inspiration that came with them.

The time in the desert was filled with potential. It was a time of journey and exploration, a time when the identity and character of the Jewish people—and each of us along with them—were being shaped.

But there is a second level to this text and experience. Those who recently suffered a trauma or the death of a loved one understand this text much differently. Following my father's death, as I stood in prayer the day after the reading of the Torah, my eyes welled with tears. As much as I wanted the days of old to return, I knew that it was no longer possible. The world, my world, had changed—permanently. Thus, these words were formed into a blessing for me as I acknowledged that I stood in a different place than I did only a short time before. And as I continue to cling to the memories of the desert experience of my people as recorded in the Torah, I cling to my father's memory as well. I pray that we may feel once again as we once did in the days of old.

Deliverance

OCTOBER 17

May it be your will, Adonai, my God and God of my ancestors, to deliver me today and every day from impudent individuals and from insolence, from an evil person, a bad companion, and a bad neighbor, from an evil occurrence and from the destructive adversary, from an oppressive lawsuit, and from a hard opponent be that person a person of the covenant or not.

FROM THE MORNING BLESSINGS

When we awaken each morning, we really don't know what the day ahead has in store for us. Sometimes we wake with excited anticipation, ready to confront the day anew. Sometimes we wake fearful and trembling, terrified by the many things we have to face. Just as all of our morning prayers can be a centering experience for us and provide focus and direction for the day ahead, this particular blessing acknowledges all of our fears and states them quite clearly. We put them all out there and ask for God to help us get beyond them.

There are many people who can cause our day to spin out of control. But it is we who allow it to happen. If we know that God will always be there to support us, to strengthen us, against our adversaries, then we can approach them—and our day—without fear.

Paying Attention

OCTOBER 18

It is better to go to a house of mourning than to a
tavern, for every human being ends there [in the house
of mourning]. Let everyone alive pay attention.
ECCLESIASTES 7:2

The book of Ecclesiastes is read each year on Sukkot. Like the holiday, which is a celebration of the fall harvest, Ecclesiastes is the harvest of one person's life. Some may find the book—and such sentiments as the text here suggests—depressing, because it takes a realistic look at the world around us. Others, like me, find it inspiring, because it is able to see the world clearly and critically and offer guidance for living.

This particular text teaches us the powerful lesson that is contained in the house of mourning. While we find community there—for friends and relatives come to support the mourner who has experienced a loss—it also teaches us that nearly all else is eclipsed by the shadow of death. We have an obligation to visit and comfort the mourner. As we do so, we are reminded of what is really important—and the work that needs to be done and not put off until tomorrow. For we know not what tomorrow will bring. So we look for the blessing that is today and not wait for it at another time.

Covenantal Light

OCTOBER 19

I, Adonai, have called you to do right, and have taken you by the hand, and kept you and established with you a covenant to be a light to the nations.
ISAIAH 42:6, FROM THE HAFTARAH FOR SHABBAT BEREISHIT

In case there was any question as to what our role in the world should be, Isaiah makes it quite clear. He is a prophet who, according to Jewish tradition, speaks on God's behalf. While he may not have written this at the beginning of the Jewish year, the Rabbis wanted to make sure that we understood the import of his lesson. So they made sure that it was read at the beginning of each year's Torah cycle. While the text reflects the obligation of the entire Jewish people, it makes our individual responsibility no less important. The Jewish people can't fulfill its obligation as a collective whole unless we do so as individuals.

Our obligation emerges from our relationship with God. This relationship has purpose and direction. God called us— God calls each of us—to do what is right in the world and to demonstrate to the rest of the world by our example what is right. Then we can be a blessing to all people—and to ourselves.

The Blessing of a Common Person

OCTOBER 20

Do not underestimate a common person's blessing.
BABYLONIAN TALMUD, *BERAKHOT* 7A

When we think of words of blessing, we usually think of lofty phrases that have been wordsmithed by poets, writers, and rabbis over the centuries and wherever the Jewish people has wandered in its journey through history. Many of these blessings are included in the fixed liturgy of the prayer book or recorded elsewhere in the sacred literature of the Jewish people. As a result, we are often diffident about shaping our own words of blessing. We worry that our words may not be as beautiful or as eloquent as the words of others. And so we refrain.

But this text from the Talmud, which is attributed to Rabbi Ishmael ben Elisha, reminds us that we should never underestimate words of blessing, regardless of who may offer them. We never know who may be hiding in the clothes or being of the common person. It may be Elijah the prophet, waiting to usher in the messianic era. And if we do not take his words seriously, we may miss the opportunity once again.

Working at Spirituality

OCTOBER 21

Blessings from above descend only when there is some substance not just emptiness below.
ZOHAR 1:88A

As the central mystical text in Judaism, the *Zohar* is quite frank in its direction concerning spirituality. The notion is simple. Spirituality is serious business. It doesn't just happen. We have to work at it. So this notion of emptiness is not a slight against those who believe that we have to empty ourselves in order to connect to the Divine. Rather, the *Zohar* is teaching us that Jewish spirituality—and the blessings that come from it—makes demands on us. Study, prayer, and ritual are not just the company line. They are required if we are to form the foundation for a dialogue with the Divine.

Nevertheless, there are many ways in, depending on our own personal interests, talents, and background. Start simple. One prayer. One blessing. Or one ritual. Engage it fully. Don't rush to take on another one. Then once you have mastered it, or at least feel comfortable with it, you can add a second and a third. Don't forget music and art—if that is your nature. Both can beautify the act of ritual. Then from such substance will come blessing.

Lifting Up the Load

OCTOBER 22

I will carry the load if you help me lift it.
BABYLONIAN TALMUD, *BAVA KAMMA* 92B

This is both a practical notion and a powerful spiritual teaching. It is difficult to navigate the world alone. So whether this text refers to God or a friend or both, burdens are diminished when they are shared. And we are never alone when we acknowledge God's presence in our lives.

Loads are lighter when more than one person lifts them, no matter how heavy the burden. And it takes far more energy to lift than it does to carry. But help and support do not always come on their own. We have to ask for them, as difficult as it may be to do so, as reluctant as we may be to ask for such help. The reality is that we can't do it alone. There are critical elements in Jewish life that require a community (a minimum of ten), because there is a recognition that particularly the really hard stuff cannot be done alone.

So don't be afraid to ask for help. You never know the form in which angels appear on earth—bringing God's blessing from afar.

Holy Ground

OCTOBER 23

*The bush burned with fire,
and the bush was not consumed.*
EXODUS 3:2

This is a well-known text from the Bible. It describes a significant incident in the spiritual journey of Moses and thereby becomes an important model for all of us. Artisans have re-created it, and authors have written about it. And yet, no one has fully captured its essence—nor will they probably ever be able to do so. This is part of the seductive mystery of the bush.

What does this teach us about our life and our effort to shape a life of blessing for ourselves? The bush burned, but it was Moses who noticed that it was not consumed. There were other bushes in the desert, but this particular bush demanded his attention. Others might have walked by the bush or seen it burning from afar, but apparently didn't notice it or its unique character at all.

We live a life that is filled with blessing. Even the moment we awaken in the morning is a blessing. Yet, too often we go about our daily lives without noticing—even when there is so much that calls out to us, so much that demands our attention. Like Moses, open your eyes. Then tread carefully. You are on holy ground.

Watching the Wind

OCTOBER 24

The one who watches the wind will never sow,
and the one who gazes at the clouds will never reap.
ECCLESIASTES 11:4

This reads like Ecclesiastes' spin on Cervantes' *Don Quixote*. The author, called Kohelet in the text, was a practical man. He understood what it took to make things happen in the world. So he denigrated most everything that did not have what he perceived as real substance. And there was little that he considered real substance. For Ecclesiastes, most of life is ephemeral, without any real substance. But in this selected text from his writings, Kohelet is not being critical of dreams. Rather, he is just critical of the dreamer who spends an entire life immersed in dreams, dreams that paralyze the person from moving forward, dreams that prevent the individual from bringing blessing into the world, into the life of others.

Perhaps this lesson from Ecclesiastes could better be read as "The one who [just] watches the wind will never sow, and the one who [only] gazes at the clouds will never reap." So watch the wind, for it is God's spirit whose force it embodies. And gaze at the clouds, for they are amidst God's heavenly abode. And continue to dream. Then go out and do the work that is needed to make the dreams real.

Becoming a Blessing

OCTOBER 25

*First become a blessing to yourself before you can
become a blessing to others.*
SAMSON RAPHAEL HIRSCH

This common wisdom is found in numerous places and said
in various ways. Sometimes it is phrased, "You can't love others unless you love yourself." No matter how it is said, the sentiment is the same. We may want to change the world, but we
have to begin with ourselves. One blessing will lead us to the
other.

What does it take to become a blessing, the kind that leads
us to be a blessing for others? Most of us are way too hard on
ourselves. We make mistakes. Some may harbor any guilt or
pain that goes along with it. But mostly, when we err, we compare ourselves with others—angry that we can't do something
that someone else can easily do. This can lead to a gradual self-
destruction of the ego. Who we are and what we have become
as a result start with what we have been blessed with, including our shortcomings. Sometimes I like to refer to these as the
dark side of our personalities. Even the brightest of light can
cast a shadow.

So let go of who you are not and become fully who you were
meant to be. Such a posture will lead you to a life of blessing.
On the way to bringing blessing to others, you will bring blessing yourself as well.

Feeling the Divine Presence

OCTOBER 26

The divine presence is everywhere.
BABYLONIAN TALMUD, *BAVA BATRA* 25A

What more needs to be said? God's presence is everywhere. No matter where you are, no matter what you do, the potential to experience God is ever present. So if that is the case, why are our experiences with the Divine sometimes so limited? Perhaps it is because we do not readily open ourselves to such experiences. We take a rational, critical approach to the world, always ready to dismiss the mystery of the unknown. We place filters on our interactions with the world, which severely limits our experience with it.

Let down your guard. Get rid of the filters. Open your heart, your head, and your hands to God so that you may find the divine presence that surrounds you. To fully experience the Divine, we have to begin with the acknowledgment of the statement from the Talmud quoted here: God's presence is indeed everywhere. To feel it, to acknowledge it is a blessing. Let it envelop and lift you.

Sacred Speech

OCTOBER 27

*Sometimes one person speaks in one corner of the
world and another person speaks in another corner of
the world or one person speaks in one century and
another person speaks in another century,
and God, who is above time and space,
hears the words of them both and connects them.*

RABBI NACHMAN OF BRESLOV

While it can happen at any time, what Rabbi Nachman is describing is something that I have experienced in rare moments during the study of sacred text. It is then that I fully understand the blessing derived from study. The comment of another that helps me to understand is not relegated to the printed word or to a distant place or time. Rather, it speaks directly to me. It is not *as if* the person who made the comment is in the room with me. That person has indeed joined me in my study and is speaking directly to me. I have also felt that notion in prayer as the words of others rise off the page and are whispered into my ear, allowing me to speak words of prayer that may not have come to me otherwise.

It is the acknowledgment of God's presence, especially in study or in prayer, that brings these words to me, that allows me to hear them, that permits them to enter my soul. Otherwise they might just be suspended in time and I would be unable to hear them at all.

Words of Blessing

OCTOBER 28

We are prohibited from deriving benefit from the world without speaking words of blessing.

BABYLONIAN TALMUD, *BERAKHOT* 35A

Perhaps this teaching from the Talmud should be the frontispiece for this entire volume. After all, a book about blessing is really a guidebook as to how we fully engage the world around us. We participate in this world. We encounter its riches. And we express our thanks to God for the many blessings that we enjoy. Joy is not possible without an expression of gratitude and thanksgiving. These are the two emotions that are often framed by our words of blessing: joy and gratitude.

Maybe it is the absence of words of blessing that leads people to depression and despair or, at least, to an absence of joy in their lives. So if you are sad, or in order to prevent sadness from creeping into your life, utter a blessing. Begin with something small, perhaps over a piece of fruit or a glass of wine. The fruit will taste better and the wine will more readily gladden your heart. Both will change your outlook in the hour ahead and the days that follow.

Divine Light

OCTOBER 29

The sun will no more be your light by day,
neither for brightness will the moon give light to you;
but God will be to you an everlasting light,
and your God your glory.

ISAIAH 60:19

While this verse from the prophet Isaiah is also contained in one of the haftarah readings between Tisha B'av and Rosh Hashanah and therefore contains words of consolation and comfort, such words are welcome any time of year—particularly as those of us who live in northern climes begin to enter the winter months. The weather changes. It gets light later in the morning and gets dark earlier in the evening. But we don't have to worry, because divine light will provide us with guidance, direction, and insight.

The Rabbis introduced these words from Isaiah into the fixed reading cycle of the synagogue because they knew that such inspiration was needed at specific times during the year. Perhaps reading them aloud in the context of a community afforded each person the opportunity to offer a blessing to one another and give each other mutual support. By saying it aloud one time a year and drinking in its meaning, we can transfer its inspiration to other times of the year when we might be motivated to say these words as well.

It may be dark outside but there is always a light illuminating the world. May you always be able to discern that light and find your way.

Sacred Travel

OCTOBER 30

Blessed will you be in the city and
blessed will you be in the country.
DEUTERONOMY 28:3

Some of the classic rabbinic interpreters of this verse suggest that it means that your home should be close to a synagogue, whether it is in the city or in the country. However, it seems that the Torah is trying to teach us something else by specifically including it in a list of blessings that an individual is to gain as a result of following the divine path in life. Some commentators suggest that our behavior—irrespective of whether we find ourselves in the city or the country—should be the same. The assumption is that we might feel compelled to act differently when no longer in closer proximity to the synagogue—that is, no longer in the midst of or in close proximity to the synagogue community. It would seem that the more distant we are from our community, the less influence the community—and its standards—would have on us.

It doesn't matter where we reside or travel. Accrued blessings accompany us. That is, in fact, probably why we call them blessings and not something else. Wherever we go, whatever we do, the blessings that emerge from a relationship with the Divine travel along with us.

God's World

OCTOBER 31

You. Everything is You.
RABBI LEVI YITZCHAK OF BERDITCHEV

This simple phrase of Levi Yitzchak actually reflects a rather profound theology. It was captured in a well-known Yiddish song that I remember from my childhood. And even though it is not sung in the morning minyan (prayer quorum) in which I regularly *daven* (pray), I get the feeling that it animates many of the people who participate in it. I feel it in the air, in the mumble of the prayers of individuals that elevate my own. It is what seems to motivate a group of people to rise early in the morning, when many others are still asleep or just starting their day, to come together as a community to pray.

Developing a pattern of expressing blessing—whether using the traditional Jewish formula of blessing or one that we have devised on our own—is all about shaping and maintaining an ongoing dialogue with the Divine. The challenge that Levi Yitzchak places in front of us is to understand that all dialogue is reflective of our relationship with God. For him, this is both a description of reality and a goal to be reached. Whatever we do, whatever we say—everything reflects the sacred relationship with God. In so doing, we are able to see God in all aspects of the world, even in an everyday routine that may seem void of God and even humanity. But that is the point. When we see God wherever we go in the world, we are able to raise humanity as well.

NOVEMBER

Holding Onto the Holy

NOVEMBER 1

*A person should always set a table after Shabbat
even if one is quite full and satisfied.*

BABYLONIAN TALMUD, SHABBAT 119B

This is the text that is cited to justify what has come to be called a *M'lavei Malkah* (a Saturday evening collation to usher out the Shabbat bride). The text specifically makes a reference to the individual being full from *cholent*, a slow-cooked stew-like dish.

On Friday night, with a great deal of anticipation, we joyously usher Shabbat into our lives. This is especially true if we gather with our families, after a hard week where all have gone their separate ways. For some, it might be the only time we come together for a meal. We imagine Shabbat as a queen, a royal presence in our midst, whose beauty fills our homes and our hearts. We look forward to her blessings. We even braid our Shabbat *challah*, imagining it to be the hair of the Sabbath queen, ever conscious of the special nature of the day and the meal. Although we know that she will be with us just for a day, we hold onto her an extra hour on Saturday night (making Shabbat a twenty-five-hour day, the only one all week). Eventually we are forced to let her go.

But still we resist. Just as Friday night is dedicated to welcoming her into our midst, we commit our Saturday night to ushering her out with due honor. As a result of her special nature and our relationship with her, we just can't say goodbye. Even the *Havdalah* ceremony seems insufficient, inadequate. So Saturday night takes a different form. It becomes a party that offers us meaning rather than entertainment. What defines Saturday night is the transition from Shabbat to the rest of the week. It is not the theater we attend or the social gathering in which we participate. Saturday night is a blending of the holy and the profane, the sacred and the secular.

So we'll party, but it will be a different kind of party. Perhaps it will be different because we have mixed feelings about leaving Shabbat behind and being forced to return to the tasks of daily living. Perhaps it will be different because even those tasks have changed since our experience of Shabbat. Just as love changes our view of everything, even the most mundane of tasks, our relationship with the Sabbath queen changes our view of the world, even the most routine of daily living. On Shabbat, we have tasted what is possible. We have glimpsed into the world-to-come, even as we desperately try to maintain our hold on it. So Saturday night becomes a celebration of the potential in this world—and in us.

This party will also be flush with gratitude. It will be a feast of David, who, according to tradition, was supposed to die over Shabbat. Since he didn't, he offered thanks to God on Saturday night. Like him, cognizant of what it means to be grateful for life, we express our thanks to God as well. We are thankful for the week that has just passed—the fact that we were alive to experience it. And we are thankful for the gift of Shabbat that we have just been given. Even more so, and this is what the *M'lavei Malkah* teaches us, we are thankful for all we have yet to experience in the week ahead.

Moving Forward

NOVEMBER 2

Jacob dreamed of a ladder standing on the ground and reaching to heaven. This means: We never stand still. We either ascend or descend.

HAFETZ HAYIM

This is a reference to the well-known story in Genesis (28:10–12) about Jacob. After leaving his father's home, during his travels from Beersheva to Haran, Jacob rested along the way. While he slept, he dreamed of a ladder extending itself to heaven, with angels ascending and descending on it. The Hafetz Hayim saw in this story a lesson for our daily living. Jacob's predicament describes our lives. We are never in the same place. We are constantly in motion—even when we think we are not. We may think that we are not getting anywhere but we are all moving quickly in our lives. The challenge is to make sure that we are going in the right direction.

So what will it take to make sure that we are moving forward and not losing ground? First, we must recognize that we are not standing still, that we are constantly in motion. Then all it takes is to place one foot forward, one foot in front of the other. It is a blessing to be able to step forward. Small steps take us forward just as do large steps. What is important is that we move forward.

Making Miracles

NOVEMBER 3

*May the One who wrought miracles for our ancestors,
redeeming them from slavery to freedom, redeem us
soon and gather our dispersed from the four corners of
the earth in the fellowship of the entire people Israel.*
FROM PRAYERS USHERING IN A NEW MONTH

Our wish for divine intervention in our lives, either as individuals or as a collective whole, is based on two things: the relationship of our ancestors with God and God's deliverance of the Jewish people from Egyptian slavery into freedom. We ask for the blessing of redemption. For the writer of this prayer, redemption implies a new world. As the Rabbis envisioned messianism, this would include the gathering of Jews into the Land of Israel.

There are critical moments in our lives when we take a real accounting of our souls, what the Rabbis call *cheshbon hanefesh*, or life review. We often do it in anticipation of—or shortly after—major life events, whether they are personal or part of the life of the community. When the new moon and new month arrive, we think back on our lives—and about what the future holds. Thus, the occasion to think about what we can do to bring about a redemptive future is ushered in each month. And it is contextualized within the ongoing dialogue between the individual and God. Seize the opportunity. Do something that will bring the day of our redemption closer.

Directing the Heart

NOVEMBER 4

If an individual is sitting on a boat or a wagon or a raft [and the time for reciting the Amidah—*the central prayer of Jewish worship—comes], the individual should direct the heart toward the Holy of Holies.*

MISHNAH BERAKHOT 4:6

This is part of an entire series in the Mishnah about what to do when we are traveling and it is time to say our daily prayers. Since the relationship between the individual and God—and the dialogue that fosters it—should not be a burden to the individual, the Rabbis have carefully considered a variety of occasions when such a dialogue—and thereby the nurturing of that relationship—might be at risk. So what do we do when traveling on a boat—which can't easily be stopped—and it is time to pray? We stop what we are doing, unless we are responsible for the boat and the welfare of others, and we pray.

A second level of the discussion, which is picked up by the Talmud, has to do with the direction you face while praying or if you are unable to stop and pray. If you are traveling by car or even a boat, it may not be so easy to determine the direction to face for prayer. Or you may be physically unable to do so.

Knowing where you are in this world is indeed a blessing. When in doubt, whenever in doubt, simply turn your heart toward Jerusalem.

Getting to the Top

NOVEMBER 5

*Adonai will make you the head, not the tail; you will
always be at the top and never at the bottom—if only
you obey and faithfully observe the sacred instructions
of Adonai your God that I enjoin upon you this day,
and do not deviate to the right or to the left from any
of the sacred instructions that I enjoin upon you this
day and turn to the worship of other gods.*

DEUTERONOMY 28:13–14

This is a fascinating statement that comes near the end of
Moses's oration to the people prior to their entry into the
Promised Land. It is at the end of their journey in the desert. It
is as if Moses is telling the people, "I hope that you learned
something during your desert wanderings. If you listen to God,
then you will be blessed. But if you deviate from the path that
God has set in front of you, you will encounter trouble along
the way."

Some people will dismiss this notion as an unrealistic
reframing of the reward and punishment theology of Rabbinic
Judaism. But that would make it too simple. The Bible is teaching us that if we follow God's direction for our lives, then we
can never be the tail, we can only be the head. We will never
be at the bottom and will always be on top. It is a direct result
of our relationship with the Divine.

Righteous Memory

NOVEMBER 6

The memory of the righteous is a blessing.
PROVERBS 10:7

This is a somewhat ubiquitous phrase. It is the kind of text that we share with one another as a way of comforting someone whose loved one has died. The words sound right, but I am not always sure what such texts actually mean. Perhaps this verse from Proverbs is more straightforward than we realize. It means that when a person dies, we are blessed with the memories of the individual.

But this is not a statement about Judaism's perspective on life after death. True, the text teaches us that a person may have left us in body but not in spirit. And the blessing we receive from people who have died is our memory of them and the good works that they did on earth—the blessings that they bestowed on others including us. This is particularly true of those who have lived righteously and done right, as the text suggests. But the message is quite simple. Memory itself can be a blessing when we permit it to enter our hearts and provide us with comfort.

Stepping-stones to the Divine

NOVEMBER 7

God
Like stones across the river
Carry me across
You are my Rock
And my Redeemer.

RABBI KARYN D. KEDAR

God is called many things in the Jewish tradition. Some theologians argue that God should not be described at all, because all such words are limiting. So instead of increasing our understanding of the Divine, we actually come to know less. Even the four-letter name of God is not to be pronounced. The notion of God as Rock and Redeemer is found frequently in Jewish sacred texts, nonetheless, and is sometimes used as a way to conclude our prayers.

This short statement by Rabbi Kedar is quite uplifting and insightful. As we attempt to navigate the difficulties of life, God is there to support and guide us. Thus, God provides the stepping stones so that we may know how to move forward. God helps us to keep our balance as we make our way across. And when we lose our balance and fall, God is there to pick us up, to bless us, and to help us make it across the river.

Healing Words

NOVEMBER 8

*May God be with you, may health and strength sustain
you. May nothing harm you, may wisdom and kindness
enrich you. May you be a blessing to this world and
may blessings surround you now and always.*
RABBI NAOMI LEVY

This blessing can be offered by parents to children, children
to parents, and friends to one another. It contains what we
would wish for anyone close to us. As my mother used to tell
me as I was growing up, when you have your health, you have
everything. While never wealthy, and fighting cancer at a
young age, she understood this notion far better than I did at
the time. It was an idea that I had to grow into. The recognition and understanding of such an idea does indeed provide us
with strength and fortitude. So Rabbi Levy's blessing is not just
for health. It is also for an understanding of the power of such
knowledge.

Such an understanding is real wisdom—it comes from the
experience of living and, too often, of encounters with the
angel of death who threatens our well-being and the health of
those we love. And when we bring such an understanding to
others, we will indeed feel blessed and offer the world blessing,
as well.

The Blessing of Indignation

NOVEMBER 9

May we all be blessed by God's shalom,
the awareness that righteous indignation has its place
but is deeply misplaced when manifested as an attack.
May we remember that our vulnerable selves are holy
and that the wholeness we seek
is sought too by the Holy One.

RABBI MENACHEM CREDITOR

It seems odd to place words like "righteous indignation" and "attack" in the context of a blessing. But the Jewish tradition seldom sugarcoats life, so why should its blessings be devoid of a foundation in reality? Rabbi Creditor contends—by placing *shalom* at the beginning of his list—that *shalom* is the most important part of being blessed. *Shalom*, usually translated as "peace" is really more about tranquility, completeness, and fulfillment. It is what has been called by some "feeling centered."

"Righteous indignation" motivates us to act in order to protect those who are less fortunate, who may not be able to act on their own. But becoming "holier than thou," as implied by this blessing, is not appropriate. And neither is being indignant about certain inequalities, yet unwilling to act accordingly in other areas of one's personal life. To be ritually observant and yet not apply an awareness of God's presence—and God's judgment of our personal lives—in our work, for example, is not acceptable.

We are all holy selves, and we are all vulnerable to the attacks of others—no matter how hard-shelled we appear to be. Seek wholeness for yourself and for others. It is something that God seeks for us, as well.

A Wise Heart

NOVEMBER 10

*May it be good in Your eyes to give a wise heart to
whomever we elect today and may You raise for us a
government whose rule is for good and blessing to
bring justice and peace to all the inhabitants of the
world and to Jerusalem, for rulership is Yours!...
May You give to all the peoples of this country, the
strength and will to pursue righteousness and to seek
peace as unified force in order to cause to flourish,
throughout the world, good life and peace and may
You fulfill for us the verse:*
*"May the pleasure of Adonai our God be upon us, and
establish the work of our hands for us, may the work
of our hands endure" (Psalm 90:17).*
FROM A PRAYER FOR VOTING BY RABBI DAVID SEIDENBERG

This is really a blessing for the democracy for which we are
grateful. Implicit in these words is also the notion that we are
aware of all those whose lives are not as free as ours. And thus
we pray that they may be released from their bondage. As we
enter the voting booth during any election, whether it has local
or national consequences, we ask for guidance for insight—
both for ourselves and for those whom we elect. We understand that such insight comes from the same Source.

While the prayer for our country has been a fixed part of
our liturgy for a long time, taking different forms depending
on where we have found ourselves as a people, few have considered the need for a blessing or prayer for voting. But
Rabbi Seidenberg's prayer expresses what we all feel: Please
God, bless the work of our hands—and the work of our
leaders.

Sufficient Blessings

NOVEMBER 11

Pour you out a blessing,
that there shall be more than is sufficient.
MALACHI 3:10

This text offers us some parameters for the reward of a blessing. To be blessed is not to be overwhelmed in abundance. To be blessed is to have our needs met, to have sufficient food to eat, to have a home that is sufficient to shelter us, to have sufficient clothes to cover us and protect us from the elements. Our challenge is to determine what is indeed sufficient to meet our needs—and then to understand that is indeed a blessing.

The prophet Malachi teaches that such blessings pour out from the heavens, that God is the Source of such blessings. So when you are poised to buy something new, to expand your home, to "super-size" your meal, remember the words of this prophet. Then such blessing can extend to others, as well.

Life's Trajectory

NOVEMBER 12

The days are long, but the years are short.
FOLK SAYING

Adults—especially those in the throes of middle age—readily comprehend this truism, for they live it. Our daily tasks constantly threaten to overwhelm us. How often we say to ourselves, "There are just not enough hours in the day to get everything done." It is ironic that the very electronic devices that were designed to save us time seem to busy us even further.

And they tether us even more inextricably to our jobs—so much so that our workdays seem never to cease.

Well before the modern age of electronics, the psalmist understood this predicament. It was this same notion that motivated the psalmist to write, "So teach us to number our days—that we may gain a heart of wisdom" (Psalm 90:12). Those who lived in the ancient world had a profound appreciation for the limited days we are granted on this earth and our challenge to do something meaningful with them—to leave the world a better place than it was before we entered it because we have entered it. This is the blessing of a fulfilled life.

Whenever I appear to be working too much, too hard, or too long, my friend Rabbi Leonard Kravitz always says, "Slow down. You work too hard. No one is going to build you a *goldeneh matzevah* [a golden headstone for your grave]." It is his way of saying that there are things beyond our work that provide transcendent meaning for our lives. And these are really what matter most. These are all that really matter. Family, friends, love, truth, and God. These alone give meaning and length of days to our lives.

Opening the Heart

NOVEMBER 13

Adonai your God will open up your heart and the hearts of your offspring to love Adonai your God with all your heart and soul, in order that you may live.

DEUTERONOMY 30:6

This statement from the Torah is a striking example of the logic of Jewish spirituality.

If we express our love for the Divine, God will open up our hearts so that we may love God even more. And a result of that loving relationship is a life filled with the holy and sacred. But the expression of our love for the Divine must be deep and profound, just as we would hope God's love is for us. It must be more than a passing interest or attraction. This is why the text here suggests that we must involve "heart and soul"—our entire being. This is the true blessing of God's love for us and for the world.

This is a statement about our spiritual lives, rather than our physical lives. Our spiritual lives are nurtured and sustained through our ongoing relationship with the Divine. For me, Jewish spirituality is about that relationship, and our spiritual actions—such as study, prayer, and ritual—are designed to bring the individual closer to the Divine.

Finding the Path

NOVEMBER 14

The one who is wise will consider these words,
The one who is prudent will take note of them.
For the paths of Adonai are smooth;
The righteous can walk on them,
While sinners stumble on them.
HOSEA 14:10

The prophet Hosea tells us all that we need to know. God has set out a path for our lives. If we follow that path, we will discover a life of blessing. It is the path itself that offers us the blessing—rather than any reward for which we may be waiting. How do we know? Our wisdom comes directly from our experience—and the experience of others.

A smooth road doesn't mean that the path will be easy. Nor does it mean that it will be straightforward. We may all lose our footing. And others will stumble and fall.

But a life in dialogue with the Divine just means that we will know where we are going and the path will unfold itself in front of us.

God's Goodness

NOVEMBER 15

Give thanks to Adonai, for God is good.
RECURRING TEXT FROM THE PSALMS, SUCH AS PSALM 106:1

This is the month in which a variety of emotions coalesce, particularly for North Americans who live in winter climes. Thanksgiving, which has its roots in the fall harvest festival of Sukkot, as described in the Bible, colors the month for many of us. The emotional mélange of Thanksgiving gives us pause. As we gather with our family and friends around the table, we are mindful of the many blessings for which we are grateful—even if we are aware of those no longer sitting around the table, who may be estranged, or distant, or no longer with us. Nevertheless, there are many things for which to be thankful.

We are also keenly aware of the dependability of nature—and of God as its Source—as we witness the change of seasons. Even as winter threatens and the cold begins to bite at us, and we realize how fragile are our lives, we feel an incredible sense of warmth and well-being. May we always know such joy.

Embracing the Moment

NOVEMBER 16

As a Jew I believe the meaning of life is trying to embrace each moment by having a keen awareness of the moments, especially the blessings, in our lives. Therefore we have an obligation to bring blessings to others' lives as well. As a Jew I believe that life is about family, friends, and community and that we must find ways to embrace and foster connections with one another.

RABBI RACHEL AIN

For Rabbi Ain, the meaning of life is tied to an awareness of the blessings in our lives. In order to recognize our bounty, we have to embrace each moment, for they are all filled with blessing—even when, or perhaps especially when, we don't realize it. But to simply enjoy our own life of blessing would be selfish and too limiting. We have to share our life of blessing with others. This is the math of spiritual logic. When we share our blessings with others, our own blessings increase rather than diminish.

Blessings can be found in the relationships that we nurture with others. But these need to be fostered. They don't just emerge on their own. We have to work at them—whether the relationship is with family, friends, or members of our community. The philosopher/theologian Martin Buber once said that "all life is meeting." It is in the context of meeting that life can be found. And it is in the context of that meeting of two individuals where blessing can be found, as well.

Running after Righteousness

NOVEMBER 17

You should run after righteousness with your words;
with your mouth you should speak
only what is in your heart.
TZENAH URENAH ON DEUTERONOMY 16:18B

This text comes from one of my favorite commentaries on the Torah. While originally written in Yiddish, it was designed to be easily accessible. For this author, righteousness is not just about deeds, for the author understands the power of words. It is also about the words by which we live. So it is the righteousness that accompanies our words that can potentially reach our hearts—and the hearts of others.

It is also important to run after things that are important, to pursue them aggressively with the understanding that there is an urgency about them. There are many times during which walking is the appropriate posture—such as on Shabbat, when we intentionally slow down our world and are not in a rush to go anywhere or do anything. But justice cannot afford such an approach.

So speak up and run ahead. And bring blessing in your wake.

Finding the Blessing

NOVEMBER 18

V'zot hab'rakhah—*"This is the blessing"*
with which Moses, the man of God,
bade the Israelites farewell before he died.
DEUTERONOMY 33:1

Besides the formalized words of blessing of our tradition that can be found in a prayer book, we aren't always privy to our final words, especially when they come in the form of a blessing, spoken just prior to our death. No one wants to think about death, and yet it is a real part of life. We are reminded of it when we least expect it. And we are reminded of it when we indeed expect it—when someone close to us dies. And so we seek blessing from their lives through the process of memory.

Moses's words of blessing to the people were recorded. Perhaps part of the blessing was that he, in fact, spoke to the people and offered them insight, encouragement, and guidance. For Moses, the journey was over. But for the people, the journey continued.

Nevertheless, what is missing from Moses's final words is what he said to his family and close friends. When the time comes, and it comes for all of us, what words of blessing will you leave?

Bearing Witness

NOVEMBER 19

I am a witness to the beauty and value of Judaism.
LYDIA KUKOFF

I have always been intrigued by the notion of "witness," something relatively foreign to the everyday language of Judaism except in the context of legal issues such as witnessing the signing of a *ketubah* (marriage contract) or a dip in the *mikvah* (ritual bath) for the purpose of conversion. But it means that we stand as living proof that something exists or has occurred and that we are ready to testify to that effect. It is a blessing to be such a witness.

So Lydia Kukoff is suggesting—and I concur—that Judaism has inherent value and beauty. It is ours to discover. And once we do, we can become its witness for others. Perhaps she is also suggesting that sometimes the value and beauty of Judaism can be found through the eyes of other people before we can identify it for ourselves.

So look for someone to lead you on your way. And once you have found it, grab someone else's hand and take them there, as well.

The Purpose of Death

NOVEMBER 20

Death is merely moving from one home to another.
The wise person will spend his or her main efforts in
trying to make the future home the more beautiful one.
RABBI MENACHEM MENDL OF KOTZK

The Kotzker Rebbe, as Menachem Mendl of Kotzk is known, was probably speaking about the relationship between this world and the next world, the world of the unknown, in an effort to limit our fears and provide us with some direction for our lives. If we live properly in this world, we merit the blessing of being able to live in the next world. This seems like an unusual position, since Judaism is generally focused on the here and now and not as worried about what happens after bodily death.

It is not the Kotzker's way of suggesting that we should never move to new homes or places. According to Rabbi Avi S. Olitzky, it was the Kotzker's way of challenging us to work daily on renovating our homes, that is, beautifying what we do on the inside. For if we don't do any interior renovation, we will not be able to find a home in the afterlife. So get started today. Break down the walls and start renovating now.

Sacred Instructions

NOVEMBER 21

Loving deeds of kindness are equal in weight to all the mitzvot *[sacred instructions].*
JERUSALEM TALMUD, *PE'AH* 1:1

Why is it that the Talmud accords such weight to the loving deeds of kindness that we perform? Perhaps it is what makes all the mitzvot worthwhile. For me, mitzvot are all about bringing individuals closer to God. But one of the best ways to get close to God is to get closer to other human beings—who are made in the image of God. How do we get close to them? By performing loving deeds of kindness, particularly important in a world that is marked by violence, loneliness, and pain.

While I usually translate *mitzvot* as "sacred instructions," because I believe that we enter a voluntary covenant with the Divine, most translators use the word "commandments." This certainly quickly raises the activity to a sacred dimension. But it is really we who transform these acts into a level of sacred activity by the unconditional love with which we do them. It is we who can transform everyday actions into deeds that carry blessing with them.

Whether you enter the covenant voluntarily or you feel commanded to do so, perform your actions out of love and kindness.

Gentle Guidance

NOVEMBER 22

*God, when my soul is low, help me raise it up.
When my heart empty, fill it.... Help me God to live
up to all the goodness that resides within me.
Give me the humility to learn from others
and learn from my mistakes—
to grow, to age, to mellow and ripen.*

RABBI ALEXANDER DAVIS

This is a personal blessing, as expressed by Rabbi Davis. It can be said during several holidays, in the midst of formal liturgy, or as a personal *kavvanah* (sacred mantra) on its own. It reflects an intimate relationship between the individual and the Divine. It also acknowledges the power that God has to help us, to nurture us, and to fill our soul to overflowing.

The prayer also acknowledges our essential self as good, even if we sometimes go off course and become less than humble, often at the expense of others. Finally, these words of Rabbi Davis's help us to understand that the process of becoming human—which is why I often speak of "humans becoming" rather than "human beings"—often comes with age and experience. But it doesn't come on its own. We have to work at it. And with the gentle guidance of the Divine, we may grow, age, mellow, and ripen.

God's Judgment

NOVEMBER 23

The Rock, God's work is perfect,
for all God's ways are justice;
a God of faithfulness and without iniquity,
righteous and just is God.

DEUTERONOMY 32:4 (ALSO PART OF THE *TZIDDUK HADIN*,
SAID AT THE CEMETERY FOLLOWING BURIAL OF THE DECEASED)

These are not easy words to say, especially when someone whom we love has died. Yet we recite these words as a reflection of our faith in God even as we suffer the pain of loss. The verse above is part of a longer prayer, probably written during the Talmudic period, that emphasizes the relative worthlessness of humans as compared to God. By reciting this prayer, the mourner declares his or her acceptance of God's harsh decree: the death of a loved one. It is also an acknowledgment that the mourner has realized the limitations of life, something we sometimes forget in our pursuit of the everyday. We are reminded of such things—particularly our own finitude—in the face of death. All else is eclipsed, and often loses meaning, in the presence of death. But in the face of death we are also taught the blessing of our life.

God is known by many names in Jewish tradition. Usually these names are based on our relationship with the Divine. Unlike humans, rocks are eternal. They do not have limited life spans. They were there prior to our death and will be there long after we are gone. But rocks are solid and supportive. Likewise, especially at the time of loss, we depend on God—as a Rock—for support. We lean on God to hold us up when we feel weak and uncertain of ourselves.

Celebration

November 24

*Praised are You, Adonai, whose mitzvot add holiness
to our lives and who gave us the sacred instruction
to recite the* Sh'ma *[prayer].
We celebrate Your sovereignty with a whole heart and
willingly [acknowledge] Your Oneness
and happily serve You.*

Ancient Jewish blessing, found in the Cairo Genizah

This blessing was found by Rabbi Solomon Schechter in a genizah in Cairo, Egypt. It is a blessing that offers praise and gratitude to God for instructing us to recite the prayer known as the *Sh'ma*. Like most blessings, it first establishes a relationship between the individual and God through the use of the traditional Jewish formula for blessing. Then it mentions the act that we are instructed to do, in this case the reciting of the *Sh'ma*. But this blessing continues. First, it reminds us that engaging in regular prayer adds a dimension of holiness to our lives. Second, it implies that saying the *Sh'ma* is a celebration of God's sovereignty. Such a willing acknowledgment actually brings happiness to our lives.

The next time you recite the *Sh'ma*, first recite this introductory blessing. Don't rush into the *Sh'ma*. Allow for some minutes of silence and reflection. Then say the words slowly and thoughtfully. Breathe slowly. Make yourself aware of each breath and the connection of breathing to life. And after your prayers, then you can rush out to serve God in all that you do.

Core Beliefs

NOVEMBER 25

Sh'ma Yisrael Adonai Eloheinu Adonai Echad.
Hear, O Israel, Adonai is our God, Adonai is One.
THE FIRST LINE OF THE *SH'MA* PRAYER

The tradition tells us to repeat this text twice formally in the liturgy (morning and evening) and to recite it before going to sleep at night. Sometimes I feel like shouting it from the rooftops. At other times I like to quietly reflect upon it in silence and solitude. While it may not technically be a blessing, it is nevertheless a core statement for my personal faith. It is the one statement that holds it all together. Some people believe that this statement reflects the entire essence of Judaism. That is perhaps why we are to say the statement aloud, in order to make sure that others hear along with us.

I like to translate it this way: "Listen, O people of Israel. Adonai the God with whom we have a personal relationship through history and Adonai the God of the world is one and the same." This helps me to realize that the God I wake up to in the morning, the God who makes for the rising of the sun and the order of the universe that I come to expect each day, is the same God to whom I give my soul for cleansing and restoration each night before I go to sleep.

Stargazing

November 26

*When I look up to the heavens, the work of Your
hands, the moon and the stars that You set into place,
[I wonder] what is the human that You should
remember us, mortals that You would care for us?*
PSALMS 8:4–5

As we look upward into the sky, especially on a clear night,
we readily appreciate the majesty of the heavens, and we are
awed by their sheer beauty. We may think about how small we
are compared to how great are the skies and all that they contain. The psalmist reminds us that it is easy to understand
God's concern for the vastness of the skies, the sun and the
moon, and their pattern of motion. It is far more difficult to
understand, in comparison, why God should have any interest
in us as mere humans. We are tiny in comparison to the vastness of nature that surrounds us.

Amidst the psalmist's wondering about why God should be
interested in us is the recognition that God does, in fact, care
for us and show concern for us. While the psalmist understands that we are small in comparison to all that surrounds us,
implicit in the psalmist's comment is that we are charged with
maintaining the world around us. We may share the same
Creator, but we have been charged with the co-stewardship of
the world. It may be a big job, but its reward is that we are
blessed to continue to share in its beauty.

The Source of Light

NOVEMBER 27

Humans are no mere reflections of the Above.
They are a source of light.
ADAPTED FROM RABBI ABRAHAM JOSHUA HESCHEL

Rabbi Abraham Joshua Heschel certainly believed in the light that comes from a divine source. He understood its transformative power for those able to bathe in it. Rabbi Heschel even had a term for the human encounter with the Divine: "radical amazement." But Heschel also understood that there are other sources of light in the world. We can bathe in such light; we can feel blessed by such light. And one of the most powerful of those sources is humans, especially when their light is joined together one to the other. Heschel demonstrated such light himself when he marched for civil rights in the South in the 1960s. He called it "praying with my feet."

But human light can also be muted and distorted. It is directly limited by what we do with that light. The activity of humans can prevent such light from shining forth, or it can actually create such light. When we do things that allow human light to shine, it will indeed shine brightly. Perhaps through the joining of human light we can actually help bring divine light into the world. God and humans walking and working together can provide an intensity of that light that can illumine the world.

It really is a simple plan. Just let your own light shine forth, so that it can align with others and with God. Just let it shine.

Traveling with Ourselves

NOVEMBER 28

Wherever we go, we take ourselves along.
RABBI SIDNEY GREENBERG

This is a reminder especially for people who aren't always happy with who they are or what they have become. Even when we change, when we renew ourselves, we still bring our past with us wherever we go. And as difficult as it might be to accept it, that is OK. Wherever the Israelites journeyed in the desert, they carried the ark of the covenant with them. Inside the ark, along with the tablets were the shards of the tablets that Moses shattered. Even when we are whole, we carry our brokenness along with us. Carrying shards of our past with us is what makes us whole. We can't separate ourselves entirely from who we once were. We can only transform it with what we do today. What we have become is a result of what we once were. It is the blessing of being broken and made to feel whole once again.

So wherever you go, don't forgot to follow yourself. Then you will be sure to be heading in the right direction.

Beautiful Work, Beautiful Words

NOVEMBER 29

This is my God and I will praise God.
EXODUS 15:2

While the text sounds a little bit more poetic in its Hebrew original, this text from the Bible is the source for what is called *hiddur mitzvah*, the embellishment or beautification of a mitzvah. It is the textual reference that is called upon for taking a ritual object and transforming it into a work of art, making it beautiful and thus beautifying the ritual with which it is connected. While almost anything can be used for ritual purposes, the regard we have for doing a particular ritual can often be found in the object we choose to use to engage the ritual.

There is something special about making a blessing and using a beautiful piece of art for wine or candles or anything else that is relevant. But this notion of *hiddur mitzvah* transcends the limitations of a ritual object. It is also about transforming ourselves and our home for a particular holiday.

Getting Muddy

NOVEMBER 30

If you want to help a friend out of the mud,
don't hesitate to get a little dirty.
BAAL SHEM TOV

Don't hesitate to get a little dirty. Not only is it often unavoidable, but Baal Shem Tov, as the founder of Chasidism was known, is telling us indeed to get a little dirty. It is important to get close to someone whom we are helping, to feel the pain of our friend, to be in the situation in which we find ourselves. In so doing, we may have to get dirty. This is Baal Shem Tov's profound wisdom. He used the mud as a metaphor because it is hard to help someone out of it without dirtying ourselves. Too often we are afraid of getting too close, fearful that we may be contaminated by the mud. But that is the posture we should assume whenever we reach out to help someone in need.

Mud is dirty. It is a mixture of dirt and water. But water, half of the substance of mud, can also be used as a purifying and cleansing agent. It can be used as a substance for blessing and transformation. So it seems the solution to our problems can often be found in the problem itself. When we separate out the water from the mud, then we are able to find the solution we are seeking and we can get cleansed at the same time.

DECEMBER

Lighting the Way

DECEMBER 1

*May the light of our Hanukkah candles burn through
the gloom of the lonely and cold parts of our world,
and may it be our mission to warm those
held captive by the dark night.*

RABBI AVI S. OLITZKY

Often we pause momentarily from our busy lives to light
the Hanukkah candles and then continue on with our holiday
celebration, thinking little about those whom we may have
left behind in the darkness. The Hanukkah lights are there to
illumine the darkness. We may take their light for granted,
but they are lit to offer light especially to those who feel
lonely and cold. The lights remind us of our past and the religious freedom wrought by the victory of our Maccabean
ancestors.

But the Hanukkah lights also point us toward the future. We
have an obligation to extend the light to others, especially
those held captive by the dark. So as you light your Hanukkah
candles, carry the light forward into the dark night so that you
may bring their blessing deeper into the world.

Natural Beauty

DECEMBER 2

May I express there everything in my heart, and may all the foliage of the field, all grasses, trees, and plants, awake at my coming, to send the powers of their life into the words of my prayer so that my prayer and speech are made whole through the life and the spirit of all growing things, which are made as one by their transcendent Source.

FROM A PRAYER BY RABBI NACHMAN OF BRESLOV

Sometimes it is hard to feel God's presence in our everyday routine, especially for those of us who live in an urban environment, often separated from the wonders of the natural world. It may take a journey into nature for us to realize God's transcendent power and the presence of the Divine in our lives. Often, when we are confronted by the beauty of nature or its unbridled awesome power, we are motivated to express ourselves to God through blessings and prayer.

When you open yourself to nature, open yourself to God, as well. Use the natural environment to help raise your prayers heavenward, even as it lifts you at the same time.

Changing Ourselves

DECEMBER 3

Prayer is less about changing the world than it is about changing ourselves.

RABBI DAVID J. WOLPE

What is it that we pray for, and why do we pray? Prayer is part of an ongoing dialogue between God and the individual that takes a multiplicity of forms. Usually we think of prayer solely as an act of petition. We want or need something and think that God can provide it for us. But Rabbi Wolpe is teaching us that we may think that prayer will lead to a change in the world but instead it has the potential to lead to a change in ourselves.

Perhaps that change comes from the relationship between the individual and God that is established through prayer. Maybe it emerges in the dialogue itself. Or perhaps it comes from a realization of what is important in life, what really matters, when we begin to isolate those items for which we pray. Few of us will pray to win the lottery. But we may pray for our health or the well-being of those whom we love. And so we let go of those things that matter less. Change can bring blessing. It is the process of prayer that helps us to make the change.

Deep Prayer

DECEMBER 4

Deep, soulful prayer, prayer worth staking your life on, prayer that makes life worth living, is rooted on two things that every one of us can access: heartache and gratitude.
RABBI SHARON BROUS

For me, this is the ultimate goal of prayer—to help us soar heavenward, to bridge the gap between the individual and the Divine. It may be a short one-line traditional formula for blessing or the poetic prayer of the heart or those fashioned by the liturgists of the past. This is the kind of prayer that our spiritual lives depend on, so it is indeed the kind of prayer on which we would stake our lives. Some will say, therefore, that prayer demands a dismissal from the rote, speed praying that sometimes occurs in the synagogue community. But for some, it is that kind prayer environment that enables us to pray. The "white noise" of a praying community may be the context in which we might be able to pray. Others demand a different kind of environment, one in which each word is carefully articulated and thoroughly explored, often through song.

Regardless of the model, both have one thing in common—the potential for intensity of the prayer experience. And that intensity emerges from the soul because of a deep heartache or an overflow of joy and gratitude. Both are powerful motivators for prayer. The posture that we take for prayer that emerges from profound joy or deep gratitude should inform the prayer of our everyday.

The Value of Questions

December 5

We place more value in questions than in answers.
Rabbi Rolando Matalon

While Rabbi Matalon's comment reflects his perspective on the synagogue he leads, it is also his outlook on Judaism that is made manifest in that synagogue. And it is in the synagogue that the religious ideology of Judaism is expressed. For him and for his understanding of Judaism—a perspective with which I heartily agree—it is important to seek out answers and to struggle with them rather than to expect them to come easily. So it is the questions that are important—and the personal struggle that accompanies them—much more than pat answers.

But how does the individual know what questions to ask? Questions emerge out of everyday living, out of confrontation with the reality of the world around us. They surface out of our interactions and relationships with others. And they help us to focus on the ultimate values of life. So think deeply and reflect. Then ask your questions. And don't expect the answer to come quickly or easily. For it is in the deep struggle with the question that faith emerges and we may be blessed by it.

Finding What We Seek

DECEMBER 6

If you think you know what you will find, then you will find nothing. If you expect nothing, then you will always be surprised. So it is with setting out on the path of liberation, leaving everything.

RABBI LAWRENCE KUSHNER

It may sound hackneyed, but our lives are journeys. And they are made up of the individual journeys that we travel each day, one blessing at a time. Some of these daily excursions take us long distances. Others barely move us at all. But when they don't move us forward, even when we are standing still, we seem to be moving backward—because the world continues to move forward even if we are not prepared to do so. Nevertheless, part of the journey includes standing still at times and not moving at all. It is part of learning how to appreciate the present as a blessing without rushing forward or being wistful about the past.

And at other times, as Rabbi Kushner suggests, we have to let go of the past in order to find that something in the future that we are seeking. But the critical element is not to look for it. Simply continue your journey forward with open eyes and an open heart. That's when you know that you will arrive at your destination.

The Nature of the Wilderness

DECEMBER 7

The Torah invites us, again and again,
to contemplate the nature of the Wilderness.
We are asked to picture ourselves there—in a place
where we are lost and powerless and frightened.
Into that core place in our lives comes the Torah,
bringing divine truth and wisdom and perspective.

RABBI AMY EILBERG

Why would the Torah want us to contemplate the nature of the wilderness as Rabbi Eilberg suggests? Because it is there where the Jewish people emerged. It is there where the collective memory of the Jewish people was born. It was there where the people came in close contact with the Divine. It was there where we were each blessed, one individual at a time. And it was there where Torah was revealed. It is in the wilderness, in the desert, where one's vision is unimpeded, where we see most clearly. And it is there where we found our way from servitude to freedom, from slavery to a land brimming with promise.

But Rabbi Eilberg takes this teaching to a far deeper level. It is in the wilderness where we are most vulnerable, where we are most exposed. It is there where the layers that we have built up to protect us are disassembled. And it is there, as a result, where we can come to know the Divine and our essential selves.

Ancient Blessing

DECEMBER 8

*Praised are You, Adonai our God, Sovereign of the universe,
who has made us holy with the sanctity of Aaron
and instructed us to bless the people Israel with love.*

SAID BY THE DESCENDANTS OF THE PRIESTS
PRIOR TO BLESSING THE COMMUNITY

This process of blessing, known as *dukhenen* (or *Birkat Kohanim*), takes place in the synagogue on festivals (although descendants of the priestly class of ancient Israel do it each morning in synagogues in Israel). For me, the pivotal element in the entire blessing—and why the blessing is recited prior to the actual offering of blessing—is the notion that it must be given in love. There are no conditions with such a blessing. There are no stipulations. Perhaps that is how all blessings should be defined—by love.

There have been many debates about the offering of the Priestly Blessing in this way, particularly about who is entitled to offer it and whether "the sanctity of Aaron," that is, a descendant of the ancient priesthood, is relevant any longer, especially as we try to break down barriers between people. What is most powerful about the blessing of the *kohanim* (the descendants of the priests) is that it demonstrates that one individual can indeed bless another—and within that blessing is a great deal of power and love.

An Intimate Statement of Faith

DECEMBER 9

*Praised are You, Adonai our God, Sovereign of the universe,
who has made us holy with mitzvot and
instructed us concerning the mitzvah of tzitzit.*

BLESSING SAID UPON PUTTING ON THE FOUR-CORNERED
SMALL *TALLIT* UNDERGARMENT IN THE MORNING

This blessing should not be confused with the blessing said when wrapping yourself in a large *tallit* for prayer. This blessing is for the smaller *tallit*, usually called a *tallit katan* (literally, "*small tallit*") or *arba kanfot* (four corners). Since it is usually worn as an undergarment (although there are some who wear it as an outer garment), I consider the blessing and the wearing of such a *tallit* to be very personal and to reflect an intimate relationship with the Divine.

While there are many acts of faith that are public, it seems that the transcendent moments are often those that are private. So as I dress in the morning, in the privacy of my bedroom, I put on the *tallit katan* as a personal statement of faith. It may seem like a simple act, similar to putting on socks and shoes. For me, it symbolizes a moment of intimacy that I share with the Divine each day—which helps to ready me for the day ahead and all the challenges that I will inevitably encounter.

Protecting Angels

DECEMBER 10

May Michael be at my right hand and
Gabriel at my left. Before me is Uriel.
Behind me is Raphael,
and the divine presence is above my head.
FROM THE *SH'MA* PRAYER
SAID AT NIGHTTIME BEFORE GOING TO SLEEP

It is dark, late at night. We lie down and prepare for sleep after a long day. Regardless of our age, we feel vulnerable and unprotected. We feel weary, spent, lonely. We yearn to be refreshed, renewed in a way that only comes from a good night's sleep. Particularly when that sleep is elusive, we crave it.

This blessing which accompanies the recital of the nighttime *Sh'ma*, emerges out of a midrash. As we lie down to sleep at night, we imagine these four angels surrounding us, those who are closest to God protecting us. And because we can't imagine these four angels without God present, God's sheltering presence is with us, as well. And so we sleep at night, unafraid and protected. This itself is a blessing.

Kindness

DECEMBER 11

May kindness surround the one who trusts in Adonai.
FROM THE WEEKDAY TORAH SERVICE FOR FESTIVALS

With the Torah unfurled in front of us, the symbol of revelation and our connection with the Divine, we offer these words—a blessing for others. What is the relationship between kindness and our trust in God? Integrity. Those who have a relationship with God, who trust in the Divine, must treat others with kindness, as well. They, like us, are made in the image of the Divine. A relationship of meaning cannot exist between the individual and God without a similar relationship with other human beings.

This statement emerges at this time in the prayer service as a reminder. It could just as easily be said when the Torah is not in front of us, when we are not celebrating a holiday or festival. The Torah reminds us that God demands kindness from us. The holidays remind us that we will encounter many others during our own pilgrimages, our own journeys. And our only response is to treat them with kindness, particularly if they are strangers.

Blessing the People

December 12

May Adonai our God be with us, as God was with our ancestors. May God never abandon or forsake us.
1 Kings 8:57, from the blessing by King Solomon of the people Israel as part of the dedication of the ancient Temple in Jerusalem

Following the completion and dedication of the Temple in Jerusalem, Solomon blessed the people. While it might seem appropriate, or even effortless, for a king or any sovereign ruler to bless the people, it is not an easy thing to do. Blessings are intimate acts that are often made more difficult when offered in public. Nevertheless, blessings are powerful experiences both for the people who offer them and for those who receive them. People may die, but the blessings we receive from them live long after they have left this earth.

So rather than just reciting words of blessing that solely reflect the relationship that you have with the Almighty, try harnessing the strength of that relationship in order to offer words of blessing to someone else: a child, a parent, a friend. And don't wait for a special occasion to do so—although Jewish tradition has numerous fixed occasions for such exchanges, particularly on Shabbat. Offer what is in your heart. It is really the only gift that will continue to give throughout your life and beyond.

Courage

DECEMBER 13

Strengthen the hands that have become weak.
Make firm tottering knees.
Say to the anxious of heart,
"Be strong. Do not be afraid."
ISAIAH 35:3–4

There are times in our lives—we all have them—when we become disillusioned and weary. The burdens of daily living overwhelm us. As the prophet suggests, we feel weak and anxious even about simple things. When that happens, we may turn to God for support and strength. But sometimes all it takes is someone else saying to us, "Don't worry. It will be OK." Rabbi Eliot Malomet is fond of saying, particularly after someone has experienced the loss of someone close to them, "It won't be the same. But it will be OK." It is his way of both acknowledging the loss and recognizing that somehow we continue to live even with the burden of grief that we carry forward with us into life. We somehow feel the power of blessing behind these words.

The modern Hebrew idiomatic equivalent is *yiyeh tov*, "it will be good." Some may dismiss this notion as trite, but there is profound spiritual power in the affirmation of this notion expressed quite simply. When we experience transitions in our lives, we are indeed anxious. Not only are we unsure of what the future holds, we are also unsure about our ability to navigate it. Do we have the capacity to do what needs to be done? Can we be successful in our new stage in life? Do we have the skills and personal fortitude? This is where Isaiah's words inspire us once again to step forward, knowing that we are not alone: "Be strong. Do not be afraid."

Righteous Giving

DECEMBER 14

Tzedakah *is not about giving.*
Tzedakah *is about being.*
RABBI BRADLEY SHAVIT ARTSON

It is easy to make money. It is harder to give it away. This seems counterintuitive, but it is another principle embedded in the nature of spiritual living, which is why Rabbi Artson's statement is so important. *Tzedakah* is not merely the righteous act of charitable giving, it is also a state of being. Rich or poor, we are only temporary stewards of our personal wealth. Eventually we have to give it all away. Through *tzedakah* we have the opportunity to give it away in order to make the world a better place—and we become better people for doing so. Through *tzedakah*, we have the power to bring blessing to others.

There is also a bit of active theology implicit in the giving of *tzedakah*. Some see God as the Source of reward and punishment in the world and perceive those who are wealthy to be rewarded by God for goodness. But *tzedakah* places broader demands on us. Human beings can be partners with God through *tzedakah* by righting the imbalance of wealth, especially when those who are righteous go unrewarded.

Peering into the Heart

DECEMBER 15

Adonai sees into the heart.
1 SAMUEL 16:7

I always like to say, "Think with your heart. And if you can't think with your heart, then think with your head." Most people assume that the act of thinking is primarily connected to the head rather than to the heart. But in relationships and in navigating this life, the heart often comes first. That is why the insight of the biblical prophet Samuel is so important. God sees into the heart. God knows when we are thinking with our heart and when we are thinking with our head and when we are not thinking at all.

But don't leave all this seeing to God. Take a hard look at your own heart. What is there that may be limiting your ability to think with it? Once you identify those things that may be blocking your ability to think with your heart, set them aside. Then continue thinking. That's when there will be something that you may finally want God to see. And that is when God may be prepared to offer you a blessing.

The Blessing of Hospitality

DECEMBER 16

A good guest says, "Blessed is my host."
JERUSALEM TALMUD, *BERAKHOT* 9:1

Usually we think of hospitality and welcoming as being the responsibility of the host. But this text from the Talmud teaches us that part of the responsibility is with the guest. When a guest appreciates all that is being done and expresses that to the host, the host feels gratified and is motivated to welcome other guests as well. So when we enjoy a good time as the guest of another, many others benefit. It is part of the spiritual logic that helps me to understand the world around us.

I learned this lesson many years ago from the parents of a friend. Whenever we were invited to their home, they taught us how to celebrate Shabbat and the Jewish holidays to the maximum extent possible. Good food. Good conversation. Words of Torah. Acts of blessing. And as a result, many years later, we now do the same for others.

If I forgot to say thank you to them then, I do so at this time—and with every guest that I invite into my home from this day forth.

Watching Out for Yourself

December 17

Blessed be the hands that take for themselves.
YIDDISH FOLK SAYING

While this might read like a rather selfish statement, it is not that way at all. We have to gain insight into the Yiddish psyche in order to understand it fully. It might be rendered into an American idiom as "God helps those who help themselves," or perhaps into the well-known statement from *Pirkei Avot* (1:14), attributed to Hillel, "If I am not for myself, who will be for me?" It is like living in the tension between expecting a miracle and not anticipating one at all. We can't expect God to act if we are not willing to do so.

This Yiddish statement undergirded a lot of my father's homespun philosophy. Blessings did not come through the hands of others, only through our own doing. He felt that we always had to look out for ourselves, because no one would be looking out for us. But I understand the statement a little more broadly. It is only when we look out for ourselves that others will be willing to look out for us, as well.

Rejoicing in Our Own Portion

DECEMBER 18

So I saw that there is nothing better than for a person to rejoice in what one does, for that is one's portion. Who can enable one to see what will be afterward?
ECCLESIASTES 3:22

This might be described as the blessing of the present. Kohelet was a sober realist. For him, the only time is the present. And the only reality is the one that we are currently experiencing. This is why we have to rejoice in it. It is too easy to get lost in the fantasy of the lives of others—what they have, how they live, what they do. Just as we are not able to see what may come next for them, we are also unable to see what may come next for us. It certainly could be worse. It might be better.

This lesson didn't come early in the life of Kohelet. It was a learning that emerged after a great deal of life experience. The benefit of the text of Ecclesiastes is that we can learn from what Kohelet experienced rather than having to do so on our own. This is what makes it wisdom literature. So enjoy the present. It is a gift that we have been given.

Sacred Work

DECEMBER 19

Sometimes work can change your luck.
HAYYIM NAHMAN BIALIK

We usually think of luck as something that we cannot control. It is just something that happens, although the origin of our understanding of luck has something to do with the alignment of the stars and the interpretation of the symbols of the Zodiac. In Jewish theology, with God as the Source, there is no luck. Nevertheless, there are indeed events that happen that we can neither understand nor explain.

Bialik wants us to understand that sometimes we make our own luck. In other words, we can influence the outcome of events by what we do. Often things don't just happen on their own. We can't just say things and they happen. We have to work to bring them to be. This understanding is captured in the blessing for the study of Torah, "Praised are You, Sovereign of the universe, for making us holy with mitzvot and instructing us to busy ourselves with the words [and work] of Torah."

The Fruit of Our Labors

DECEMBER 20

Praised are You, Adonai our God, Sovereign of the universe, who creates the fruit of the earth.
BLESSING RECITED UPON EATING THINGS
THAT GROW IN THE GROUND

Like blessings for other produce of nature, this blessing is recited upon eating things that grow in the ground. While it may be taken for granted by some people, especially as we have grown accustomed to eating things irrespective of the time of year or the location in which they are grown, blessings such as these help us to be cognizant of the things on which we depend for sustenance—and of the Source of all. I particularly appreciate this blessing, because it helps me to feel grounded, attached to the earth on which I stand.

Part of the discipline of reciting blessings when we benefit from them is so that we don't take the gifts of our life—or of our world—for granted. This is the case with the blessing over fragrant oils as well: "Praised are You, Adonai our God, Sovereign of the universe, who creates fragrant oils." How many of us recite such a blessing when we place oils on our bodies? Yet we are cognizant of them, especially when they adorn another and bring beauty into the world of senses.

Standing for Prayer

DECEMBER 21

A person should stand to pray only in a reverent frame of mind. The pious ones of old would wait an hour before praying, in order to direct their hearts to God.
MISHNAH BERAKHOT 5:1

This is the source cited for the verses of song (*P'sukei D'zimrah*)—mostly psalm texts that provide the warm-up and introduction to the fixed liturgy of the morning service. I get up early in the morning, rush to synagogue, and then get intentionally lost in the words of the psalmist. Sometimes I speed through the words so that I may speak them all. At other times, I get stuck on a line or two and hold onto them for many moments—even as my fellow worshipers have sped ahead. I do whatever I can to get ready for prayer even while I am praying.

It is also important that I stand at the beginning, reminding me before whom I stand and why I am there in the first place.

So perhaps I am not as pious as those who came before me. I am in too much of a rush most times to take an hour in order to prepare myself to pray. But I get it. If I expect to emerge from my prayers feeling flush with its words of blessing, then I can't expect it to happen on its own. I have to ready myself for prayer—today and every day.

Reverence and Love

December 22

God of days and years, Author of life, our times are
in Your hand. We thank You for the blessing of life
and for all that enriches our lives.
We gather today in special thankfulness to share in
the happiness of [enter name].
Be with him (her) always as the joy of his (her) life.
May he (she) be blessed with health and happiness, and
with the strength to overcome sickness and sorrow.
May we have the joy of coming together for many
more years, united by mutual reverence and love.
Then will our lives be filled with abundance and blessing.

Birthday blessing by Rabbi Chaim Stern

While there are a variety of rituals and ceremonies associated with birth, birthdays are really not celebrated in Jewish tradition. Instead, the anniversary of the death of an individual is marked (called a *yahrzeit* among eastern European and North American Jews). Thus, there are no actual blessings prescribed for birthdays, although it is the custom among most of us to celebrate them in any case. Instead, people are encouraged to recite the *Shehecheyanu* blessing (see entry for February 3). It was probably the influence of Western culture that motivated Rabbi Stern to pen the blessing here.

Embedded in this blessing is profound gratitude for being alive. There is no "lying about one's age," as popular convention often suggests. People who have danced with the angel of death understand the absurdity of such a proposition. We should celebrate each passing year, each year that we grow older, with fervor and enthusiasm and be thankful for each day that we have lived, for each day that we have learned, for each day that we have loved.

Earthly Pleasure

DECEMBER 23

Delight yourself with pleasure
and God will reward you with this very pleasure.
DEUTERONOMY RABBAH 3:1

In context, this is a statement about Shabbat and the sheer joy and pleasure that it can bring to an individual. Many people see the traditional observance of Shabbat as a burden. Jewish tradition sees it as joy. My personal experience attests to the validity of such a notion. It really provides us with a taste of the world-to-come. We sit. We eat. We enjoy one another. And we express our thanks to God for all that life has given us during the week that has passed and the years that have accumulated.

Since Shabbat is a paradigm for pleasure in Judaism, this statement also helps us understand a basic philosophy in Judaism. Judaism advocates for personal pleasure and does not shy away from it. And just to make sure that there is no misunderstanding, the Rabbis who wrote this passage tell us that there is a reward for pleasure and it is God who is offering it to us. Now that is a blessing!

Divine Delight

DECEMBER 24

*"I am Adonai, who exercises mercy, justice,
and righteousness on the earth.
I delight in these things," says Adonai.*
JEREMIAH 9:23

Jeremiah is one of my favorite prophets. He leaned toward the dramatic in order to make a point. This is why he is often pictured bent over from the weight of a yoke he placed around his neck to emphasize that the king of Babylon would defeat the ancient Jewish people and send them into exile. We look at the innocent who suffer—and there are many—and say, "They don't deserve it." But most of us are also unwilling to say that anyone "deserves" it, especially when the prophets like Jeremiah suggest to us that God "exercises mercy, justice, and righteousness on the earth." It may be impolitic to suggest that we, in fact, may deserve to be punished for our actions, but we depend on God's mercy so that we are not punished. It is important to note the other activities of God that become divine attributes about which Jeremiah reminds us: justice and righteousness. While we may also look to God for justice, God looks to us for righteousness.

So let's continue to lead a good life and pray for mercy and hope that God delights in us, and blesses us, as well.

Nourishing Love

DECEMBER 25

May it be Your will
That the food that I cook
bring nourishment, fulfillment, and happiness
to those who eat it
and bring honor to the land
and all the people that make this meal possible.

FROM A BLESSING FOR COOKING
BY LEAH KOENIG AND ANNA STEVENSON

There are many blessings for eating various kinds of food. However, there are no traditional blessings to be recited by those who cook, with the possible exception of the blessing for separating challah. The blessing for separating challah— "Praised are you Adonai our God, Sovereign of the universe, who has made us holy with mitzvot and instructed us to separate challah"—is reminiscent of the process used of separating out some of the challah for the ancient priests in the Temple in Jerusalem. By separating the challah (which is from the word *chol*, "secular"), we are consecrating the bread—which is the staff of life—and acknowledging its Source.

Those who cook, especially with love and for others, are making a similar statement. They are nurturing both body and soul—those who will eat, as well as their own.

Concealed Acts

December 26

Concealed acts concern Adonai our God; but with overt acts, it is for us and our children ever to apply all the provisions of this Teaching [Torah].
Deuteronomy 29:28

The focus of Judaism has always been about doing rather than thinking or even saying. In short form, this notion may be described as "deed over creed." So, more than anything we say, it is actions that reflect who and what we are. And these actions should manifest what is contained in the Torah, as God's teaching. But not all actions are appropriate. Some need to be rejected. Those that are concealed, which generally refer to those things done nefariously, are not acceptable. Of course, there are certain actions that do not belong in the public sphere, such as the intimate relations between people. But we should never do anything in private that we are unwilling to have known publically.

Moreover, actions are thought through. They are intentional. They are conscious. They are our deliberate attempt to live as God instructs us to live—with a life of blessing. How we live because of this Teaching teaches our children how to live as well.

A Whole Heart

December 27

Let your heart therefore be whole with Adonai.
1 Kings 8:61

I know few people whose hearts are whole. There is too much pain in this world to make such things possible. But this text doesn't say we must have a whole heart before we can approach God. Rather, the text advises that our heart should be whole with Adonai. When approaching the Divine, we have to be open and honest with our emotions. There can be no duplicity, no hidden agendas.

But here is the blessing. When we approach God with a broken heart, a heart that has been torn asunder by disappointment or by abandoned love, it is through the relationship with God that our heart can become whole again.

Between Heaven and Earth

DECEMBER 28

The distance between heaven and earth is a journey of hundreds of years, but the distance between the mind and the heart is even greater.
RABBI MENACHEM MENDL OF KOTZK

We may be able to travel long distances in space, but what appears to be the shortest distance is much harder to traverse. It is difficult to make the connection between our head and our heart. We often know what we should be doing. We know what is the right thing to do, but for some inexplicable reason, we just can't do it. It may be that our heart can't communicate with our head. Or maybe our head just doesn't want to hear what it is our heart is saying to us. So we stay stuck, unable to move in either direction. This is particularly true when we are dealing with things that are close to our heart, especially when they concern friends and members of our family.

Undoubtedly there will be well-intentioned people who will want to give you advice as to how to move from one place to another. And some of them may be right. But as you try to make the trip from your heart to your head, listen to what both are telling you along the way. You might find that the safest route to travel is in the middle. And that is the place of blessing.

Prophetic Vision

DECEMBER 29

*All of us have an angel of God calling out to show us
the way to blessings, to clarity and to prophetic vision.*
RABBI NAOMI LEVY

I believe in angels. I am not afraid to admit it. I believe that
God sends forth messengers to bring the divine message to
humankind. The ancients saw these messengers primarily in
the form of prophets. But those messengers were not limited to
the ancient world or to prophets. They have been called forth
throughout the ages. They are sent to bring blessing into our
world. Often these messengers come in the form of friends and
family members close to us—people who are assigned particular tasks, even when they are not informed of the Source.

As Rabbi Levy suggests, these messengers call us to specific
tasks and help provide us with clarity for the work ahead of us.
But with these messengers comes the potential for blessing if
we are prepared to answer the call.

Healing Broken Hearts

DECEMBER 30

*Compassionate One, who answers broken hearts,
answer us, answer us.*
FROM THE LITURGY FOR YOM KIPPUR KATAN

The notion of a minor Yom Kippur (Yom Kippur Katan)
comes from this text in the Talmud: "Bring atonement upon
me for making the moon smaller" (Babylonian Talmud,
Chullin 60b). The mystics who introduced the idea of a minor
Yom Kippur inferred that the moon's size diminished as God

withdrew the divine presence from humanity. Thus, it is our goal to decrease the distance between God's presence and us. It is in the closing of this gap that we may find blessing. And we can do so through personal atonement.

While this mini-holiday is not observed every month for a variety of different reasons, it is observed most months the day before Rosh Chodesh. So we ask God to show divine compassion and answer our prayers, especially since they are made in the midst of our desire to change and be renewed. I include it here because these same mystics felt that we had until Hanukkah to complete the repentance we started some months ago at Yom Kippur and have yet to complete. The job of personal repentance and renewal is never complete.

Life's Journey

DECEMBER 31

*May your journey fill you with awareness,
compassion, forgiveness and empathy,
moving you to inner peace, wisdom and liberation
from all that holds you back.
Helping ourselves and each other along this journey,
may we, together, relieve suffering,
awaken new perceptions of what life might become,
encourage self-realization, enlightenment and
a strengthened connection between thought,
feeling and action.*

RABBI NINA MIZRAHI

It is the end of the secular year, a time that provides us with the opportunity once again to look at the months behind us and the year ahead. It is also one of the reasons why the day preceding each Rosh Chodesh in the Hebrew calendar is considered a Yom Kippur Katan, literally a "minor Yom Kippur." The Rabbis understood that as we marked the movement of time in the calendar, we also marked the progress of our lives and our plans for the future.

Just as the past contributed to our journey, how we got to this place in our lives, the future extends our journey forward. This is why it is important to plan for it. According to Rabbi Mizrahi, there is a whole list of items necessary for such a journey. Since we have a lot of work to do, don't hesitate. Let's get started now. The work may be difficult and the journey arduous. But we have the capacity to make it.

May the year ahead be a year of blessing for you, for those you love, and for all humankind.

GLOSSARY OF WORDS AND IDEAS

Akdamut: Liturgical poem read on Shavuot, dating from the early eleventh century in Germany as a response to the requirement by those leading the Crusades in Europe to engage in a mock "debate" with members of the Jewish community. The author, Rabbi Meir ben Yitzchak, refused to participate in such a debate.

Akedah: The Binding of Isaac, referring to the abandoned sacrifice of Isaac by Abraham in the biblical book of Genesis.

Amidah: Central prayer in all worship services around which the remainder of the liturgy is built. The word means "standing" since it is recited while standing. It is also referred to as *Sh'moneh Esreh* ("eighteen," for the number of blessings originally included in its weekday version) and *Hat'fillah* ("the prayer," that is, the central prayer).

arba kanfot: Four corners, referring to four corners of the garment and of the *tallit,* sometimes used to refer to a *tallit katan.*

aron hakodesh: Cabinet or ark where the Torah scrolls are housed in the sanctuary of a synagogue.

aufrufen: Also called *aufruf* (in the singular); premarital blessings, generally offered following an *aliyah* (calling up) to the Torah by the prospective groom (and bride, among egalitarian congregations).

Babylonian exile: The period of time, 586–538 BCE, when the Israelites were exiled from the Land of Israel and forced to live in captivity in Babylonia.

bar/bat mitzvah: Life-cycle ceremony marking the individual's transition from childhood into adulthood.

Birkat Gomel: Blessing of gratitude recited upon recovering from illness, following delivery of a child, or returning from a long journey.

Birkat Hamazon: Prayers said after eating, sometimes referred to as Grace after Meals.

b'rakhah: Blessing.

brit milah: Literally, the covenant of circumcision.

bubbe: Yiddish for "grandmother."

Chabad: While technically the intellectual brand of Chasidism, it is known for its outreach in communities and familiar mitzvah tanks. The name is an acronym for the Hebrew words meaning wisdom, understanding, and knowledge. Referred to also as Lubavitch.

cheshbon hanefesh: Literally, "an accounting of the soul." Refers to introspection and self-evaluation.

chevruta: Classic form of cooperative or partner learning model, generally employed in the study of sacred literature.

cholent: A slow-cooked stew-like dish usually eaten on Shabbat afternoon.

davening: Praying, the traditional posture for Jewish prayer.

dukhenen (alternatively, *Birkat Kohanim*): The blessing of the people by the descendants of the priestly class.

d'vekut: The mystical notion of attaching oneself to God.

genizah: A (sometimes temporary) storage place for damaged or worn-out books or ritual objects containing the four-letter divine name of God.

ger: "Stranger," sometimes also used to refer to convert to Judaism.

Haftarah: Reading from the Prophets (or Writings) section of the Bible for Shabbat and holidays, related to the theme of the weekly or holiday Torah reading.

hashkamah minyan: Early-morning prayer service, usually taking place immediately following dawn.

Havdalah: Literally, "separation." A group of rituals that mark the separation between Shabbat and holidays and the rest of the week.

hiddur mitzvah: The adornment and beautification of ritual objects, as implements of holiness.

Hineini prayer: Literally, "I am here." Traditional personal prayer of the cantor said on the High Holy Days on behalf of the congregation.

Holy of Holies: The innermost precinct of the ancient Temple in Jerusalem.

Hoshanah Rabbah: Literally, "the great saving"; a day of supplication observed on the seventh day of Sukkot.

Kaddish D'rabbanan: Prayer said in memory of teachers of Torah.

kavvanah: Spiritual intention behind prayer; also a sacred mantra.

kenanhora: A corrupted Yiddish form of *ayin hara*, "evil eye."

ketubah: Marriage contract document.

Kiddush: Blessing said over wine to consecrate the day as Shabbat or a holiday.

Kiddush L'vanah: Ritual for blessing the moon, said after the beginning of the month and when the moon appears full.

Ladino: Jewish folk language spoken by Jews from Spanish-speaking lands. Functions similarly to the way Yiddish was employed by eastern European Jews.

Maccabees: The heroes of the Hanukkah story. Best described as a national liberation movement that won freedom for the Jewish people from the tyranny of Antiochus IV Epiphanes. They went on to establish the Hasmonean royal dynasty, which ruled the Land of Israel independently from 164 to 63 BCE.

malach hamavet: The angel of death.

mashiachzeit: Yiddish; literally, "messiah time," or the messianic era.

megillah: Literally, "scroll." Five scrolls contained in the Bible from the section referred to as Writings. These scrolls are Ecclesiastes, Esther, Lamentations, Ruth, and Song of Songs.

midrash: Rabbinic parables.

mikvah: Ritual bath.

Minchah: Afternoon worship service.

mitzvah: Plural, mitzvot. Commandment, sacred instruction. Refers to the 613 commandments traditionally acknowledged to have been given by God. Colloquially used to refer to a good deed.

M'lavei Malkah: A Saturday evening collation to usher out the Sabbath bride.

muktzah: Any objects that are related to those labors prohibited on Shabbat and that therefore may not be touched.

musar: Ethical guidance and advice encouraging strict behavior regarding Halakhah, Jewish law. Beginning in the nineteenth century, *musar* developed into a full-scale literature.

niggunim: Wordless melodies that are often associated with Chasidism.

N'ilah: Closing service on Yom Kippur.

omer: A measure of barley; usually referring to the period of time between the second night of Passover and Shavuot.

P'sukei D'zimrah: Literally, "verses of song." Mostly psalm texts that provide the warm-up and introduction to the fixed liturgy of the morning service.

Purim: Spring holiday that celebrates the saving of the ancient Jewish community of Persia from destruction.

Rosh Hashanah: Jewish New Year, occurring in the fall, sometime in September.

Seder: Hebrew for "order." Refers to the table ceremony held on Passover, which celebrates the holiday and retells the Exodus using a special book called a Haggadah.

Shabbat Shuvah: "The sabbath of return"; the Shabbat between Rosh Hashanah and Yom Kippur.

Shehecheyanu: Blessing of thanksgiving, thanking God for bringing us to this time, said upon experiencing something special for the first time or at the onset of holidays and festivals.

Shekhinah: Indwelling presence of God, often described with feminine characteristics.

Sheva B'rakhot: Literally, "seven blessings." The seven blessings recited at a wedding; also used to refer to the seven days of celebration (and attendant meals) following the wedding.

Sh'ma and Its Blessings: The nearest to a creedal statement in Jewish liturgy and the prayers that surround it in the fixed liturgy of the prayer book.

Sh'moneh Esreh: See *Amidah*.

shuckle: Yiddish term referring to swaying motion of the body expressed in prayer.

sukkah: Temporary booth built for the holiday of Sukkot.

tallit: Prayer shawl.

tallit katan: Small tallit, usually worn as an undergarment by traditionally observant Jewish men.

T'fillat Haderech: Traveler's prayer.

t'fillin: Prayer boxes, phylacteries.

Tisha B'av: A holiday in late July or early August that marks the destruction of both Temples in ancient Jerusalem and other tragedies in Jewish history.

t'khines: From the Yiddish for "prayers of supplication," these are personal prayers traditionally offered by women at the lighting of Shabbat and holiday candles.

Torah: Also known as the Five Books of Moses or the Pentateuch, this is the first five books of the Hebrew Bible, including Genesis, Exodus, Leviticus, Numbers, and Deuteronomy.

t'shuvah: Repentance, a return to the ways of God. While one is supposed to do *t'shuvah* all year long, it is also reflective of the mood of the High Holy Days and of the month that precedes them.

Tu B'Shevat: The fifteenth day of the Hebrew month of Shevat, the Festival of the Trees, the Jewish Arbor Day. It connects us to Israel because it is the day when the sap begins to run in Israel's trees, promising spring.

tzedakah: Charitable giving; literally, "righteousness."

Tzidduk Hadin: Literally, "justifying the judgment." Text including Deuteronomy 32:4 that is read generally after the eulogy (although some do so beforehand) and generally after the casket has been lowered into the ground and covered with earth.

tzitzit: Fringes on the four corners of the *tallit* (prayer shawl).

Un'taneh Tokef: Literally, "Let us proclaim." Prayer recited on the High Holy Days whose imagery forms the heart of the essential posture of prayer for the holidays period—"who shall live and who shall die?"

World-to-Come: A reference to the world as it will be following the coming of the Messiah.

yahrzeit: Yiddish term marking the anniversary of someone's death, among Ashkenazic Jews. The term *anos* is used among Sephardic Jews to refer to the same period of time.

yissurim shel ahavah: Literally, "chastisements of love." This is a theological explanation for the punishment of individuals.

Yom Ha'atzmaut: Israel Independence Day, observed in the spring, on 5 Iyar.

Yom Hashoah: Holocaust Remembrance Day, observed in the spring, usually in April or May, on 27 Nisan, which is eight days before Yom Ha-atzmaut.

Yom Hazikaron: Israel Memorial Day for fallen soldiers and victims of terrorism, observed in the spring, on 4 Iyar, the day before Yom Ha-atzmaut.

Yom Kippur Katan: Literally, "minor Yom Kippur." A minor day of atonement that occurs on the day before Rosh Chodesh most months in the Hebrew calendar.

Yom Yerushalayim: Day that celebrates the unification of Jerusalem and therefore Israeli control of the Old City of Jerusalem (since 1967). It takes place in the spring, usually in May, on the date that corresponds to 28 Iyar.

OUR TEACHERS: AUTHORS OF QUOTED TEXTS

Texts are the touchstone of Jewish spirituality. The authors of individual texts become our teachers as we study their writings.

Aaron ben Zvi Hakohen: Editor of Baal Shem Tov's *Keser [or Keter] Shem Tov* originally collected by Rabbi Jacob Joseph of Polonnoye.

Rabbi Rachel Ain: Spiritual leader of Congregation Beth Sholom-Chevra Shas in Dewitt, New York.

Rabbi Ammi (third century): Talmudic rabbi who lived in the Land of Israel and in Babylonia.

Rabbi Melanie Aron: Spiritual leader of Congregation Shir Hadash in Las Gatos, California.

Rabbi Bradley Shavit Artson: Dean of the Ziegler School of Rabbinic Studies at the American Jewish University in Los Angeles and author of several books, including *The Bedside Torah: Wisdom, Visions & Dreams.*

Baal Shem Tov (1700–1760): Literally, "master of the good name"; also called the Besht. The name Baal Shem Tov was used by the founder of Chasidism, Israel ben Eliezer, a charismatic leader who became known through the oral tradition of his students who handed down tales of his travels and good works.

Bachya ibn Pakuda (mid-eleventh century): Moral philosopher who lived in Muslim Spain. His major work, *Duties of the Heart*, was written in 1000. He exerted a major influence on Jewish pietistic literature.

David Ben Gurion (1886–1973): Pioneer builder of the Jewish state and its first prime minister. He played an important role in the struggle for the establishment of the State of Israel. As prime minister and minister of defense during the formative years of the state, he can be credited with many of its achievements.

Hayyim Nahman Bialik (1873–1934): Recognized as Israel's national poet, he participated as a pioneer in the revival of the Hebrew language.

Rabbi Terry Bookman: Senior rabbi of Temple Beth Am in Miami, Florida. His most recent book is *God 101*. Widely published in a variety of religious journals, he is well known for his online spiritual forum through which he offers spiritual workouts and guidance to participants each day.

Edgar M. Bronfman: Community leader and mega-philanthropist, former president of the World Jewish Congress who has made his philanthropic mark by supporting the reimagining of communal projects such as Hillel: The Foundation for Jewish Life on college campuses around the world.

Rabbi Sharon Brous: Spiritual leader of Ikar, a synagogue in Los Angeles based on social justice and spirituality. She was the first recipient of the Los Angeles Jewish Community Foundation's Inspired Leadership award.

Martin Buber (1878–1965): Austrian philosopher, theologian, and educator (who later immigrated to Israel) best-known for his notion of covenant theology described as "I-Thou." He was also a cultural Zionist.

Rabbi Shlomo Carlebach (1926–1994): Rebbe, teacher, musician, and composer who touched the hearts of many Jews through his outreaching efforts to bring them back to Judaism.

Rabbi Norman J. Cohen: Provost and professor of midrash at Hebrew Union College–Jewish Institute of Religion and author of numerous books, including *Voices from Genesis: Guiding Us through the Stages of Life* (Jewish Lights).

Paul Cowan (1940–1988): *Village Voice* writer and author of several books, including *An Orphan in History* (Jewish Lights).

Rabbi Menachem Creditor: Rabbi of Congregation Netivot Shalom in Berkeley, California. He is the founder of Shefa Network, co-founder of Keshet

Rabbis, and author of The Tisch, an electronic commentary on Jewish spirituality. He is also one-half of Shirav, a Jewish folk-music group.

Rabbi Alexander Davis: Senior rabbi of Beth El Synagogue in St. Louis Park, Minnesota.

Alan Dershowitz: An American lawyer, jurist, and political commentator. He is the Felix Frankfurter Professor of Law at Harvard Law School, and is known for his extensive published works, career as an attorney in several high-profile law cases, and commentary on the Arab-Israeli conflict.

Rabbi Eliyahu E. Dessler (1892–1953): Teacher of ethical piety (*musar*) and leader of the Ponevitch Yeshiva in Lithuania.

Rabbi Amy Eilberg: The first woman ordained as a Conservative rabbi by the Jewish Theological Seminary of America in 1985 and nationally known as a leader of the Jewish healing movement.

Albert Einstein (1979–1955): World-renowned scientist best known for his theory of relativity. His name later became a synonym for "genius."

Rabbi Eleazar ben Judah of Worms (1160–1238): Mystic, Talmudist, and codifier. He was coauthor of *Sefer Hasidim*. His many writings are the greatest collection of documents on medieval German Chasidism.

Eliezer ben Hyrcanus: One of the most prominent sages of the first and second centuries.

Rabbi David Ellenson: President of Hebrew Union College–Jewish Institute of Religion and Anna Grancell Professor of Jewish Religious Thought. He is the author of numerous books, including *After Emancipation: Jewish Religious Responses to Modernity*.

Eli Evans: Former president of Revson Foundation, American Jewish historian, and author of numerous books and articles on southern Jewish history, including *The Lonely Days of Summer: Reflections of a Jewish Southerner*.

Rabbi Edward Feld: Ordained rabbi and teacher at the Jewish Theological Seminary of America. He formerly served as the spiritual leader of the Society for the Advancement of Judaism in New York City and as the executive director of the Hillel Foundation for Jewish Life at Princeton University.

Rabbi Michael Feshbach: Reform rabbi who leads Temple Shalom in Chevy Chase, Maryland.

Rabbi Louis Finkelstein (1895–1991): Scholar and administrator who was chancellor of the Jewish Theological Seminary of America. He was generally considered an influential personality in supporting traditionalist elements within Conservative Judaism.

Debbie Friedman: Contemporary Jewish folk singer, particularly well known for compositions such as *Mi Sheberach* (for healing).

Rabbi Laura Geller: Senior rabbi of Temple Emanuel in Beverly Hills, California who is noted for her writings on feminism.

Rabbi Jonah Gerondi (ca. 1180/1200–1263): Moralist who was most famous for his work *Gates of Repentance*. He came from Girona in Catalonia, Spain. Initially an intensely vocal critic of Maimonides, he eventually regretted the position he had taken and attempted to make amends for it.

Rabbi Shefa Gold: Rabbi in the Jewish Renewal Movement, well known for her application of chanting practice to the liturgy and the worship environment.

Leah Goldberg (1911–1970): Leading Hebrew poet, translator, and researcher in Hebrew literature.

Rabbi Arthur Green: Rector of the Rabbinical School of Hebrew College in Boston. Author of numerous works on Jewish mysticism and Chasidism, including *Ehyeh: A Kabbalah for Tomorrow* (Jewish Lights); former president of the Reconstructionist Rabbinical College; and former faculty member at Brandeis University.

Blu Greenberg: Orthodox feminist, writer, and poet.

Rabbi Irving "Yitz" Greenberg: Formerly president of Jewish Life Network, a Judy and Michael Steinhardt Foundation, and founder of CLAL: National Jewish Center for Leadership and Learning. Rabbi Greenberg has published articles on Jewish thought and religion and on American Jewish history. His books include *The Jewish Way* and *Living in the Image of God: Jewish Teachings to Perfect the World*.

Rabbi Sidney Greenberg (1917–2003): Rabbi of Temple Sinai in Philadelphia (later Dresher) for more than fifty years prior to his retirement. An author of over twenty books, he was a major writer on the topic of prayer.

Hafetz Hayim: Literally, "the one who desires life," the pen name of Rabbi Yisrael Meir Kagan (1838–1933), a Polish rabbi, after the name of the book he wrote about Jewish laws of speech and slander.

Rabbi David Hartman: Pluralist Orthodox rabbi who founded the Shalom Hartman Institute in Jerusalem following a long and successful career in the congregational rabbinate in Toronto. He is the author of *A Heart of Many Rooms: Celebrating the Many Voices within Judaism* (Jewish Lights), among other books.

Rabbi Hayyim Halberstam of Zans (1793–1876): Founder of the Zans Chasidic dynasty in western Galicia in the mid-nineteenth century.

Theodor Herzl (1860–1904): Hungarian journalist and founder of modern Zionism and the chief architect of the modern political Zionist movement; author of *Der Judenstaat* (*The Jewish State*) and *Alteneuland* (*The Old New Land*).

Rabbi Abraham Joshua Heschel (1907–1972): Philosopher who attempted to illumine the relationship between God and people, encouraging people to see God in the world with "radical amazement." He also was known as someone who "prayed with his feet" and participated in social justice activities as a reflection of his theology.

Hillel: Talmudic rabbi of the first century CE known for his more lenient teachings, which became adopted in most cases of Jewish law. He position was usually juxtaposed with the position taken by Shammai.

Samson Raphael Hirsch (1808–1888): German rabbi, considered by many the architect of modern Orthodox Judaism, who coined the term *Torah im Derekh Eretz* (Torah and the way of the land), which was his way of expressing a posture that allowed Jews to practice traditional Judaism and engage with the secular world.

Rabbi Lawrence A. Hoffman: Professor of liturgy at Hebrew Union College–Jewish Institute of Religion, New York; senior academic fellow of Synagogue 3000, which he established (with Ron Wolfson); and author of numerous books on Jewish prayer and liturgy, including the award-winning *My People's Prayer Book: Traditional Prayers, Modern Commentaries* series.

Moses ibn Ezra (ca. 1070–ca. 1150): Shortened name of Rabbi Moses ben Jacob ibn Ezra, Spanish philosopher, linguist, and poet. Also known as Ha-sallah (the writer of penitential prayers).

Rabbi Karyn D. Kedar: Senior rabbi of Congregation B'nai Jehoshua Beth Elohim in the Chicago area and the inspiring author of several books, including *God Whispers: Stories of the Soul, Lessons of the Heart* (Jewish Lights).

Rabbi Ron Klotz: Reform rabbi and longtime director of Myron S. Goldman Union Camp Institute in Zionsville, Indiana.

Leah Koenig: Writer, editor, and blogger, especially about foods; editor in chief of the blog The Jew and the Carrot.

Rabbi Abraham Isaac Kook (1865–1935): Religious thinker and first chief rabbi of pre-statehood Israel. He identified himself with the pioneers and exerted a great influence on the younger generation of his time.

Rabbi Michael L. Kramer: Reform rabbi of Temple Solel in Bowie, Maryland.

Lydia Kukoff: Author of *Choosing Judaism* and first director of the outreach program of the Union for Reform Judaism. Currently, she consults on synagogue change.

Rabbi Harold Kushner: Rabbi Laureate of Temple Israel in Natick, Massachusetts, where he served as spiritual leader for twenty-five years, and author of many books, including the best-selling *When Bad Things Happen to Good People.*

Rabbi Lawrence Kushner: Senior Scholar at Temple Emanu-El in San Francisco, California, and formerly rabbi of Beth El Temple of the Sudbury Valley in Massachusetts. Leading mystical teacher in the Reform Movement and author of many books, including *God Was in This Place & I, i Did Not Know* (Jewish Lights).

Levi Yitzchak of Berditchev (1740–1810): Chasidic rabbi who was the disciple of the Maggid of Mezritch. His was known for his great compassion. Levi Yitzchak's chief work was titled *K'dushat Levi*, a commentary on many aspects of Judaism, sacred writings, and teachers and arranged according to the weekly Torah reading.

Rabbi Naomi Levy: Founder and spiritual leader of Nashuva, a Jewish outreach organization based in Los Angeles. She is also author of *To Begin Again* and *Talking to God*.

Rabbi Isaac Luria (1534–1572): Mystic who made his way to Safed in 1570. There he schooled his disciples in his unique kabbalistic system, which came to be known as Lurianic Kabbalah. Also known as the Ari, the "sacred lion," an acronym made from his name.

Moses Maimonides (1135–1204): Moses ben Maimon, also known as the Rambam. He is considered one of the greatest thinkers in all of Jewish history. Trained as a physician, he was also a commentator and philosopher. Under the influence of Aristotelian thought as articulated by the philosophers of the Middle Ages, he was best known for his *Guide for the Perplexed* and his *Mishneh Torah*, an "easy-to-use" compilation of Jewish law.

Rabbi Eliot Malomet: Spiritual leader of Highland Park Conservative Temple and Center–Congregation Anshe Emet in Highland Park, New Jersey.

Rabbi Rolando Matalon: Spiritual leader of Congregation B'nai Jeshurun on the Upper West Side of New York City.

Rabbi Daniel Matt: Leading scholar on Jewish mysticism and translator of the *Zohar*, its primary text. He is annotator and translator of *Zohar: Annotated and Explained* (SkyLight Paths).

Rabbi Israel Mattuck (1883–1954): Born in Lithuania and trained in the United States, he was the first liberal rabbi in the United Kingdom and founded the World Union for Progressive Judaism.

Rabbi Menachem Mendl of Kotzk (1787–1859): Also known as the Kotzker Rebbe; Polish Chasidic rebbe. His religious intensity was considered so extreme that it bordered on madness. He isolated himself from everyone for the last twenty years of his life.

Rabbi Nina Mizrahi: Director of the Pritzker Center for Jewish Education of the Jewish Community Center of Chicago.

Sir Moses Montefiore (1784–1885): British philanthropist who devoted his resources to Israel. He introduced a textile mill and the printing press to Israel. He was also the inspiration behind several agricultural settlements, as well as the Yemin Moshe colony just outside of the Old City of Jerusalem.

Rabbi Nachman of Breslov (1772–1810): The great-grandson of Baal Shem Tov and founder of the Breslover Chasidim. One distinctive Breslov practice is *hitbod'dut* which means "being in solitude." In addition to daily prayer, Bresolver Chasidim try to spend time each day in meditation. Reb Nachman, as he is often called, is still considered the leader of the Breslover Chasidim. His followers believe that no other leader can follow as his successor.

Carol Ochs: Director of the Graduate Studies Program at Hebrew Union College–Jewish Institute of Religion, New York, where she is also visiting professor of philosophy. She is the author of numerous works on spirituality, including *Jewish Spiritual Guidance* (with Kerry Olitzky).

Rabbi Avi S. Olitzky: Assistant rabbi at Beth El Synagogue in St. Louis Park, Minnesota.

Rabbi Jakob Petuchowski (1925–1991): Professor of theology at Hebrew Union College–Jewish Institute of Religion, Cincinnati, and author of numerous books, including *Ever Since Sinai*.

Marge Piercy: Novelist and poet, she has been a key player in many of the major progressive political battles of our time. Piercy is one of the most published and quoted contemporary poets in North America.

Ellis Rivkin: Professor emeritus of Jewish history at Hebrew Union College–Jewish Institute of Religion, Cincinnati, and author of numerous books on Jewish history, including *The Shaping of Jewish History* and *What Crucified Jesus?*

James B. Rosenberg: Rabbi emeritus of Temple Habonim in Barrington, Rhode Island.

Rabbi Israel Salanter (1810–1883): Israel ben Ze'ev Wolf, founder of the *Musar* movement (for ethical piety).

Rabbi David Saperstein: Reform rabbi and lawyer who is the executive director of Reform Judaism's Religious Action Center in Washington, D.C., which does lobbying and political education.

Rabbi Zalman Schacter-Shalomi: Spiritual leader, motivating force behind the Jewish Renewal movement, and author of *First Steps to a New Jewish Spirit: Reb Zalman's Guide to Recapturing the Intimacy and Ecstasy in Your Relationship with God* (Jewish Lights), among other books.

Rabbi Natan Schafer: Prison chaplain in Massachusetts.

Rabbi Solomon Schechter (1847–1915): While born in Moldavia, he was a British scholar who was most famous for his roles as founder and president of the United Synagogue of America, chancellor of the Jewish Theological Seminary of America, and architect of the movement for Conservative Judaism in North America.

Rabbi Harold M. Schulweis: Rabbi emeritus of Valley Beth Shalom in Encino, California. He is the founding chairman of the Jewish Foundation for the Righteous and the author of *For Those Who Can't Believe* and *Conscience: The Duty to Obey and the Duty to Disobey* (Jewish Lights), winner of the National Jewish Book Award. Rabbi Schulweis has been instrumental in the development of synagogue programs such as the Synagogue Havurah Program (since adopted nationally) and the program for para-rabbis.

Rabbi David Seidenberg: Creator of NeoHasid.org. He is a graduate of the Jewish Theological Seminary, where he received rabbinic ordination and his PhD. He also received ordination from Rabbi Zalman Schacter-Shalomi. He writes extensively on ecology and Judaism and teaches about Jewish mysticism.

Shammai (first century BCE): Talmudic rabbi who took a more rigorous and stringent point of view on Jewish law than did his contemporary, Rabbi Hillel.

Rabbi Rami Shapiro: Sometimes writing under his Hebrew name Reb Yerachmiel ben Yisrael, Rabbi Shapiro is a poet and essayist, who has written over a dozen works of poetry, liturgy, short story, and nonfiction, including

The Sacred Art of Lovingkindness: Preapring to Practice and *Ethics of the Sages: Pirke Avot—Annotated and Explained* (both SkyLight Paths). Formerly a congregational rabbi, he now directs the One River Foundation.

Richard Siegel: One of the coauthors of the *Jewish Catologue* and former executive director of the Foundation for Jewish Culture, he is interim director of the School of Communal Service, Hebrew Union College–Jewish Institute of Religion, Los Angeles.

King Solomon: Biblical king, well-known for his wisdom, who built the First Temple in Jerusalem and who began his rule in approximately 967 BCE. He was the son of King David.

Rabbi Elie Kaplan Spitz: Spiritual leader of Congregation B'nai Israel in Tustin, California, and author of *Does the Soul Survive? A Jewish Journey to Belief in Afterlife, Past Lives & Living with a Purpose* and *Healing from Despair: Choosing Wholeness in a Broken World* (both Jewish Lights).

Rabbi Paul Steinberg (1926–2005): Longtime dean and later vice-president of Hebrew Union College–Jewish Institute of Religion who was responsible for its presence in New York City for much of the second half of the twentieth century.

Rabbi Chaim Stern (1930–2001): Longtime spiritual leader of Temple Beth El in Chappaqua, New York; author, poet, biblical scholar, and leading liturgist in the modern Reform Movement.

Anna Stevenson: Farm manager at Adamah: The Jewish Environmental Fellowship. She also works with Hazon on curriculum materials about Jews and food.

Rabbi Uri of Strelisk (d. 1826): Early Polish Chasidic master, known for his style of prayer filled with fervor and enthusiasm. He believed that people should forgo their lust for money and live in poverty.

Vilna Gaon (1720–1797): Elijah (Eliyahu) ben Shlomo Zalman, known as the Gra, was a talmudist, kabbalist, and authority on Jewish law.

Ezer Weizman (1924–2005): Seventh president of Israel who served from 1993 to 2000. Previously, he had been commander of Israel's air force and minister of defense.

Rabbi David J. Wolpe: Spiritual leader of Sinai Congregation in Los Angeles, California, and author of numerous books, including *The Healer of Shattered Hearts: A Jewish View of God* and *Why Faith Matters*.

Herman Wouk: American novelist who has written numerous best-sellers, mostly set in the context of wars, including *The Caine Mutiny*, *Marjorie Morningstar*, *The Winds of War*, and *War and Remembrance*. His memorable *This Is My God* is a nonfiction polemic written in defense of Orthodox Judaism.

Natan Zach: Israeli poet, critic, editor, and translator who exerted a great deal of influence on the development of modern Hebrew poetry.

Rabbi Schneur Zalman of Liadi (1745–1812): Also known as the Alter Rebbe (literally, "older rabbi") or the Rav, founder and first rebbe of the Chabad branch of Chasidism and author of the *Tanya*, a classic text of Chasidism, and the *Shulchan Aruch HaRav*, a code of Jewish law.

Rabbi Sheldon Zimmerman: Spiritual leader of the Jewish Center of the Hamptons in East Hampton, New York, and former president of Hebrew Union College–Jewish Institute of Religion.

Sources of
Quoted Texts

While the texts I have shared in these pages provide the reader with a great deal of insight and inspiration, it is important to realize that most of them come from larger works. These are described below.

Avot d'Rabbi Natan: Small tractate that provides an expansion to the tractate of *Avot*. It is ascribed to Rabbi Nathan the Babylonian.

Babylonian Talmud: The first source book of Jewish law, with over two thousand scholarly contributors. It is comprised of the Mishnah, a six-volume work written in Hebrew and edited by Judah the Prince (200 CE), and the Gemara, which explains the Mishnah, completed in approximately 500 CE and written in Aramaic.

Bava Kamma: Literally, "first gate," this is the first in a series of tractates in the Talmudic order of *N'zikin* that deal with damages and torts. This tractate focuses on specific damages and compensation.

Beitzah: Literally, "egg," one of the tractates in the Talmudic order of *Mo'ed*. It focuses on the rules of the holidays.

Ben Sira: Short for the Wisdom of Ben Sirah (or Sirach), a book of wisdom, from the so-called intertestamental literature (the Apocrypha), sometimes referred to as Sirach, by Ben Sira, also known as The Wisdom of Jesus son of Sirach, The Wisdom of Ben Sira, or Ecclesiasticus.

Berakhot: The tractate of the Talmud dealing with blessings.

Deuteronomy: Fifth book of the Torah, also known as *D'varim*.

Deuteronomy Rabbah: The fifth book in a collection of midrashic parables to the Pentateuch and the five *megillot* (scrolls).

Ecclesiastes: Also known as *Kohelet*, book of wisdom literature, one of the five scrolls, from the third section of the Hebrew Bible known as the Writings.

Even Sh'leimah: A compendium of wisdom by the Gaon of Vilna, gathered by Rabbi Shmuel of Slotzk.

Exodus: Second book of the Torah, also known as *Sh'mot*.

Genesis: First book of the Torah, also known as *B'reishit*.

Genesis Rabbah: The first book in a collection of midrashic parables to the Pentateuch and the five *megillot* (scrolls). Also known in Hebrew as *B'reshit Rabbah*.

Hallel **psalms**: A series of psalms (113–118) of praise recited on special holidays, as well as during the Passover Seder and on the first of the beginning of the Hebrew month.

Isaiah (741–701 BCE): Prophet in Jerusalem. In the book of Isaiah, the prophet protests strongly against moral laxity. His famous vision speaks of a time when "nation shall not lift up sword against nation, neither shall they learn war anymore" (Isaiah 2:4). Modern scholars speak of several Isaiahs contained in the biblical book.

Jeremiah (seventh century BCE): Prophet belonging to a priestly family near Jerusalem. He witnessed the tragic events in the history of Judea that ended in the destruction of Jerusalem. His prophecies foretell the doom of his people as punishment for their sins. Jeremiah is the second of the major prophets.

Job: Third book in the biblical section called the Writings. The theme of Job is divine justice and the problem of suffering of the righteous. In the end, Job learns that people can never really understand the mystery of God's ways. The magnificent poetic descriptions of Job's trials and his patient faith, together with the lofty descriptions of divine power, make the book of Job one of the great wisdom books of the Bible.

Jonah: One of the so-called minor prophets. Unlike the other prophetic books, this is not a recording of the prophet's words. This simply tells the story of a reluctant prophet. This book is read in its entirety in the synagogue on the afternoon of Yom Kippur.

Lamentations: Third of the five scrolls of the Writings section of the Bible. It contains five chapters of mourning over the destruction of Jerusalem by the Babylonians. The book is attributed to Jeremiah and is read in the synagogue on Tisha B'av.

Lamentations Rabbah: One of the books in a collection of midrashic parables to the Pentateuch and the five *megillot* (scrolls).

Leviticus Rabbah: The third book in a collection of midrashic parables to the Pentateuch and the five *megillot* (scrolls).

Makkot: Hebrew for "stripes." Fifth tractate in the Mishnah order of *Tohorot*, dealing with the laws of ritual impurity in connection with foods that are susceptible to such impurity when wet.

Mekhilta: Midrash that functions as a commentary to the book of Exodus, focused more on Jewish law than on Rabbinic parable.

Mishnah: Legal codification of Oral Law, compiled by Rabbi Judah the Prince in the early third century.

Mishneh Torah: Code of Jewish law prepared by Moses Maimonides 1170–1180.

Niddah: Seventh tractate in the Mishnah order of *Tohorot*, dealing with women's menstruation and ritual purity.

Numbers: Fourth book in the Torah, also known as *B'midbar*.

Numbers Rabbah: The fourth book in a collection of midrashic parables to the Pentateuch and the five *megillot* (scrolls). Also known as *B'midbar Rabbah*.

Pesachim: The tractate of the Talmud dealing with laws related to the Passover offering and the observance of Passover.

Pirkei Avot: Collection of pithy sayings by the Rabbis and included in the Mishnah.

Proverbs: Collection of moral sayings included as the second book in the Writings section of the Bible.

Psalms: First book in the Writings section of the Bible. It consists of 150 psalms traditionally ascribed to King David.

P'sikta d'Rav Kahana: Central collection of Rabbinic midrashim emerging out of sermons for special Sabbaths and holidays.

Shabbat: First tractate of twenty-four chapters in the order of the Mishnah and Talmud called *Mo'ed*. It deals primarily with labors that are prohibited on Shabbat.

Shirat Yisrael: Literally, "the poetry of Israel," written by Moses ibn Ezra.

Song of Songs: First of the five scrolls incorporated into the third section of the Bible, called Writings. It consists of a collection of poems about sexual love and courtship. The composition of the book has been attributed to King Solomon.

Song of Songs Rabbah: One of the books in a collection of midrashic parables to the Pentateuch and the five *megillot* (scrolls).

Sotah: One of the Talmudic tractates in the order of *Nashim*. It focuses on the ritual of the *sotah*, a woman suspected of adultery.

Sukkah: The tractate of the Talmud dealing with the laws of Sukkot and the ritual objects associated with the festival.

Tamid: Ninth tractate of the order *K'doshim* in the Mishnah and Talmud. It describes in detail the preparation and sacrifice of the *tamid* (continuous) offering.

Tanchuma: Ninth-century midrash on the entire Torah.

Tosefta: From the Hebrew word meaning "supplement," this material is supplementary to the Mishnah. It is considered less authoritative, but the material dates from the same period of time and was complied around 200 CE, by Rabbis Chiya and Oshaiah, according to Jewish tradition.

Tur, Orach Chayim: *Tur* is a shorthand reference to a legal work called *Arbaah Turim* composed by Yaakov ben Asher in the thirteenth century in Spain. Each of its four sections is called a *tur*. *Orach Chayim* deals with the laws of prayer and the synagogue, as well as Shabbat and the holidays.

Tzenah Urenah: Formerly referred to as "the women's Torah," Yiddish commentary on the Bible, written by Yaacov bar Yitzchak of Yanova (d. 1628), with women as the target reader audience.

Ya Comimos: A poetic Judeo Spanish or Ladino prayer said after the recital of *Birkat Hamazon*.

Zohar: Central Jewish mystical text, written as a commentary on the Torah. While probably a thirteenth-century work of Spanish scholar Moses de Leon, it is ascribed to the second-century Rabbi Shimon bar Yochai, who was said to have hidden in a cave for thirteen years studying Torah with his son, during which time the prophet Elijah inspired him to write the *Zohar*.

BLESSINGS INDEX

Theme Index

About Jewish Lights

People of all faiths and backgrounds yearn for books that attract, engage, educate, and spiritually inspire.

Our principal goal is to stimulate thought and help all people learn about who the Jewish People are, where they come from, and what the future can be made to hold. While people of our diverse Jewish heritage are the primary audience, our books speak to people in the Christian world as well and will broaden their understanding of Judaism and the roots of their own faith.

We bring to you authors who are at the forefront of spiritual thought and experience. While each has something different to say, they all say it in a voice that you can hear.

Our books are designed to welcome you and then to engage, stimulate, and inspire. We judge our success not only by whether or not our books are beautiful and commercially successful, but by whether or not they make a difference in your life.

For your information and convenience, at the back of this book we have provided a list of other Jewish Lights books you might find interesting and useful. They cover all the categories of your life:

Bar/Bat Mitzvah	Life Cycle
Bible Study / Midrash	Meditation
Children's Books	Parenting
Congregation Resources	Prayer
Current Events / History	Ritual / Sacred Practice
Ecology / Environment	Spirituality
Fiction: Mystery, Science Fiction	Theology / Philosophy
Grief / Healing	Travel
Holidays / Holy Days	12-Step
Inspiration	Women's Interest
Kabbalah / Mysticism / Enneagram	

Stuart M. Matlins

Stuart M. Matlins, Publisher

Or phone, fax, mail or e-mail to: **JEWISH LIGHTS Publishing**
Sunset Farm Offices, Route 4 • P.O. Box 237 • Woodstock, Vermont 05091
Tel: (802) 457-4000 • Fax: (802) 457-4004 • www.jewishlights.com
Credit card orders: (800) 962-4544 (8:30AM–5:30PM ET Monday–Friday)
Generous discounts on quantity orders. SATISFACTION GUARANTEED. Prices subject to change.

**For more information about each book,
visit our website at www.jewishlights.com**